FABRIC
SURFACE
DESIGN

FABRIC
SURFACE
DESIGN

CHERYL REZENDES

Photography by John Polak

Storey Publishing

For my parents, Constance LaPointe, Dennis Rezendes, and Beau Rezendes,
and for their unwavering belief in who I am as an artist since the time I was very small.

The mission of Storey Publishing is to serve our customers by
publishing practical information that encourages
personal independence in harmony with the environment.

Edited by Gwen Steege
Art direction and book design by Mary Winkelman Velgos

Cover photography by Mars Vilaubi (front), © John Polak (back), and © 2010 Lee Ann Barker (author)
Interior photography by © John Polak, except as noted on page 308
Illustrations, page 241, by Missy Shepler

Indexed by Nancy D. Wood

Storey Publishing
210 MASS MoCA Way
North Adams, MA 01247
www.storey.com

Printed in the United States by Quad/Graphics
10 9 8 7 6 5 4 3 2 1

Library of Congress Cataloging-in-Publication Data

Rezendes, Cheryl.
  Fabric surface design / by Cheryl Rezendes.
      pages cm
  Includes index.
  ISBN 978-1-60342-811-8 (pbk. : alk. paper)
  ISBN 978-1-60342-872-9 (e-book) (print)
  1. Textile crafts. 2. Textile design. 3. Textile finishing. I. Title.
TT699.R49 2013
746.6—dc23
                        2012027709

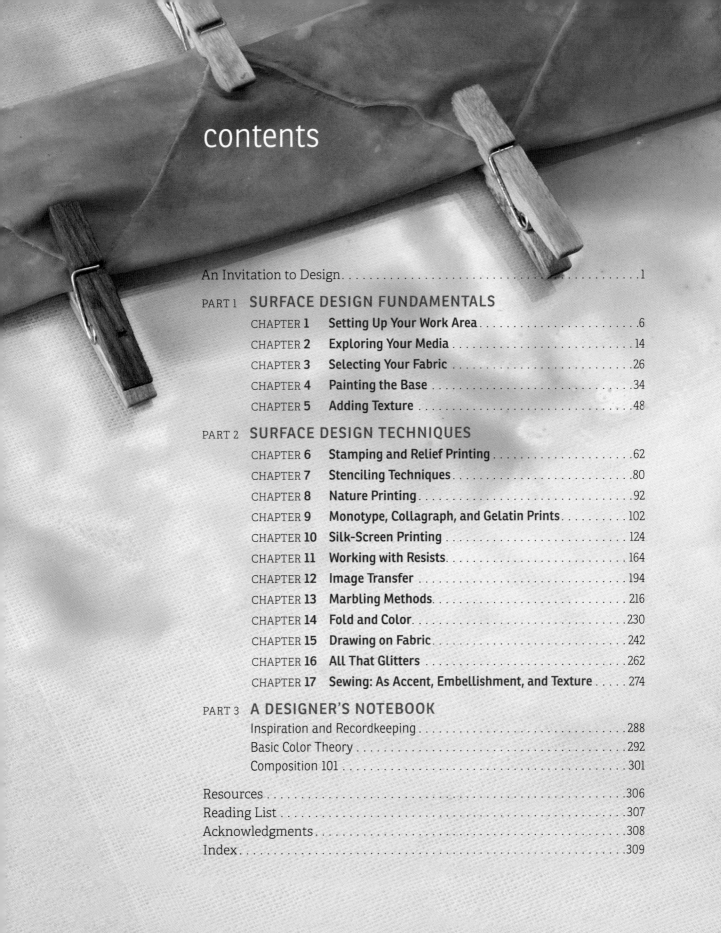

contents

An Invitation to Design

Designing your own fabric opens up a whole world of possibilities, and in this book you'll find a wide range of techniques that you can use for just this purpose. Keep in mind that this book was written for you and your creative process. It is not about me, my artistic sensibility, or even the techniques I use and love, although I included most of them in these pages. I've also presented the work of a variety of fiber artists whose aesthetics encompass a wide range of imagery as well as personal taste and style, so that you can see the endless possibilities these techniques offer you.

Why Choose Paint Instead of Dyes?

I chose to write about using paint on textiles rather than dyes simply because paints are easy to work with. There are no complicated recipes to follow and no toxic chemicals or fumes to worry about. Paints are quick and easy to set up. Cleanup is also a breeze, because it can be done simply with just soap and water. If your studio is the family kitchen table, and your time frame is the length of your youngest child's afternoon nap or the couple of hours you have between dinner and bedtime, then paint is the way to go.

It's my belief that many of the techniques accomplished with dyes on fabric can also be executed with paint. The only real restriction is size, although I successfully stretch and paint 3 yards of fabric at a time on a regular basis. Even more impressive, textile painter Mickey Lawler stretches vast quantities of fabric in her backyard to paint yards of incredible skyscapes. (For an example of her work, see page 46.)

Techniques and Creativity

Although the step-by-step instructions in this book are written with beginners in mind, experienced surface design artists will value the information as a reference or reminder of techniques they may have forgotten. You can take all of these techniques much farther than the specific instructions here: use my guidance as a kickoff to your own investigation. Think of each technique as a big experiment where you have to uncover the meaning and scope of its capability. The reality is that you could work with any one of the techniques for months on end before even beginning to tap into its full potential.

For those of you who are just starting out as a creator of art, think of the work you do from these exercises as samples of the techniques you are learning; chances are they aren't going to be masterpieces at first. For more experienced users, remember that masterpieces come only after many ho-hum pieces. More simply great or wonderful or even just nice pieces are out there than there will ever be masterpieces. And even a masterpiece is never perfect. Rather, each masterpiece is only a stepping stone (albeit a rather large stepping stone) to the next piece or, more than likely, to the next direction your work takes you. And each time you turn in a new direction, you are a beginner again.

Masterpieces aside, even good work needs your permission to emerge. You, as the artist, grant that permission by allowing yourself to experiment without judgment. As you work, you need the spontaneity and wonder of a child before you can achieve provocative artwork. You need to learn to let go of the visual idea in your head as to what "good" art really looks like.

If you are the sort of person who tackles each new project with a steadfast idea in your head, remember that what happens on the piece of cloth in front of you has a mind and a direction of its own. What it becomes is often far more exciting, or at least just as exciting, as the original idea.

One of the most important tools we need as an artist is one we all possess: our eyes. Using our eyes to truly observe the world around us is a critical step in learning to be an artist. The next time you sit down to draw something from life, take note of how much time you spend looking at the object in contrast to how much time you spend looking at your drawing. Often people spend more time looking at the drawing and then are frustrated because the drawing doesn't accurately represent the object they're trying to draw. How can it? The artist doesn't really know what it looks like, because he or she has been drawing based on a preconceived notion of what the object looks like, rather than what it actually looks like.

Similarly, to succeed at fabric surface design, it's important to develop the ability to observe our work as it unfolds and not be locked into a visual preconception of what we want it to look like. When we come at it with an open mind, we are able to see our unique and personal creations as the successes they truly are, not as failures because they turned out different from what we had intended, or pre-imagined, them to be. Promise yourself that from now on you will take a thoroughly objective look at what you are creating. Give your materials and your instincts (yes, you do have them) the right to guide your hands as they discover new tools, new mediums, and new results. Pay attention

to what your piece truly looks like, as well as to what you intended it to be.

Be forewarned that even experienced artists go through a period of doubt with each and every piece they have created. Often an art piece looks awful simply because it hasn't had time to evolve. Keep working and push yourself through the doubt. If you really just can't stand the piece, put it aside for a month or so before throwing it out. You may see its potential after you have had a little distance from it. I often hang an unfinished piece where it will be the first thing I see when I enter the room the following day. (For more suggestions on evaluating your work, see page 10).

I love what Leonardo da Vinci said: "Painting is poetry that is seen rather than felt, and poetry is painting that is felt rather than seen." Whether you're decorating a length of fabric to sew into a tote bag or creating an art quilt, go about your work as the artist that you are. Know that you are participating in the great act of creativity. Be proud and honor yourself for the work you are creating and for the courage you have to create it.

Thinking about Color

I very purposely put color theory in part 3 of this book. For many people it is a complicated subject that requires a lot of focused thought to fully grasp. While planning this book, it was very important to me that no one would be overwhelmed from the get-go. I have come to understand from years of teaching that some brains just can't wrap themselves around the color wheel very easily. It's nothing to be embarrassed about. It's just like algebra (yikes!) or reading maps. Some of us can do it without effort, and some of us have to work really hard at it. So in lieu of color theory, I suggest that for your first fabric surface designs, you use colors you are already familiar with and like. Chances are pretty good that they go together nicely.

How to Use This Book

You can, of course, start from the beginning of this book and very methodically make your way from chapter to chapter. If that just isn't your style, however, feel free to hop around. Each chapter is self-contained and can be adapted to whatever stage your project is at.

The advantage of starting at the beginning is that this is where I cover ideas and techniques for preparing your fabric for other surface design, in other words, how to create a fabric base that you can add onto. Almost all the techniques covered in part 2 (stamps and prints, block printing, stenciling, monoprinting, and so on) will be most successful if you apply them to a piece of fabric that already has some background texture or color, however subtle you may choose to paint it. I personally love hand-painted fabrics that give an illusion of depth. Because of this, I have presented the techniques in an order that's logical for creating this kind of fabric.

However you choose to approach this book, make sure to have fun! Be a kid again! And believe in the power of your own creativity!

A WORD ABOUT RECORDKEEPING

Some of us do a great job of keeping records, but many of us don't. We think we will never forget how we did something, especially when we love it. But we do forget.

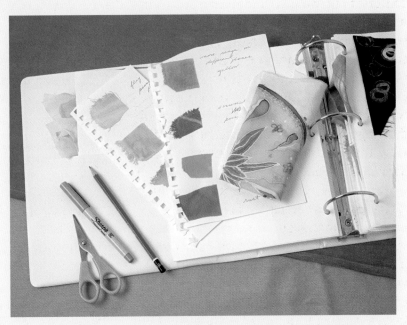

The easiest and most pain-free method is to keep a sample piece of fabric close at hand. Every time you come up with a new design, technique, or tool for any given project, use it on your sample piece of fabric. If you think you won't remember how you did it, jot down a few notes about it as well.

I use a 3-inch loose-leaf binder to store my samples. I staple them to 8½-by-11-inch sheets of heavy white paper, making notations of anything I think I may forget, including color names and/or numbers and the recipes for any colors I mixed myself. I brush a swatch of each individual color I used directly on the paper, then brush on the final color they made when mixed together. I am frequently very grateful to have this notebook at hand, and for many of my projects, it has been invaluable to me. It can also serve as a great source of inspiration when my creativity bank feels empty. (For more about journals and recordkeeping, see page 288.)

PART ONE

Surface Design Fundamentals

CHAPTER 1

Setting Up Your Work Area

It's always easier to have a space to work where you can leave your projects and materials out, but whether you have a beautiful studio space separate from your home or you're using your kitchen table, it's still possible to have great results from your artistic efforts. With the addition of roll-away storage cabinets for art supplies, and a portable work surface and design board, the sky's the limit for what you can accomplish even in a limited amount of space and time.

Creating Your Work Surface

For most of the techniques covered in this book, your work surface should be firm with a little padding. I made my worktables by mounting ¾-inch plywood on adjustable, industrial workbench legs ordered from an industrial-supply catalog (see Resources for sources). I used a full sheet of plywood, which measures 4 by 8 feet for the top. If your space isn't large enough for that size, however, have the plywood cut down to the size you can manage, at the lumberyard or at your local home-improvement center.

Cover the plywood with 2-inch foam insulation, which comes in 2-by-8-foot sheets with tongue-and-groove cutouts on the two long sides. Using a long bread knife, you can easily cut the foam to fit the dimensions of your plywood. Use good-quality duct tape if you need to butt any of the cut ends together to fit your table.

I put several layers of white craft felt on top of the foam. I like the brightness of the white felt as a background for my work. On top of the felt, I lay 6 mm plastic sheeting, purchased at my local hardware store. The sheeting is long enough to come down the sides of the foam and then fold up to the underside of the

A portable work surface. This lightweight work surface consists of a layer of white craft felt on top of 2-inch foam insulation, which is then covered with plastic sheeting, held in place with duct tape.

plywood. I then use duct tape to secure the plastic to the plywood.

This foam, felt, and plastic padding provides a firm surface with a little give, which is ideal for stamping and silk-screening, with the added bonus that if you need to hold down the edges of your fabric while you work, you can push straight pins right down into the foam. When you start to see color coming through to your white felt (because of all the pinholes), you'll know that it's time to change the plastic. But if your plastic is just paint covered, you can easily wash it clean. My mom, who often helps me out in the studio, has washed my plastic-covered tabletops many times with Bon Ami and a sponge with great results.

If you can't set up a permanent work surface in the space you have, don't despair. Have a piece of plywood cut down to a size that fits on top of an existing table in the area. As long as you don't sit on the edges of the plywood, it can easily extend beyond your existing table by as much as 6 inches on all sides. Cut the insulation foam to fit the plywood, adhere them to each other with self-adhesive Velcro, then cover with the felt and plastic as described above. Be sure to protect the finish on your table by covering it with a pad or blanket before laying the plywood down. When you're finished working, you can simply pick up this portable tabletop and store it in your basement or garage. If you live in a small apartment, stash it under your bed or behind a tall piece of furniture.

If you're happy with the overall size of your existing table, you can skip the plywood and lay the foam insulation directly on your table. If you are careful, the foam can extend a few inches beyond the table to extend your working surface. You can also use carpet foam for the padding. It's not very thick, so you can't pin into it as you work, but it's easy and convenient because you can roll it up to store it.

WHEN PLASTIC CAUSES PROBLEMS

With many of the techniques in this book, the fabric can become pretty saturated with water and paint. If the fabric lies directly on the plastic, it can affect the end result after the paint has dried. Experience will tell you whether or not you like this change. If you don't, putting a muslin drop cloth between the plastic and your fabric will solve the problem. When you're through working, you can put the drop cloth through the washer and dryer for future use. After several uses as a drop cloth, these pieces of fabric often have a wonderful spontaneous look to them that you couldn't plan if you tried. I love repurposing these gems by using them as the back fabric for my art quilts.

Alternatively, you can put another piece of white fabric under the piece you are working on. If your top piece of fabric is fairly thin, the paint will seep through to the bottom piece of fabric, giving you a bonus painting for a base fabric. Sometimes the piece underneath is more exciting than the one you were actually working on.

Organizing Your Tools

Keep your tools organized in plastic bins, on shelves, or in drawers. Label all the bins so you can find things easily and quickly while you work. If you have to put everything away when your work session is over, plastic drawer units on wheels work beautifully. When you're done, you can simply roll them away to a closet, garage, or basement.

The Value of a Design Board

It's extremely helpful to have a place where you can hang up your work while you're still creating it. Even small pieces look very different when you view them hanging, compared to looking down at them from the short distance between your nose and the table. You can use an ordinary bulletin board for this purpose. I have a 4-by-8-foot sheet of Homasote nailed to my wall. This is made of compressed paper fiber used for insulation and for sound control, which you can buy at a lumberyard or home-improvement center. Alternatively, the same 2-inch-thick insulation foam you used for your tabletop can also be used as a portable design wall. Two sheets will give you a design wall that is 48 inches wide by however high you want it to be. Fit the tongue-and-groove sides together, then use duct tape down the length of the seam. Paint it white or use spray adhesive to cover it with white felt or a piece of flannel cut to size. The beauty of covering it with flannel or felt is that your fabric pieces will adhere to the flannel without using pins. Use the duct tape like a hinge to simply fold the wall in half before putting it away.

If you don't have a wall or a bulletin board to use as a design board, or if your piece is too wet or has too many unattached layers to hang up, then carefully place it on the floor. With even more care, stand on a stool or your chair to get some visual distance between you and your artwork. Do this frequently while you work. I am still surprised at the difference this viewpoint can make.

Using a design board. I pinned this work-in-progress on my design board so that I could see how the various pieces work together and where I can add new elements, such as the small stones at the lower left.

Equipment Needs
. . . and Niceties

Every technique in this book requires a specific list of necessary supplies. But just as a recipe book might include a list of ingredients that every cook should have on hand in their pantry closet, there are basic supplies that every surface design artist should have on hand as well. Think of these as your pantry closet staples.

- **Several gallon-size containers and buckets or pails.** Easy access to water is important, but before I had the benefit of running water in my studio, I used plastic gallon containers and buckets. I filled the gallon containers with water and kept them close at hand for mixing with paint and to fill smaller containers for brush washing. I dumped the gray water into the pails or buckets to be hauled off to the kitchen when full. Remember to give all your brushes a good wash under warm running water and soap when you are done.

- **Small plastic containers with covers.** These are useful for saving mixed paint.

- **Spray bottles.** Be aware that all spray bottles are not alike! Some spray in a fine, even mist, while others dribble all over everything. Both have their appeal and uses. You can buy small spray pump bottles at drugstores, dollar stores, and beauty- and art-supply stores, as well as from catalogs and online.

- **Brushes of all kinds and shapes.** There's no limit to the kinds of brushes you can use, including watercolor brushes, stencil brushes, foam brushes, Chinese wash brushes, inexpensive bristle brushes, and basting brushes for cooking. I even use feather dusters from the dollar store as brushes.

- **Plastic spoons.** These are useful for scooping out paint.

- **Palettes for mixing paint.** Many flat, white surfaces work for this purpose. For instance, the disposable foam trays that meat comes on work very well, and you can feel good about making extra use of them before sending them to the landfill. I also like to use small, square, ceramic plates sold at kitchen-supply stores, or look for white plates and bowls at the local Goodwill, Salvation Army, or other secondhand stores as well as tag sales. It's important that the surface you spread and mix your paint on be white or a neutral gray, as any other color will change the appearance of your paint color.

- **Sponges.** You can use the synthetic type found at the grocery store, as well as small natural sponges available in the pottery section of your local art-supply or craft store.

AVOIDING MOLD

Don't store the gallon jugs of water in a dark area, such as under the table, or mold will grow on the inside upper edges where, of course, you can't reach to wash!

- **Scissors.** At the very least, you'll need one pair of scissors for paper and one pair for fabric; small embroidery scissors come in handy, too.

- **Rotary cutter.** I've been very happy with the Olfa brand rotary cutters, which are available at fabric and craft stores.

- **X-Acto knife.** I like using one with a #1 handle and a size 11 blade.

- **Self-healing cutting mat.** Often used by quilters, these cutting mats are marked with a helpful grid for guidance when you need to measure. Get as big a size as your budget allows and one that fits nicely on your work surface. These are available at fabric and craft stores.

- **Brayers.** The Rollrite Multi-Purpose 4-inch foam brayer, model #94B from Testrite Visual Products is the best for the techniques in this book. These are available at Dick Blick art-supply stores (see Resources for Dick Blick online store).

- **Plexiglas.** Have on hand several sheets of Plexiglas measuring approximately 8 by 10 inches. Your local glass, hardware, or home-improvement store will have this.

- **Permanent markers (such as Sharpies).** Supply yourself with both regular and fine-point markers.

- **Pencils and white plastic or kneaded erasers for use on paper.** There are never enough! Soft pencils work best on fabric because you can draw a very light line. In general, pencil is very hard to remove from fabric, so if you don't want the pencil lines to show at all, use a pencil designed for use on fabric, such as one made by Fons & Porter; this also comes with an eraser.

CARING FOR YOUR BRUSHES

Clean up your palette and brushes with Ivory soap and warm water. Gently swirl the bristles of your brushes over a bar of Ivory soap. Holding the brush between your thumb and forefinger, work the soap into the base of the brush, then rinse. Repeat until the soap and water are clear. Set aside to dry.

- **Plastic sheeting (4 mil).** This comes either in a roll or folded and is available at your local hardware, paint, or home-improvement store. Some of the techniques in this book are messier than others. Plastic sheeting will protect your work surface, but you may also want to lay down an additional piece of plastic sheeting that measures slightly larger than your fabric. When you're finished with an especially messy project, you can use the added layer of plastic as a sort of tray for transferring your wet work to another location for drying, thus freeing up your work surface for the next project.

- **Painter's tape.** I prefer the blue variety because it's easy to remove, doesn't leave a sticky residue, and is easy to find on a tableful of supplies!

- **Baking parchment paper.** Available at grocery and kitchen-supply stores, this will be used to protect your iron while heat-setting paint and fusing fabric.

- **Chocolate and dry-roasted almonds . . .** of course! (Or your own preferred snack.)

Exploring Your Media

The determination of which textile paints to work with is a personal one. As with most art supplies, when you buy textile paints you get what you pay for. The less-expensive brands tend to have more fillers and less actual pigment, and they may not be lightfast. If you're a beginner and feel that you're "just experimenting," you might think it makes sense to start with lesser-quality supplies. It will be hard to learn from those experiments, however, if your end result lacks that extra zing simply because your paints aren't capable of producing the vivid color you're after. How will you be able to accurately determine whether the disparity is your lack of experience or whether the problem instead is inherent in your materials?

15

In addition, you never know how successful your early work will be, and if you come up with something quite striking, you may be disappointed that you didn't use the best-quality supplies you could afford. On the other hand, if you're working with kids, top-of-the-line textile paints may not be necessary. There are many brands on the market to choose from. Keep in mind that your choices of brand and paint consistency are often determined by the project you're working on, so do your homework: knowledge of a variety of paints and mediums will come in very handy as you become more experienced and more involved with your work.

In what follows, I go over those paints that I'm most familiar with and what I recommend to use when you're starting. In time, however, you should try them all. Form your own opinions. New products are surfacing all the time, and some of them, I am sure, are quite good and may rival any of my current favorites.

A WORD ABOUT METALLICS

All these paints, including metallics, can get pretty costly, but metallics (in any brand) are great to have in your palette box, even if you think you aren't someone who likes glitter. A little sparkle can go a long way in adding dimension to your pieces. To help me defer the costs of the metallics (if only psychologically!), every time I place an order for some of the basic colors, I allow myself to add one metallic. This way I slowly build up my metallic collection without spending a heap of money all at once.

Textile Paints

I predominantly use paints designed specifically for textiles on my fabric pieces. In developing these paints, manufacturers have given attention to their colorfastness, application characteristics, and color intensity, while hardly changing the hand (or feel) of the finished painted cloth. All textile paints are

RECOMMENDED START-UP PAINT SELECTION

Pébéo Setacolor. Transparent starter set, plus a bottle of lightening medium

Pébéo Setacolor Opaque Shimmer. Gold and silver

PRO Chemical & Dye PROfab. Assorted textile paint sampler kit, which includes Transparent Yellow 10, Red 35, True Blue 45, Opaque White 01, Black 60, Pearlescent Light Silver 1, and Yellow Gold 7. You'll eventually want to get yourself a jar of Transparent Base Extender as well.

Jacquard Dye-Na-Flow. A variety of colors of your choice. Dharma Trading Co.'s Dye-Na-Flow Class Kit contains a 2.25-ounce bottle of all 30 Jacquard colors, plus brushes, a bottle of water-based gutta (see page 166), salt, droppers, and bottles with tips for the resist work. It is a fantastic deal. (See Resources for website.)

Jacquard Lumiere. Optional, but these paints are so wonderful, you should choose at least a couple for your start-up supply. Jacquard also makes a wonderful line of products called Pearl-Ex Pigments, which are mica-based, metallic, powdered pigments. They come in a variety of colors and can be mixed with any liquid medium, including their colorless extender, to produce lovely, shimmering effects.

water-based acrylics, which means that not only can they be diluted and mixed with water, but they can also be cleaned up with just soap and water. And although they may have a scent, there are no fumes.

I divide textile paints into four categories: thin, transparent, opaque, and metallic. The consistency of these paints ranges from thin (like dye) to heavy (like pudding), as described below. In addition to the character of the paint as it comes from the jar or bottle, auxiliary mediums are available from all textile paint companies that greater enhance the flexibility and usage of their paints.

- **Thin.** Thin paints have the consistency of dye or water, and so they can easily be applied using a spray bottle. By nature they are always transparent. Think of these paints as being like watercolors.

- **Transparent.** These paints have some body, but they are still transparent. Even if you use them straight out of the bottle, you can see through them. This means that they will not completely cover existing paint on the surface of your piece; you will always see through them to the painted or printed fabric below, even if only faintly.

- **Opaque.** Opaque paints have body, too, but you cannot see through them, and they should cover any existing paint you have already put on your piece. They are best used on dark fabrics.

- **Metallic and pearlescents.** These paints have not only body but also sheen and/or bits of metal.

This may seem overly complicated at first. If you find it too overwhelming, think of this information as something you can come back to after you become familiar with the different processes and mediums. You may want to just skip through all the details that follow and simply use my recommendations for how to get started in the box above.

The brands of textile paints that I am most familiar with are distributed by Pébéo, Jacquard, and PRO Chemical & Dye. (For websites, see Resources.) I trust these companies to produce consistent, quality paints. The chart on the following spread includes the paints I use regularly.

Comparing Textile Paints

	Thin	Transparent	Opaque	Metallic
Jacquard	**Dye-Na-Flow**	**Textile Colors**	**Neopaque**	**Lumiere**
Characteristics	• Beautiful, strong color • Can be diluted (1 part water to 4 parts paint)	• Medium body • Can be diluted (1 part water to 3 parts paint)	• Medium body • Can be diluted (1 part water to 3 parts paint)	• Gorgeous metallics and pearlescents • Heavy body • Can be diluted (1 part water to 3 parts paint)
*Auxiliary		• Colorless Extender: to create more transparency	• Neopaque Flowable Extender: to make a paler shade	• Lumiere Flowable Extender: to make a paler shade
Uses	• Spray painting • Serti silk technique • Salt effects • Faux tie-dye and batik	• Hand painting • Stamping • Stenciling • Silk-screening *When diluted with water:* • Spray painting • Salt effects • Serti silk technique • Watercolor techniques • Faux batik and tie-dye • Sun painting	• Hand painting • Stamping • Stenciling and silk-screening on dark-colored fabrics *When diluted with water:* • Spray painting • Salt effects • Marbling • Serti silk technique • Watercolor techniques • Faux tie-dye and batik	• Hand painting • Stamping • Stenciling and silk-screening on dark-colored fabrics *When diluted with water:* • Spray painting • Salt effects • Marbling • Serti silk technique • Watercolor techniques • Faux tie-dye and batik
Pébéo	**Setasilk**	**Setacolor**	**Setacolor Opaques**	**Setacolor Shimmer**
Characteristics	• Vibrant color • Thin body	• Medium body; can be diluted (1 part water to 1 part paint)	• Medium body	• Medium body
*Auxiliary	• Pébéo Lightening Medium: to make paler shades	• Pébéo Lightening Medium: to make paint sheerer	• Pébéo Lightening Medium: to make paler shades	• Pébéo Lightening Medium: to make paler shades
Uses	• Spray painting • Serti silk technique • Salt effects • Sun painting • Watercolor techniques • Faux tie-dye and batik	• Hand painting • Stamping • Stenciling • Sun painting *When diluted with water:* • Spray painting • Salt effects • Serti silk technique • Watercolor techniques • Faux batik and tie-dye • Sun painting	• Hand painting • Stamping • Stenciling and silk-creening on dark-colored fabrics *When diluted with water:* • Spray painting • Salt effects • Marbling • Serti silk technique • Watercolor techniques • Faux tie-dye and batik	• Hand painting • Stamping • Stenciling • Silk-screening *When diluted with water:* • Spray painting • Watercolor technique • Faux batik

	Thin	Transparent	Opaque	Metallic
PRO Chemical & Dye		**PROfab Transparent**	**PROfab Opaque**	**PRObrite Pearlescent**
Characteristics		• Luscious, puddinglike consistency • Wonderful for color mixing • Heavy body	• Luscious, puddinglike consistency • Wonderful for color mixing • Heavy body	• Luscious, puddinglike consistency • Wonderful for color mixing • Heavy body
*Auxiliaries		• PROfab Transparent Base Extender: to make a paler shade • PROfab Paint Thinner: for thinning • PROfab No Dri: to prevent paints from drying too quickly when silk screening	• PROfab Opaque Base Extender: to make a paler shade • PROfab No Dri: to prevent paints from drying too quickly when silk-screening	• PRObrite Neutral Base Extender: to make a paler shade • PROfab No Dri: to prevent paints from drying too quickly when silk-screening
Uses		• Hand painting • Stamping • Stenciling • Silk-screening	• Hand painting • Stamping • Stenciling and silk-screening on dark fabric	• Hand painting • Stamping • Stenciling and silk-screening on all fabrics, including dark ones

*Auxiliary refers to a medium or product used to change the inherent characteristics of the paint.

Artist Acrylic Paints

Many textile artists use artist acrylic paints on their fiber art pieces with great success. The secret to converting traditional acrylics to a paint that works well with cloth is a product called *textile medium*. Textile medium makes the paint a bit more fluid, with the result that it's easier to apply and is less likely to crack when dry; the painted fabric is also more flexible. I am most familiar with Liquitex and Golden Artist Colors acrylic paints and mediums. Golden has extensively tested their acrylic paints on fabric, and consequently they have the largest variety of paint and mediums recommended for use with textiles, depending on the technique and desired end results. Both lines include a variety of mediums recommended for use with textiles, depending on the technique and the end results that you desire. I have found these products to be unsurpassed in quality. See Golden Artist Colors Acrylic Paints on the next page for advice on what products to use for which purposes.

If you choose to use artist acrylic paints on fabric, keep in mind that some products require that the painted fabric be heat-set, while others do not. Follow the individual manufacturer's directions.

I also recommend several additional products from Liquitex and Golden for some of the techniques in this book: Liquitex Fabric Medium and Flow Aid, and Golden's GAC 900 fabric/textile medium and Silk-Screen Fabric Gel. Without question, if you are going to buy only one textile medium, go for Jacquard Textile Color Colorless Extender.

Acrylic Inks

Everyone loves the effect acrylic inks have when used on fabric. The products I recommend are Liquitex Acrylic ink! and Daler-Rowney FW Acrylic Artists' Ink. Because of their color options, color intensity, and the thicker consistency of the ink itself, my favorite is the FW Acrylic Inks. The manufacturer recommends that these inks not be heat-set for permanency, however, so they are not a good choice for any projects that will be washed. On the other hand, Liquitex inks can be heat-set and mixed with water or Liquitex Fabric Medium to make them easier to apply. If you are using them for faux dyeing or staining techniques, Liquitex Flow Aid is another medium that greatly enhances the blendability of colors, thus behaving in much the same way that dyes do. Use them for outlining with a fine brush straight out of the bottle, as well as for layering techniques using an airbrush or inexpensive spray bottle. These inks are a great addition to any fiber artist's paint box of supplies.

GOLDEN ARTIST COLORS ACRYLIC PAINTS

Although textile paints are generally my first choice for most of the techniques in this book, these are my favorite artist acrylic paints to use on fabric.

- **Hand brushing.** Any Golden Heavy Body paint mixed with an equal part GAC 900 fabric/textile medium or Silk-Screen Fabric Gel when thicker applications of paint are desired.

- **Spraying.** Golden Fluid Acrylic Colors mixed with equal parts Airbrush Medium and GAC 900 fabric/textile medium. Increase Airbrush Medium as desired to facilitate spraying and to increase transparency of color.

- **Marbling.** Golden Airbrush Colors or Golden Heavy Body paints mixed equal parts with GAC 900 fabric/textile medium.

- **Tie-dyeing and staining.** Golden Airbrush Colors mixed equal parts with GAC 900 fabric/textile medium. Prewetting the fabric with water and adding Golden Acrylic Flow Release to the paint mixture can help the paint to penetrate through the fibers of your cloth.

- **Silk-screening.** Heavy Body Acrylics mixed equal parts with GAC 900 fabric/textile medium or Silk-Screen Fabric Gel.

Heat-set all fabrics that have been treated with GAC 900 fabric/textile medium by ironing on the reverse side for 3 to 5 minutes, or run them in the clothes dryer set on high for 40 to 50 minutes. If you don't intend to wash the fabric, heat-setting is not necessary.

A BREATH OF FRESH AIR

Keep in mind that many paints have odors, even if they are nontoxic and safe to use without a mask. When working with any art materials, it makes sense to ensure that you have proper ventilation. Work by an open window if you find that the odors bother you.

Liquitex Professional Acrylic ink!

	Straight out of the bottle	When mixed with Liquitex Fabric Medium	When mixed with Liquitex Flow Aid
Characteristics	• Huge selection of deep, vibrant, and highly pigmented colors	• Increased ease of blending colors • Prevents dragging • Creates a softer hand (feel) to the fabric once it is dry • Aids in the adhesion of paint to fabric surface	• Dyelike consistency • Transparent and translucent colors work best • Dries with a soft finish
Uses	• Brush work • Stenciling • Stamping • Painting with a sponge or spray bottle	• Brush work • Stenciling • Stamping • Painting with a sponge or spray bottle	
Instructions	• Heat-setting unnecessary • Wait 4 days before washing; can be washed in the washing machine	• Start with a ratio of equal parts, then add more medium as needed.	• Mix 1 part Flow Aid to 20 parts distilled water.

Liquitex Artist Acrylic Paints

Liquitex Soft Body Artist Acrylic Paint can be mixed with Liquitex Fabric Medium and water to achieve a good consistency for working with fabric.

The manufacturer recommends the following fabrics: cottons, cotton-polyester blends, woven, knitted, felt, terry cloth, silk, velvet, velveteen, corduroy, flannel, suede, leather, and most synthetics.

Heat-setting. Protect your ironing board cover by placing a piece of parchment paper between the fabric and the ironing board. You may wish to use protective paper on top of the fabric as well.

After the Painting Is Done: Heat-Setting

Once painted, most of your fabrics will need to be heat-set. If you use acrylic paints, follow the manufacturer's directions. Heat-set textile paints by ironing the fabric with a dry iron or by putting it in a clothes dryer set on high for 30 to 45 minutes. (Don't do this until the paint is dry!)

Ironing the Finished Fabric

Iron on the reverse side of the fabric with a dry iron set on the highest setting your fabric allows. You may want to protect your ironing board cover by placing a piece of baking parchment paper between the fabric and the ironing board. In addition, some paints require that you place another piece of parchment paper (or a press cloth) between the iron and the fabric. This protects the bottom of your iron and allows the iron to glide more smoothly across the fabric. Ideally, hold the iron in one spot for a count of 10, then move it to a new location. This procedure is definitely a study in patience, as counting to 10 a gazillion times actually takes a very long time. I do the best I can to cover the surface in this manner, and then I throw the fabric in the dryer at its hottest setting for about 30 minutes. Time in the open air will set paint as well.

Most textile paint manufacturers advise that after the paint has been heat-set, the fabric can be machine washed or dry-cleaned.

I'm more cautious with my hand-painted items. I either hand wash them or machine wash them on gentle with little or no agitation. I find that metallic paint gets dull if it rubs up against other fabrics in the washer through agitation. As an added precaution, I wait about 48 hours after I've heat-set the item before washing it. If you aren't planning on making the fabric into a garment, of course, you probably don't need to wash it at all.

When You Prefer Not to Heat-Set

Jacquard makes two additives that set the paints, thus eliminating the need for heat-setting: Airfix and Versatex Fixer. Because Airfix requires ventilation when using, I prefer Versatex, which does not. Add Versatex to your textile paints only when you are ready to use them, as the chemicals remain active for only 8 to 12 hours. Mix ½ to 1½ teaspoons of Versatex into 8 ounces of paint. Do not add more than the recommended amount, as the consistency of the paints will change. If you do not use all this paint mixture during its active period, you must wait 48 hours before adding more Versatex.

A Word about Dyes

If you are interested in getting your feet wet using dyes without a lot of fuss and expensive equipment, then Jacquard Green Label Silk Colors and Jacquard iDyes are the way to go. Because the Green Label Silk Colors are in ready-to-use liquid form, you don't have to deal with mixing dye powder or chemicals: you use them straight out of the bottle. You can use them for direct painting, resist work, tie-dyeing, and any other technique that I recommend using thin textile paints for. You can steam-set the finished product just as you would traditional dyes, or you can set it with Jacquard Permanent Dyeset Concentrate mixed with water. Easy!

Jacquard's iDyes are for dyeing natural fabrics in your washing machine. Simply toss the contents of a packet of color into your washing machine along with some salt and you're good to go. With 30 vibrant colors to choose from, it couldn't be easier.

Profile: Deidre Adams

Deidre Adams's unique approach to making art quilts is inspiring. I particularly admire her artistic process and how her work is transformed by that process. Deidre randomly stitches together pieces of fabric until they are the desired size for her finished piece. She then machine quilts the piece. The last step is to paint over the entire cloth with artist acrylic paints mixed with a textile painting medium. Her focus is on the study of shape, color, texture, and mark-making, and she often paints several layers before achieving the desired effect.

A resident of Colorado, Deidre's work has been published in many books and periodicals, including Ray Hemachandra's and Karey Bresenhan's *500 Art Quilts* (Lark, 2010) and *Quilt Visions 2010: No Boundaries* (Visions).
www.deidreadams.com; www.abstractions.deidreadams.com

Deidre Adam's *Facade* (40" × 67")

Profile: Judy Coates Perez

Judy Coates Perez is an internationally award-winning textile artist whose work encompasses a rich and diverse visual vocabulary of imagery that she has drawn from the folklore, history, and nature of the many countries she lived in with her parents as a teenager. Perez has continued with her travels as an adult to teach her techniques, and she likes to refer to herself as "one part gypsy and two parts visual alchemist." Her pieces *Black and Bloom All Over* and *8 Cups* are a fascinating mix of technique and medium. Her work breathes through layers of personal and universal symbolic imagery, nuance, and mystery. Both of these pieces were painted as whole cloths with a mix of acrylic paints, textile paints, acrylic inks, stamps, and stencils.

Judy has written numerous articles for *Quilting Arts* and *Cloth, Paper, Scissors* magazines, and has made several appearances on the PBS television program *Quilting Arts*.

www.judycoatesperez.com

Judy Coates Perez's *8 Cups* (left, 24" × 60") and *Black and Bloom All Over* (right, 36" × 48")

CHAPTER 3

Selecting Your Fabric

The fabric you choose for your textile painting projects should, in most cases, be made from plant-based, natural fibers. Natural fibers are more absorbent, which means that some of the paint and water can penetrate the fibers instead of just attaching to the surface. My understanding is that a 50/50 blend of natural and synthetic fibers works equally as well, but my personal experience is with 100 percent natural fibers.

I am particularly fond of silk. Generally speaking, the application of paint transforms a shiny surface to matte, but if you keep the paint relatively thin, a slight sheen will come through. Sometimes you might want to use a length of fabric with a very shiny surface specifically to add contrast between the painted and the nonpainted surfaces, as paint has the tendency to leave a matte finish.

Experimenting with Silks and Cottons

If you are just beginning to explore fabric surface design, I recommend working with and trying the fabrics described in the chart below. They are all tightly woven with a smooth surface that will produce consistent results. As you become more experienced, you can branch off and use fabrics that are loosely woven and/or textured in some way. This can be great fun, yielding unexpected and exciting results.

You can purchase fabric from your local fabric store, as well as online. Several online companies specialize in offering fabrics that are referred to as "prepared for dyeing" (PFD). These are good choices, as they do not have any oils, sizing, or treatments of any kind that might interfere with how the paint adheres to the fiber. Before painting on your fabric, you should always prewash it in hot water with a product called Synthrapol (available at some fabric stores and online art suppliers) or a detergent that is free of any scents or fabric softeners.

It can be beneficial to settle on a fabric you like and use nothing else for a while. When you concentrate on using one surface for a variety of techniques, you have time and the opportunity to understand your medium in much more depth than if you choose a different kind of fabric for every technique. With that said, sometimes you can't help yourself, and you

SCARF FABRIC MADE EASY

Several online companies offer scarf "blanks," so called because they are plain, unprinted, undyed fabrics with rolled hems and are ready for your creative hand. With hand-rolled, hand-sewn hems already completed, these scarves come in many different sizes as well as different fabrics. They are a fun and easy alternative to doing all the sewing yourself. Once you have painted on them, they make great gifts. Dharma Trading Co., Jacquard Silk Connection, and Exotic Silks are several companies that offer silk blanks; Dharma Trading has blank garments as well. (See page 306 for contact information for these companies.)

Silks and Cottons Suitable for Surface Design

Silks

Silk habotai (also known as China silk)	An excellent starter fabric; available in three weights; very economical
Silk broadcloth	Very densely woven; matte finish gives it a lovely weight and drape; can be pricey, but my all-time favorite
Silk crêpe de Chine	Densely woven; nice matte finish; drapes beautifully
Silk organza	Very sheer; crisp finish remains even after washing
Silk charmeuse	One side matte and the other very shiny; an extremely fluid fabric

Cottons

Cotton broadcloth	Traditional quilting fabric
Cotton sheeting	Densely woven but finer than broadcloth; some nice draping qualities
Cotton sateen	Similar to sheeting but with a slight sheen to the surface
Kona cotton	Heavy and densely woven
Pima cotton	Very soft, densely woven, durable, and absorbent

just want to try everything at once. Although there's no right or wrong way, it's important to recognize your personal learning style. The journey of creativity can be so much more enjoyable if you embrace who you are as a student!

Working with Your Fabric: Stretched or Flat?

You can paint on your fabric stretched horizontally slightly above your work surface or laid flat on it — your choice. Both ways yield great results, albeit different. Stretched fabric lends itself better to spray-painting techniques and direct painting with brushes: paint doesn't pool and you can distribute it more evenly. The surface also tends to dry more evenly, and

you can even speed up the drying time with a blow dryer or fan, if you wish. On the other hand, laying the fabric right down on your work surface is the only way to go when you're stamping, stenciling, or silk-screening.

Stretching and Suspending Fabric on a Frame

You have several options for stretching your fabric, from artists' stretcher bars and even embroidery hoops to frame systems designed specifically for stretching fabric, such as Pébéo Arty's Easy Fix Fabric Stretcher Frame (see page 31). Although this product can be a bit clumsy to use at first, it's a great system. Sharp, clawlike grippers are used to attach and stretch the fabric to the frame. One of its great advantages is that as your fabric loosens up or stretches out with the weight of the paint and water, you can easily reposition the pins

Stretching tools, clockwise from top: Pébéo Arty's Stretcher Frame, artists' stretcher bars, fabric pinned over artists' stretcher bars, embroidery hoop

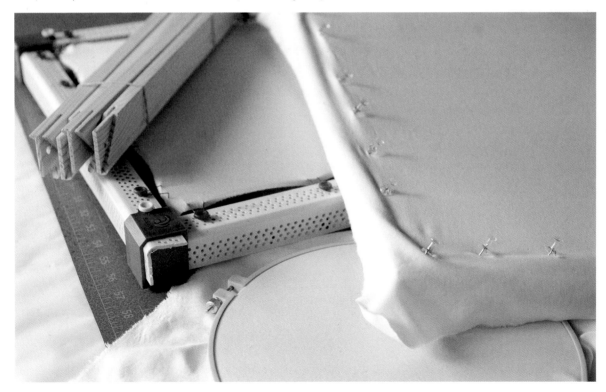

that attach the fabric to the frame. Also, the framework can be adjusted to fit different sizes of fabric, an especially nice feature if you are working with scarf blanks.

If your budget is tight, or if you are a quilter and working primarily with fat quarters, you can use the artists' stretcher bars that are designed for stretching canvases. Available at craft and art-supply stores, these are sold in pairs and are easily assembled by fitting the tongue-and-groove joints together. You can also purchase stainless-steel pushpins made specifically for stretching fabric. These pins will not leave rust spots or little holes in your fabric. There are also flat, three-pronged silk thumbtacks, but they are not made of stainless steel and may leave rust on your fabric. Additionally, these are not easy to remove if you want to restretch your fabric while you are working. Another option is Chinese fabric suspension claw hooks, which catch onto the edge of the silk so they don't get in the way when you're doing close detail work. If you plan to cut off the edges of the fabric after you've finished painting it, however, any pushpins or thumbtacks will do.

If you choose a stretcher system that involves the use of thumbtacks, please note that the three-pronged thumbtacks are specially designed to be flush with your frame once you have pushed them in. The theory behind them is that they do not get in the way of your arm as you are applying the resist. My experience, however, is that once the tack

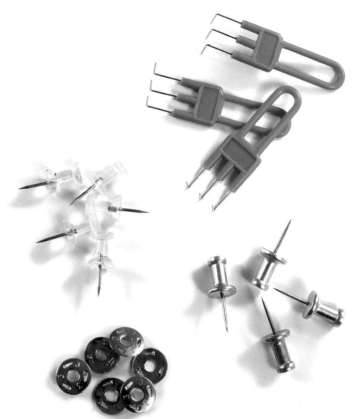

Pins for stretching, clockwise from top: Chinese fabric suspension claw hooks, stainless-steel pushpins, three-pronged silk thumbtacks, clear plastic pushpins

heads are removed, I inevitably end up dragging my arm through the wet resist. But even then, you might have to go back and fill in a missed or skipped area. Also, keep in mind that these tacks will leave rust spots on your fabric, making them a poor choice for any project that already has the hems sewn in before stretching.

FAT QUARTERS

Typically, when you ask for ¼ yard of fabric at a store, the salesperson measures out 9 inches as it comes off the bolt, so your ¼ yard measures 9 inches by however wide the fabric is. For a fat quarter, 1 full yard is cut from the bolt, then folded in half and cut; each half is again folded in half and cut. You end up with four pieces each measuring approximately 18 by 22 inches (the second measurement depends on the width of the fabric on the bolt). These pieces are known as fat quarters.

PROJECT: **Using Arty's Stretcher Frame**

SUPPLIES NEEDED

Stretcher frame pieces

Grippers

Scarf blank, or fabric cut or torn to about 1" smaller all around than the overall size of the frame

Scissors (optional)

STEP 1. Assemble the frame following the manufacturer's instructions. Cut or tear your fabric to measure about 1" narrower all around than the frame opening.

STEP 2. Starting at the corner closest to you, place the sharp pins of the gripper into the edge of the fabric, then insert the peg of the gripper into the closest hole. (If you are using a scarf blank, put the pins into the fabric just inside the hem.)

STEP 3. Turn the corner and insert another gripper in the same way.

STEP 4. Continue in this fashion down the side of the frame, spacing the grippers about 4" apart.

STEP 5. Continue on around the frame in this manner until all four sides are pinned to the frame. Pins on opposite sides of the frame should be offset in order to avoid forming ridges in the fabric.

Don't be afraid to stretch the fabric tightly. The fabric will get wet as you paint on it, and depending on how much water you use, it will sag. When this happens, just move the clawlike grippers one hole back.

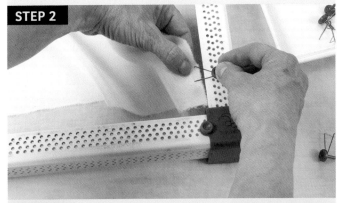

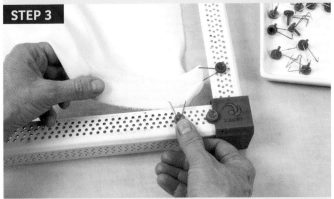

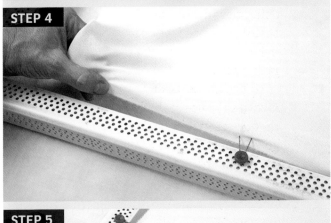

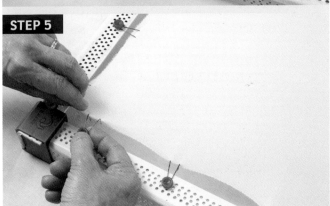

PROJECT: **Using Artists' Stretcher Bars**

SUPPLIES NEEDED

Artists' stretcher bars

Hammer

Staple gun and staples

Fabric, cut or torn to about 1" larger than the overall size of the frame

Pushpins

Scissors (optional)

STEP 1. Assemble the frame by matching up the tongue-and-groove components at the mitered corners. You might need to tap the outside of the frame with a hammer to get everything to fit snugly and to be square.

STEP 2. Using a staple gun, put a staple or two across the miter at each corner to keep the frame from slipping out of shape.

STEP 3. Place a pushpin through the fabric at the center of the side of the frame closest to you. Place pins to the left and right of the first pin, spaced about 2" apart, while pulling slightly on the fabric.

STEP 4. Turn the frame so that the opposite side is facing you and pin down the side of the fabric opposite the first, stretching the fabric as you go. To avoid ridges forming across the fabric, try to offset the pushpins from those on the first side.

STEP 5. Pin and stretch the third and fourth sides in the same manner. Stretch the fabric as you move toward the corners. The fabric should be tightly stretched. When the paint causes it to sag, you can reposition the fabric and pins to tighten it up again. Continue placing pins, alternating sides, until the entire piece is fastened down.

LAYING THE FABRIC DIRECTLY ON THE WORK SURFACE

Direct painting on unstretched fabric can give you fabulous effects as well. If you decide to try working with unstretched fabric, pin the fabric to your work surface or use painter's tape to give the fabric a little more stability. A muslin drop cloth over the plastic and under the fabric you are working on will help to absorb some of the moisture and prevent the plastic from leaving a texture. It also becomes a bonus itself: you'll have a piece of painted fabric to work with on a future project or collage!

Designing with Original Fabric

The cotton duck I used for this vest was actually a windfall: it was a piece I originally used under a piece of silk chiffon laid directly on my worktable, unstretched, while I painted it with thin textile paints using a foam brush. I finished the fabric with stamps and decorative stitching done with a sewing machine. The vest is lined with a piece of cotton lawn that was scrunched and painted with thin textile paints (Dye-Na-Flow and Setasilk).

CHAPTER 4

Painting the Base

Preparing a base fabric, then adding prints and other embellishments, allows you to create a fabric that is rich with imagery and dimension. Sometimes all you need is a little bit of mottled color to get yourself going. The easiest way to achieve this base is with direct painting and spray painting. This chapter and the next describe many ways to get started on this wonderful, creative adventure.

Direct Painting on Wet and Dry Fabrics

You can paint on dry fabric or wet it before painting. This chapter begins with a basic exercise that illustrates the difference between the two. If you have experience with water-color painting, you'll recognize the approaches, although the end results are a bit different.

Paints

In addition to medium-body transparent and thin textile paints, you can use acrylic ink, Tsukineko ink, or acrylic paints mixed with the appropriate textile medium. If you're using transparent paints, dilute several of the colors you've chosen with water at a ratio of 1 part paint to 3 parts water in plastic containers. Shake, mix, or stir until all the paint is dissolved. Preparing the paints this way allows you to grab them quickly while working. Thin paints, such as Setasilk or Dye-Na-Flow, do not need to be diluted. They can, however, be mixed with up to 25 percent water to obtain a lighter shade. Instead of water, you can use a light-ening medium, which lightens the shade of the color without compromising the pigment level and thus the intensity or saturation of color. To achieve lighter shades, mix these paints with the appropriate medium. (See Comparing Textile Paints, page 18, for information about the paints; see Liquitex Professional Acrylic ink! page 21, and Golden Artist Colors Acrylic Paints, page 20, for further information about these materials; see Basic Color Theory, page 293, for advice on mixing colors.)

Applicators

Experiment with a variety of different kinds of brushes, including watercolor brushes, sponges, inexpensive bristle brushes, basting brushes (yes, the ones you use for cooking!), feather dusters, or anything else you could substitute for a brush. For sponges, use either synthetic dish-washing sponges or natural sponges like clay artists use. You may be able to find small packages of these in the watercolor section of a craft or art-supply store.

Fabric

I like to start out painting a fairly large base fabric, so that I can later cut it down and crop it in order to use the areas of the fabric that I feel are the most successful. For your first

experiments, use tightly woven, smooth fabric measuring about 24 by 30 inches. Prewash it in hot water using Synthrapol or a laundry detergent with no scent or fabric softener. You can stretch it following the instructions on pages 31 or 32 or lay the piece directly on your prepared work surface, although it's a bit more difficult to keep it flat and stretched. Pin or use painter's masking tape on all four sides of the fabric, and stretch it as tautly as possible. You might want to lay a muslin drop cloth between your fabric and the plastic covering on your table if you decide to lay it flat.

PROJECT: **Painting on Wet and Dry Fabric**

SUPPLIES NEEDED

Work surface covered with plastic sheeting

Prewashed fabric (see page 28), 24" × 30"

Stretcher frame (optional)

Rustproof pushpins or thumbtacks or painter's masking tape

Assorted brushes and/or sponges

Medium-body transparent textile paints and/or thin textile paints

Plastic containers for rinsing brushes

Hair dryer or fan (optional)

STEP 2

STEP 3

WET SIDE

DRY SIDE

STEP 1. Stretch your fabric on a stretcher frame or lay it flat on your work surface and pin or tape it around all four sides.

STEP 2. Using a clean brush, wet one half of the fabric liberally with water; leave half the fabric dry.

STEP 3. Dip one of your brushes in paint, then draw it across the full width of the fabric, covering both wet and dry sections with the same stroke. Notice how the paint on the wet side bleeds out, but on the dry side it stays pretty much where you painted it.

STEP 4. Use different brushes and/or sponges to experiment with various strokes and other ways you can make marks on the fabric. Do the same thing on both wet and dry sides, so you can experience and compare the differences.

STEP 5. Heat-set according to manufacturer's directions, at the temperature appropriate for your fabric.

Once you have some experience under your belt, stretch another piece of fabric and try again, only this time be more purposeful with your attempts. If you liked a certain "accidental" mark or technique, do it again. Give yourself permission to experiment with the material, so that you learn what your new tools and paint can do. At this early stage, you will find it far more rewarding if you do not saddle yourself with trying to accomplish specific ideas or themes.

EXPLORING THE POSSIBILITIES:
Direct Painting

- **Capture the moment Ⓐ.** Paint continues to bleed and change as long as the fabric is wet. If you find yourself liking the way it looks before the fabric completely dries, you can halt the bleeding and capture the effect you like by using a hair dryer to speed up the drying process.

- **Paint with sponges Ⓑ.** Wet a sponge with plain water, wring it out well, and then dip it in paint. Use it like a brush to apply paint to your fabric. Or, try dabbing the paint-laden sponge onto wet fabric. You can use the sponge to remove, as well as to apply, paint.

- **Pour and push Ⓒ.** Pour the paint out of a small container directly onto the fabric, and then use a sponge to push the color around or to pick up color.

- **Blend colors Ⓓ.** Apply another color right up against the first one, and observe how much the colors mix, depending on whether they are in the wet or dry area of the fabric.

- **Try layering.** Paint a layer and let it dry. Then go back in and paint another layer on top of it.

- **Blended edges.** When you paint on the dry side, you might notice a dark-edged ring develop around the painted surface. If you don't like this, spritz a bit of water on it and work gently with a brush or sponge at the very edge of the paint to soften it a bit.

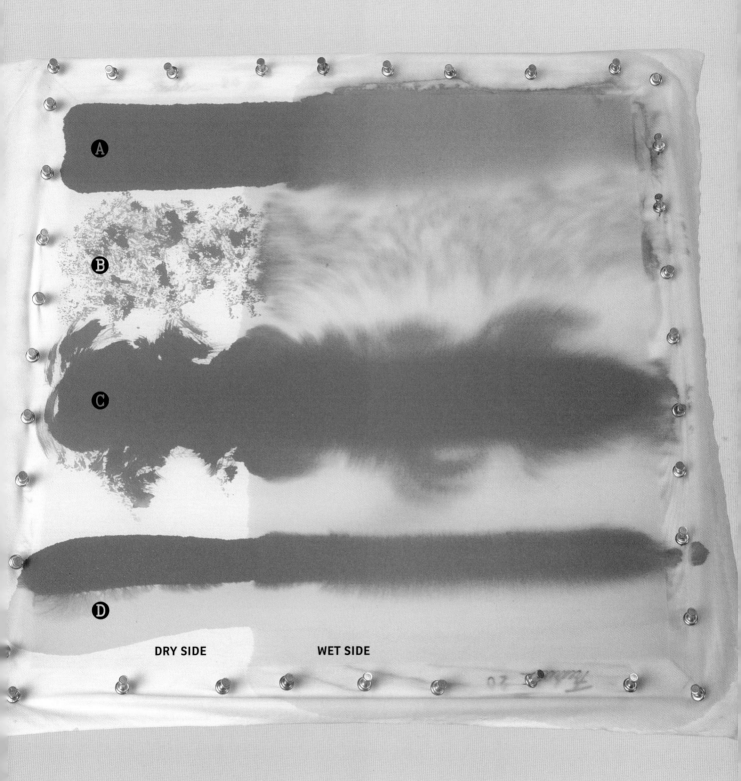

DRY SIDE   WET SIDE

EXPLORING THE POSSIBILITIES:
Color Blending

- **Shading.** Prepare at least three different shades of the same color by adding small amounts of water in succession, depending on how many gradations you want. For example, prepare one container with the color full strength; a second container with the same color diluted with water in a ratio of 1:1; a third container in a ratio of 1 part paint and 3 parts water. Continue in this manner if more shades are desired.

  Using a foam brush, paint the gradations of your prepared colors in a striped pattern, starting with the lightest shade and working up to the darkest. Each time you switch colors, overlap the first and last brushstrokes of each color. You may need to go over the overlapped areas with a semidry brush to aid the blending process. Try this on fabric that has been moistened with water, either from a spray bottle or foam brush, and again on dry fabric.

- **Complementary color blends.** Instead of using different dilutions of the same color, you may want to create a blend from one color to its complement (see Gail Callahan's Color Grid on page 294), such as green to red, as shown on the facing page. Work from the lightest to darkest color as described for blending shades of the same color. Remember to use a different brush for each color.

Spray Painting

Applying paint from small spray bottles is a great way to get the base coat of color onto your cloth.

Paints

Use thin textile paints and/or transparent textile paints diluted in a ratio of 1 part paint to 3 parts water. For lighter shades use lightening medium. You can also use acrylic ink, Tsukineko ink, or acrylic paints thinned with the appropriate textile medium. You can use just one color, or layer the colors to get a wonderful sense of depth. Keep in mind that when you spray multiple layers of wet paint, the colors will blend on the fabric as you work. If you add too many layers of paint while it's all still wet, you will get brown. If you want pure color to layer over pure color, allow the paint to dry completely before adding another layer.

Once you understand color mixing theory, you can purposely choose to mix colors directly on the fabric. For instance, you could spray yellow on your fabric, leaving some white areas. Then, while the yellow is still wet, spray on some red, trying to keep some areas just yellow. Where the red overlays the yellow, you'll get orange, but the plain yellow areas will remain yellow and plain red will remain red. Your end result will be a lovely combination of those three colors gently blending and morphing from one to the other. This makes a beautiful base for printing and other techniques, because it already has a depth and movement that solid-colored fabric does not have.

Applicators

When you're shopping for spray bottles, you'll discover that they aren't all the same. Some spray a nice even arch of color, others dribble, while still others give you a halo effect. I have found uses for all types. Look for them at drugstores, dollar stores, beauty- and art-supply stores, or online. If the spray nozzles of your bottles clog up, it could mean that the paint is too thick. Try adding some more water. If that doesn't work, unscrew the nozzle from the bottle, and place the feeding tube (the part that extends down into the liquid) in a cup of very hot water. With the tube still in the cup, start spraying. It may take a few sprays before the clog loosens up.

Method

As you work, let yourself experience the visual wonder of the colors — how they blend together and how they look when they are layered. Move your whole arm across the surface of the cloth as you spray, rather than adopting a point-and-shoot position. Think of your arm movements as those of a dancer. Or,

think of yourself as the next Jackson Pollock. Most people think that this great abstract expressionist painter simply splattered his canvases with paint in a random way, but in fact he carried out an elaborate choreographed routine. He often laid out his largest canvases on the ground outdoors. With a bucket of paint in one hand, he dipped his brush into the paint with his other, and then sprayed, dribbled, and poured the paint in an often-repeated pattern as he stepped across the width of the canvas. So, no random splattering!

PROJECT: **Working with Sprays**

SUPPLIES NEEDED

Work surface covered with plastic sheeting

Prewashed fabric (see page 28)

Stretching system

Silk thumbtacks, claw pins, or standard pushpins

3-ounce spray bottle or a plant mister filled with water

Small plastic spray bottles filled with three or more colors of paint (thinned or diluted)

Hair dryer or fan (optional)

STEP 1. Stretch your fabric on a stretcher frame as described on pages 31 or 32.

STEP 2. Spray a thin coat of water across the entire surface of the fabric.

STEP 3. Using at least three colors, spray the diluted paint on your fabric, alternating colors over the whole piece or concentrating each color in a specific area. This is your base coat.

STEP 4. Wait for the paint you applied in step 3 to dry, then add another layer of color. It is very important to allow each layer of paint to dry: paints mix when wet, often turning to an unwanted brown. If you're impatient, you can use a hair dryer to speed up the drying process.

STEP 3

STEP 4

STEP 5. Continue adding layers of color, allowing them to dry, and then applying another layer for as long you desire. If your fabric starts to sag from the weight of the water and paint, reposition your thumbtacks or stretcher pins to pull it taut again. As the layers build up, you'll start to see how each application of paint, color, and imagery adds depth and dimension to the overall piece.

STEP 6. Allow to dry, then heat-set according to manufacturer's recommendations, at a temperature appropriate for your fabric.

EXPLORING THE POSSIBILITIES: Sprays

- **Dribblers.** If you have a spray bottle that dribbles, use it on top of several layers of finer sprays or spray a couple of layers of dribbles. I especially like to apply diluted metallic paints with a spray bottle that dribbles.

- **Give it salt.** When your fabric is still very wet with paint, sprinkle kosher, rock, or table salt on the surface; you may also wish to experiment with starburst salt, a product designed specifically for use with dyes and textile paints, and available from craft suppliers. Because salt is a drying agent, each granule of salt will wick paint toward it, creating wonderful starry formations. The larger the salt crystal, the more paint gets wicked and the larger the formations.

- **Using resists.** Cover areas on the surface you're spraying with items like petals or leaves from silk flowers, plastic needlepoint screening, or motifs cut from cardboard or craft foam. Other possibilities include hair ties, washers, leaves, string, thread, and Popsicle sticks. Place these items randomly on the fabric and spray over the entire surface, then remove them either before or after the paint dries. If the paint has dried and your resist sat flush with the fabric, clean, hard edges will outline the shape of the resist; if the paint has not dried, it will bleed into the fabric where the resist was, creating a softer effect along the edges. (Resists not flush with the fabric will leave a soft, undefined image whether or not you wait for the paint to dry.)

- **Using stencils.** Cut a stencil, place it on the fabric, then spray the exposed area. (See chapter 7 for information about stenciling.)

Annette Kennedy learned traditional quilting from her grandmother and mother during the 1980s, and then moved onto making art quilts in 2003. Annette's quilts start with a photograph she has taken. She assembles the quilt top by using raw-edged appliqués that are fused to a base fabric, and then hand paints in the details and shadows.

The before-and-after series of Annette's quilts *Agave* (below) and *Stone Cellar* (see page 302)

illustrate beautifully how the subtle introduction of paint can be the culminating and transforming touch to a relatively flat but complex art quilt.

Annette's work has won numerous awards, been covered in many magazine articles, and been featured in Martha Sielman's *Art Quilt Portfolio: The Natural World* (Lark, 2012) and Joen Wolfrom's *Adventures in Design* (C&T, 2011). *www.annettekennedy.com*

Annette Kennedy's *Agave* in progress (from left to right), unpainted, painted, and quilted (17¾" × 22½")

Profile: Mickey Lawler

To me, **Mickey Lawler** is one of the first, if not *the* first textile artist to push the use of textile paints, rather than dyes, on fabric. We owe her much credit for inventing the technique she used to create her incredible *Skyscapes*, for which she painted yards and yards of cotton fabric stretched out in one long piece in her backyard.

Mickey lectures and teaches extensively and offers her one-of-a-kind hand-painted fabrics for sale. She has authored two books — *Skydyes: A Visual Guide to Fabric Painting* (C&T, 1999) and *Mickey Lawler's SkyQuilts* (C&T, 2011) — and been featured in many others.

www.skydyes.com

Mickey Lawler's *The Wall* (left; 31"×32") and Mickey at work in her backyard (below)

Profile: Pat Durbin

Pat Durbin's *Begonia Picotee Lace* (50" × 41")

Inspired by a photograph her husband took, **Pat Durbin** created this award-winning quilt by first painting the begonia and surrounding leaves with artist acrylic paints on white cotton. Once the fabric was stabilized, she used a sewing machine to go over the piece with machine thread sketching and embroidery. She added batting, then machine quilted the entire piece. Pat appliquéd a fabric border around the center image, then very successfully used beads for additional highlights. Pat likes to think of her work as bridging the gap between traditional and contemporary quilting. She certainly has developed a wonderful way of interpreting a realistic view of the natural world through the use of thread, cloth, and paint.

Pat's work has been exhibited throughout the United States, and she has received many awards, including several prestigious awards from the Houston International Quilt Festival. She lives in Eureka, California, with her husband. She has published two books: *Fabric + Paint + Thread = Fabulous* (That Patchwork Place, 2009) and *Mosaic Picture Quilts: Turn Favorite Photos into Stunning Quilts* (Martingale, 2007).
www.patdurbin.com
www.patdurbin.com/blog

47

CHAPTER 5

Adding Texture

Texture, or the illusion of texture, can add interest and dimension to your piece. Texture in a contrasting color can often be the finishing touch on a piece that needs just a little something else to pull it all together.

Basic Techniques for Achieving Texture

There are many ways to achieve the effect of textured fabric. As you explore the options, you'll no doubt discover a variety of common materials that you can use to create all kinds of effects. Let your own ingenuity take over to discover new tools and even newer ways to use them. Here are some suggestions to get you started.

- Bubble wrap, of any size; the smaller the bubbles, the better

- Rubber bands

- Scraps of burlap, or any other coarsely woven fabric

- Rubbing plates, available from art suppliers such as Dick Blick (Cedar Canyon is one brand); you may also find rubbing plates in the cake-decorating aisle of craft stores

- Plastic doilies or plastic lace

- Plastic needlepoint canvas

- Yarn or string

- Corrugated cardboard

- Crumpled plastic sheeting or plastic dry-cleaning bags

- Crumpled aluminum foil

- Plastic mesh bag (such as an onions bag)

Paints

You can use heavy-body, transparent, or opaque textile paints for textural effects, or use acrylic paints mixed with the appropriate textile medium. (See Comparing Textile Paints, page 18.)

Applicators

As well as the items suggested at left, you'll need a palette (a smooth surface to hold the paint) and a brayer to pick up the paint from the surface and apply it to the fabric. Smooth and easy to clean, the best palette is Plexiglas, available at shops that sell mirrors and glass, as well as at building-supply, hardware, and home-improvement stores. My favorite brayer is a 4-inch-wide Rollrite Multi-Purpose foam brayer, but do experiment to find the brayer that works best for you.

PROJECT: **Play with Texture**

SUPPLIES NEEDED

Work surface covered with plastic sheeting

Rubber bands in a variety of sizes

Prewashed fabric measuring about 18" × 22" (or fat quarter size)

Painter's masking tape

Paint

Plastic spoons, for scooping out the paint (optional)

Plexiglas sheet, about 11" × 13" (or other smooth, flat palette)

Brayer, for rolling out paint

STEP 1. Place an assortment of rubber bands on your work surface, and lay your fabric on top of it. Tape the fabric down.

STEP 2. Put a dollop of paint on the sheet of Plexiglas, then load the brayer with paint. The paint should evenly coat the brayer, but take care not to pick up too much paint. Dip into the paint using an up-and-down, or pouncing, motion while simultaneously rolling forward. Your goal is to spread the paint evenly on the brayer, not to spread the paint over the Plexiglas.

STEP 3. Roll the paint-laden brayer over the fabric. Avoid landing the brayer too suddenly on the fabric; this results in a sharp line where you make contact. For a softer look, use some finesse and go at the fabric with a smooth motion, striving to apply the paint gradually and evenly throughout. I think of this as "hitting the floor running." If you have a tendency to load on too much paint, roll out the brayer on another piece of fabric first. It's a good idea to wipe paint off the edges of the brayer before printing, to keep the edge of the print clean.

STEP 4. Get some visual distance from your piece before you go too far. After applying some paint, hang your piece up, and step back to take a good look at it. You'll find that a small amount of texture goes a long way, so take your time. You can always add more, but it's difficult to take paint away!

STEP 5. Allow to dry, then heat-set according to manufacturer's directions, at the appropriate heat setting for your fabric.

STEP 1

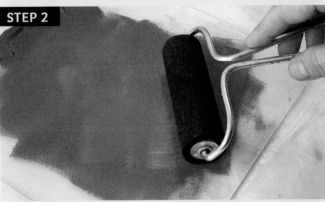

STEP 2

STEP 3

TRY THIS!

- **Use multiple colors.** Roll out several colors on the Plexiglas at once. Unless you want gray or brown, don't let more than a couple of colors mix.

- **Create different grains.** Change direction as you roll on the paint, angling the roller this way and that to achieve a variety of "grains."

EXPLORING THE POSSIBILITIES:
Texture

- **Vary the material Ⓐ, Ⓑ, Ⓒ.** Experiment with a variety of materials, including those listed on page 50 or others you discover.

- **Move around Ⓓ.** Change the position of the material you're using to achieve texture, striving for some inconsistency and/or overlapping images.

- **Use fabric crayons or Paintstiks Ⓔ.** Instead of rolling on paint, rub over the area with fabric crayons or Shiva Paintstiks. You can use the flat end or break off a piece, so you can use the side. (See pages 249 and 251 for more information on using crayons and Paintstiks.)

- **Rubber band–wrapped brayer Ⓕ.** Create a wonderful, bark-like texture by wrapping a soft brayer with rubber bands before rolling on the paint. This can be a little tricky, but it's well worth the trouble.

- **Afterthought Ⓖ.** Spread paint with a brayer on an art piece that has already been quilted. Take care that only the raised areas of the fabric get painted, while the areas with stitching do not. You'll have to experiment with different rollers and how much pressure to use. This technique can add lovely highlights and contrast to a piece that might seem too monochromatic.

- **More or less paint.** Notice how different the paint looks when the brayer is loaded compared to areas where the paint is almost gone. Use that difference to your advantage. You'll find that it adds dimension to the texture.

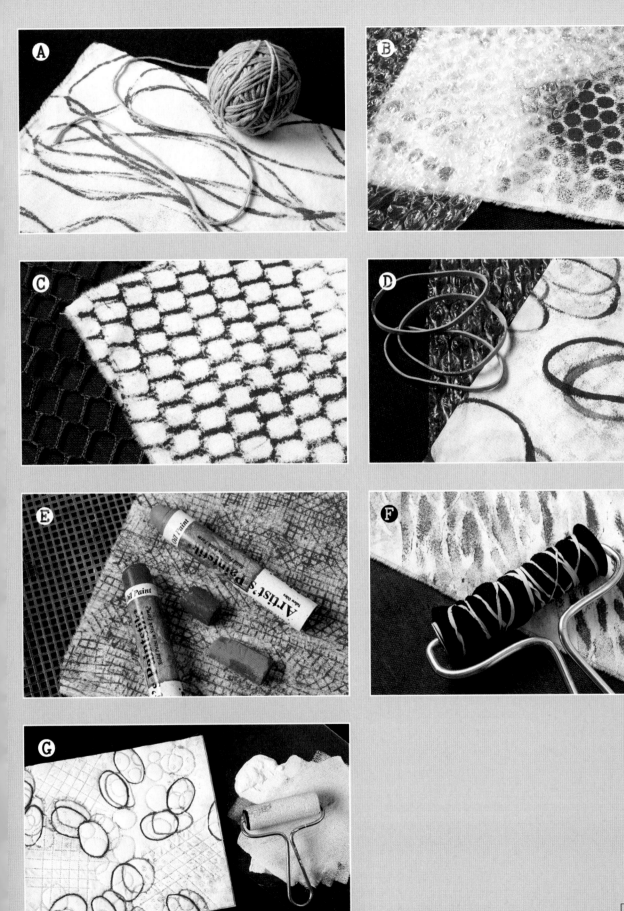

Fusible Webbing

Painting on fusible webbing is another way to add texture, along with the illusion of space and dimension, to your art piece. It often creates a veiled, mysterious quality as well. Because you can't wash a piece that you've applied fusible webbing to, or iron it without a piece of parchment paper, you can use this technique only on fabric that will not need to be washed or ironed, such as an art quilt.

I think of painted fusible webbing as one technique for creating fiber collage. The use of collage, no matter how small, cannot help but create dimension. By definition, collage elements exist on a different plane from adjacent elements, even if cut from the same piece of paper or fabric. Collage challenges the viewer to discover boundaries and to uncover multiple levels of imagery that are both one in the same and at the same time different.

Fusible Materials

Essentially consisting of glue, fusible webbing is a human-made product that melts when exposed to high temperatures, such as heat from an iron. Although the webbing was originally designed for adhering two pieces of fabric together (for such purposes as facings, appliqués, and quick hem repairs), fiber artists have discovered some intriguing ways to include it in their fiber art–making process. Note that once you iron it to your fabric, you must always lay a piece of baking parchment paper or a silicone mat over that area to protect your iron when doing any additional ironing.

My favorite brands are Mistyfuse, Wonder Under, and Lite Steam-A-Seam 2. The last two are available in packages of five 9-by-11-inch sheets at fabric stores. Some stores also sell them by the yard, and you'll find them put up both ways online. Mistyfuse, which is a very thin, wispy webbing, comes in small, rather expensive packages; for more reasonable pricing, you can purchase it online in 10-yard increments. I suggest that you buy a small amount of all three to experiment with.

Paints

Use thin textile paints, medium-body paints thinned with water, or thinned or medium-body acrylic paints. (They don't need to be as thin as dyes for this technique; see page 42 for more information.) You can apply the paint using inexpensive foam brushes or a spray bottle. Pour your paint into small, flat containers, such as disposable foam food trays, or a small cup wide enough to accommodate your brushes. You'll need one container for each color.

PROJECT: **Using Fusible Webbing**

SUPPLIES NEEDED

Work surface covered with plastic sheeting or newspaper

Paint

Small, flat containers for paint

Fusible webbing

Inexpensive foam brushes

Spray bottles (if you're working with Mistyfuse)

Hair dryer (optional)

Prewashed fabric (see page 28)

Ironing board and iron

Baking parchment paper

STEP 1. Pour your paints into containers.

STEP 2. Lay a piece of fusible webbing on your work surface. If you're using Wonder Under or Lite Steam-A-Seam 2, tear away the paper backing from one side, then lay it down with the webbing exposed (faceup).

STEP 3. Use a foam brush to apply paint to the webbing in any pattern you wish.

STEP 4. Wait for the paint to dry (or hit it with a hair dryer if you're impatient). When it's completely dry, remove the webbing from the paper backing. Sometimes it comes off in nice, clean sheets; other times it peels off in bits and pieces. Either way, the pieces are useful. You can either use the webbing as is (A) or cut or tear it into shapes (B).

STEP 5. Lay the piece of cloth you're working with on your ironing board or worktable, then place the fusible webbing where you think it might look good. Cover it with a piece of baking parchment paper, and press over it to adhere the webbing to the fabric. (Remember that even after this process, you must always cover the area with parchment paper when you iron it.)

MISTYFUSE

Mistyfuse, which doesn't have a paper backing, can be gently stretched out, giving it an even lighter and airier quality. Hold a piece using both hands, one hand on either side edge, then gently pull out. Do the same on the top and bottom edges as well. If you're using Mistyfuse, you may find it easier to apply the paint with a spray bottle.

STEP 3

STEP 4A

STEP 4B

STEP 5

EXPLORING THE POSSIBILITIES:
Painted Fusible Webbing

- **Create a web inventory.** Paint as much fusible webbing as possible, using a variety of colors and techniques. You can tap into this resource whenever you're in the heat of creating!

- **Layering.** Apply the webbing in layers.

- **Pictorial transfer.** Using acrylic paints, paint a very detailed picture on a piece of webbing, and then transfer it to your fabric.

- **Paintstiks.** Rub iridescent Shiva Paintstiks on top of the webbing after you have ironed it down. (See page 251 for information on Shiva Paintstiks.)

- **Watercolor effects.** Apply a weak dilution of paint as though you were painting a light wash of watercolor. After the paint dries, iron the webbing on an area of your cloth that already has some imagery, only partially covering the base image.

- **Stencils and stamps.** Stencil or stamp on the painted webbing with medium- to heavy-body textile paints or acrylic paints to add more dimensions. (For stenciling, see chapter 7; for stamping, see chapter 6)

- **Fabric appliqués.** After applying webbing, you can add fabric appliqués by simply laying them over the painted webbing, then ironing it again. This is particularly effective with silk organza or cotton organdy, which allows the painted webbing to show through.

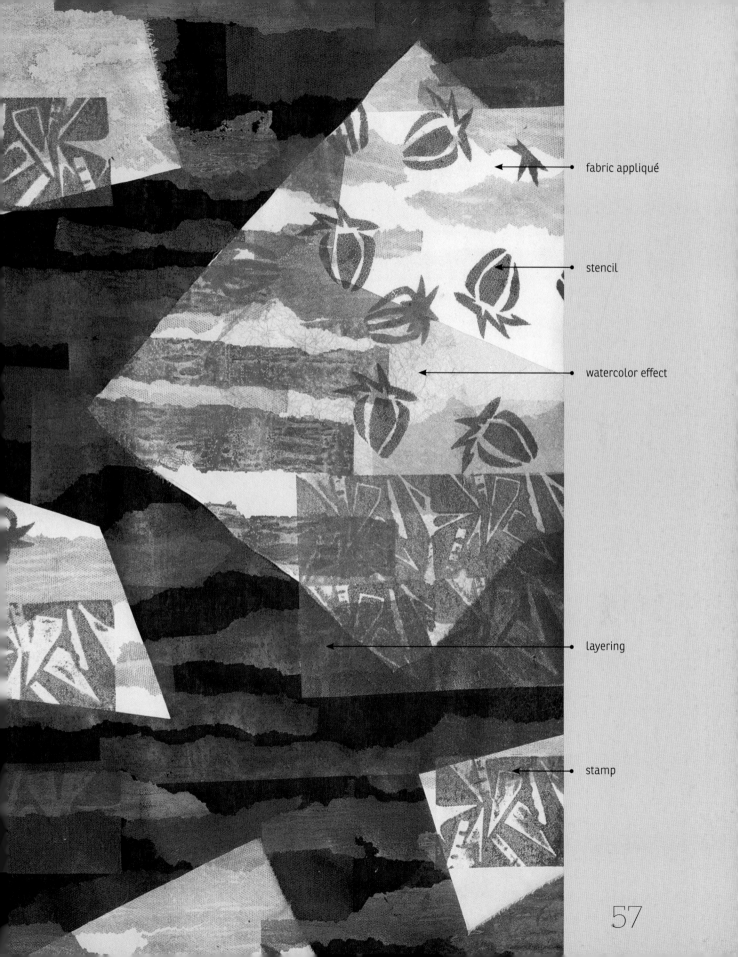

fabric appliqué

stencil

watercolor effect

layering

stamp

57

For my *Ribbon Jacket,* I stretched silk organza on a frame, then spray painted it with thin textile paints (Dye-Na-Flow and Setasilk). As I sprayed, using a different bottle for each color, I laid a plastic needle-point screen on the fabric as a resist to create the faint grid.

Profile: Linda Kemshall

Linda Kemshall lives in a small village in South Staffordshire, England, where she shares a studio with her daughter, Laura. Their textile artwork is incredibly rich with imagery and exemplifies the best of combined painting, drawing, and quilting. Linda is a master of her craft, spearheading many of the techniques we fiber artists now all take for granted. The piece shown here is a wonderful example of all that you can do with painted fusible web. I just love how she combines the embroidery work to further emphasize the high texture of the painted web.

Linda has written two books: *Color Moves* (Martingale, 2001) and, with her daughter Laura, *The Painted Quilt* (David & Charles, 2007), an impressive compilation of her techniques for painting on textiles after they have been quilted.

www.lindakemshall.blogspot.com
www.lindakemshall.com

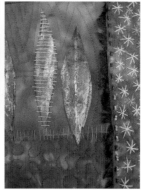

Linda Kemshall's *Jackdaw* (top; 18" × 24") and details

PART TWO

Surface Design Techniques

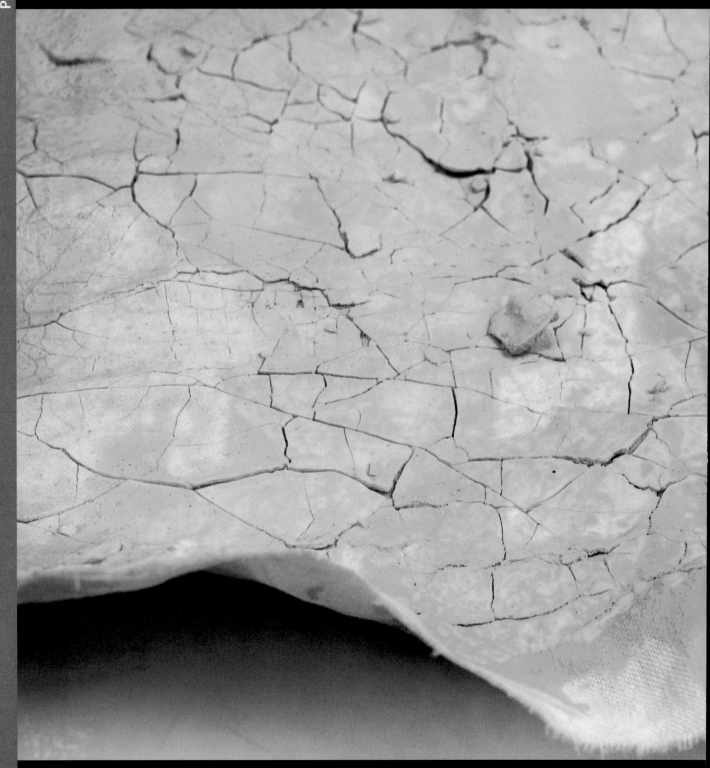

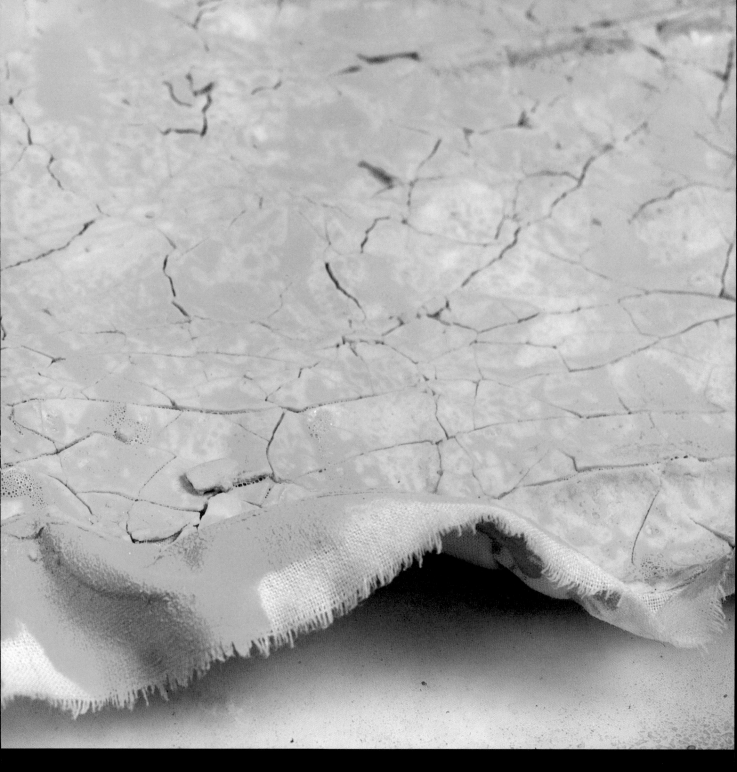

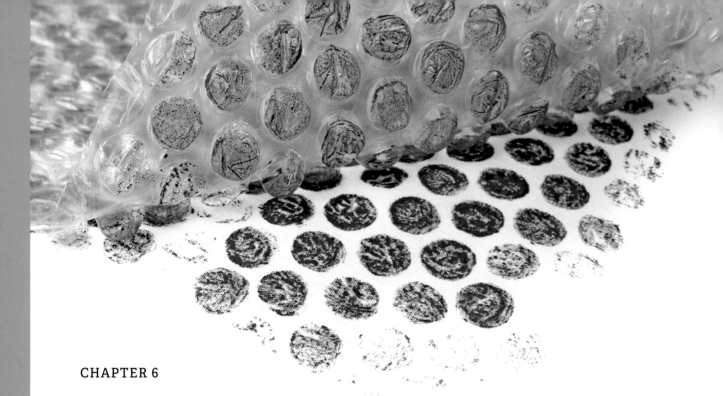

CHAPTER 6

Stamping and Relief Printing

Finding your own unique stamps is as easy as opening your kitchen drawer and pulling out an old cork, your potato masher, or the bumpy rubber thing you use to open tight-lidded jars. You can carve stamps out of wood, linoleum, erasers, and potatoes. You can also fashion them with sponges, weather stripping, craft foam, disposable foam food trays, and yarn. The possibilities are really endless. For example, a student of mine went home after a class one evening and discovered that the welcome mat at her back door had a decorative, open-weave design. So, after she wiped her feet on it, she took it inside, washed it off, and set about using it as a stamp! Anything you can spread paint on and then use to print onto your fabric can become a stamp. My personal favorite is to carve erasers, a popular technique that can be addictive!

It's very helpful to have an inventory of stamps to choose from when you're working, so spend some time thinking up designs. I like to trace several stamp-size outlines in my sketchbook, and then experiment by drawing designs within the just-the-right-size shapes. You'll soon find yourself seeing motifs and stamp design ideas everywhere you look, and even the simplest ones come in very handy. If you're in need of inspiration, take a look at pictures of hieroglyphics and Japanese woodblock prints. Dover Publishing books and coloring books have a wealth of copyright-free simple images that work well for stamps. (See Resources for suggestions.) You can copy the images you like or scan them into your computer. Many of these books come with a CD, making it a snap to download images you might want to use to your computer. As you develop your designs and ferret out sources of inspiration, don't underestimate the visual power of very simple shapes and forms.

Small stamps are easier to handle if you glue them to a base; otherwise, you often get paint on your fingertips, which transfers to your fabric when you're stamping. You can make good bases with foam core, wood, Plexiglas, or a piece of polypropylene. (The latter is a clear or white plastic that resembles corrugated cardboard and is generally used for making signs.) All of these are inexpensive and available at hardware stores and home-improvement centers. Have the Plexiglas cut into small, manageable pieces, or purchase an 8-by-11-inch sheet and use a Fletcher handheld plastic cutter to cut it into small pieces that you can glue your stamps to. Glue the stamps to any of these bases with an industrial glue like Eclectic Products' E-6000 adhesive or with hot glue.

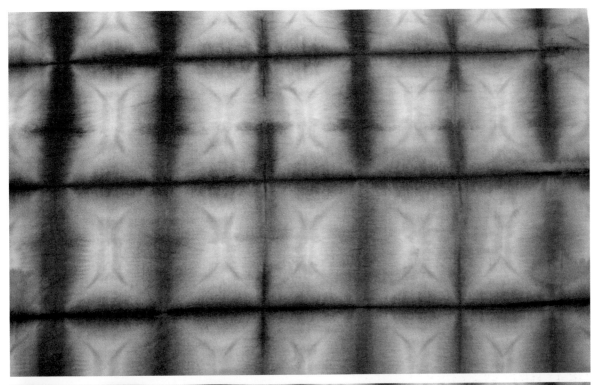

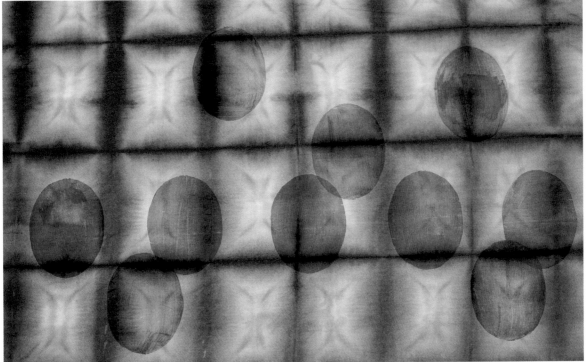

Simple shapes make excellent stamps. This garment fabric was quite striking, but I felt it needed something organically shaped to offset the grid. I used craft foam to cut the simple oval stamp; although it's so simple it may seem uninteresting, it was just the trick for making this fabric successful.

Stamps from Erasers

Staedtler Mars erasers are a very good carving material for stamps, but they can be pricey. They're readily available at art-supply and craft stores, as well as at most office-supply stores. I like carving Dick Blick's soap erasers, available by the box. They are very inexpensive and come in two sizes: 1-inch squares and 1-by-2-inch rectangles, both ⅝ inch thick. You can also use gum erasers. Their size makes them more manageable to hold, but they have a tendency to crumble more easily than the others described, which means that they have a shorter life span.

An X-Acto knife with a #1 handle and a size 11 blade is fine for carving, but fatter, rubber-type handles are also available and may be easier on your hand and finger joints.

STAMP CUTTING TIPS

- Start with easy shapes. When you feel like you're getting the hang of it, you can move onto something more complicated, such as zigzags. The reality is that you won't ever be able to cut a really complex design on erasers; they just don't hold up to a great deal of detail.

- Cut just a little bit at a time.

- When you cut along curved lines, it's sometimes easier to turn the eraser while simultaneously turning the knife blade.

- If the eraser breaks in half or in several pieces, glue the pieces to a sturdy base using an industrial glue, such as E-6000 adhesive (see page 64).

PROJECT: **Cutting an Eraser Stamp**

SUPPLIES NEEDED

Pencil

Erasers

Paper (optional)

Self-healing cutting mat or cutting board

X-Acto knife

STEP 1. With a pencil, draw the outline of your design directly on the eraser. Or, draw it on a piece of paper, and then flip the paper over on to the eraser and burnish the image onto the eraser by rubbing with your fingers. (*Note:* This gives you a mirror image of your original drawing; see page 68 for implications of this.)

STEP 2. With the eraser lying flat on the cutting mat, make the first cut with the blade of your X-Acto knife perpendicular to the surface of your eraser. Cut about one-third of the way through, deep enough so the paint won't build up too fast in the crevices.

STEP 3. Make a second cut at a slight angle to the first, and continue cutting to complete a section of your design.

STEP 4. From the side, cut horizontally in to free the piece of eraser that represents the negative space (that is, the area that will not receive paint and will not therefore print) in your image.

STEP 5. Remove cut pieces with the tip of your knife. Continue to cut away all the negative spaces in the same manner.

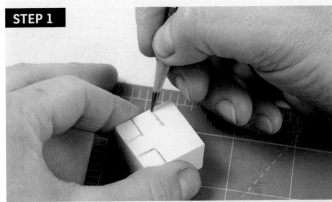
STEP 1

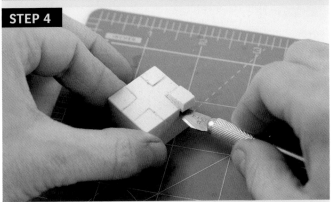
STEP 2

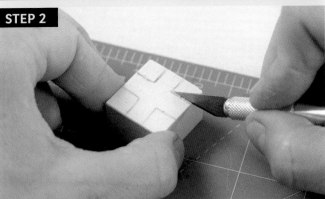
STEP 4

STEP 5

Soft Linoleum Block Stamps

Traditional linoleum blocks are hard to cut, but new products (such as Speedy-Stamp and Speedy-Carve from Speedball, E-Z-Cut, and Soft-Kut) make the work much more enjoyable. Some of these blocks have a consistency similar to that of erasers, but they're much bigger than erasers. An X-Acto knife may be hard to maneuver in the center areas of the block, so you may want to buy a set of linoleum cutters, if you plan to make a lot of large stamps. These sets come with a number of different-shaped blades, each enabling you to carve out a different-shaped groove in your block. Packages of replacement blades are also available.

THE IMPORTANCE OF DIRECT AND REVERSE IMAGES

Notice that when you use the transfer method described in step 2 on the facing page, the image on the block will be the reverse of your tracing. Your print will be like your original drawing, because when you turn it over and print, the image is again reversed. This is ideal for transferring text, as you can see in the lower print shown here. (The tracing on the left was laid facedown on the block and burnished onto the surface to create a mirror image of the R.) On the other hand, if you want your final print to be the reverse of your drawing, trace your design on tracing paper, turn the tracing paper over, and go over the image that shows through on the back side of the tracing paper. Now, place the back side of the tracing paper against the block and burnish to trace the design. Your final print will be the reverse of your drawing. Make sense? Understanding and predicting how your final image is going to look is an important part of many different printing techniques.

PROJECT: **Cutting a Linoleum Block Stamp**

SUPPLIES NEEDED

Paper (same size as block) and pencil

Blank soft linoleum block

Spoon, bone folder (a bookmaking tool; see page 207 for further information), or scoring tool (used in scrapbooking)

Set of linoleum block cutters

STEP 1. Draw your design on a piece of paper the size of your linoleum block. (You can also trace around the block and then draw your design within the space.)

STEP 2. Transfer the design by laying the paper drawing-side down on the block and burnishing (rubbing) the back of the paper with the edge of a spoon, bone folder, or scoring tool. (If you made your drawing with a soft pencil, you can simply use your finger to burnish the design.)

STEP 3. Choose the linoleum cutting blade that best fits the negatives spaces of your design, and begin to carve. (You might want to practice a bit on a smaller eraser first.)

STEP 4. When you are finished carving around the central design, cut away the material on the outside edges of the block adjacent to your design. This will help you see exactly where to place the stamp on your fabric.

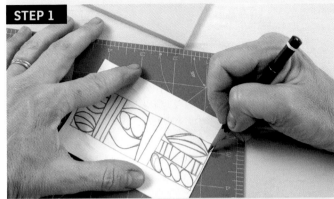

STEP 1

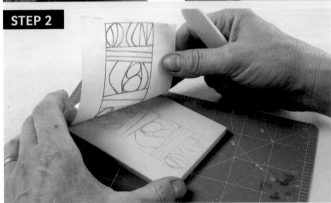

STEP 2

STEP 3

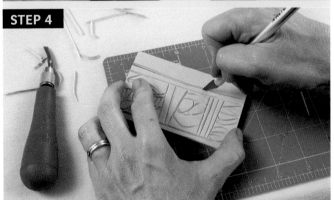

STEP 4

Using Your Custom Stamps

Try to stretch your imagination by reminding yourself that there is no right or wrong way to do most of the techniques described in this book, including stamping. As I tell all my students, my role is to help you go beyond your own visual comfort level. Be brave. Have the creative courage to do the unexpected. If you think what you've done is just horrible in the end, you can always throw it away — although I would encourage you to save even your mistakes, because a certain aspect of any one of them may be just the thing you need for a future art piece. I like to think of each piece I do as visual inventory. If collage is your love, these saved pieces will enable you to create a fiber collage sometime in the future using only your own imagery and elements you've created. If you are a beginner, keep in mind that you will learn far more from your mistakes than from your successes.

Paints

When you choose your paints for stamping, remember that unless you use opaque paints, the paint colors you already have on your fabric will show through the stamped image. This greatly adds to your goal of visual dimension.

If you've carved very detailed images on a soft linoleum block, you will have to use ink from an ink pad rather than paint. This is because even a light application of paint would more than likely fill in the negative spaces of your stamp. I recommend VersaCraft ink pads made by Tsukineko, which can be heat-set on fabric for permanence.

Work Surface

Stamping needs to be done on a flat surface with a bit of give to it. It can't be done on stretched and suspended fabric. If you haven't made a padded work surface (see page 8), you can work over a bath towel folded in half, a scrap piece of polar fleece, or a small stack of newspapers, covered with plastic sheeting.

CARING FOR YOUR STAMPS

If you take good care of your hand-made stamps, they will serve you well for a very long time. Try not to allow paint to dry on stamps; wet paint is easier to wash off than dry paint, and textile and artist acrylic paints tend to dry pretty quickly. When you finish making impressions with your stamp, wash the paint off as soon as possible. Using an old toothbrush and some soap, gently scrub away the paint.

PROJECT: **Printing Your Stamp**

SUPPLIES NEEDED

Padded work surface covered with plastic sheeting

Foam brushes or any flat brush measuring about 2" wide (or larger for big stamps)

Medium- or heavy-body textile paints, or artist acrylic paints and the appropriate textile medium (see page 18)

Stamp

Prewashed fabric (see page 28)

STEP 1. Dip your brush lightly into the paint, and brush it across your stamp. Use enough paint to make a clean image, but not so much that the paint fills in the negative spaces or squishes out the sides as you print.

STEP 2. Press the stamp onto your fabric. Take care to put pressure around the edges of the stamp as well as in the center. This is especially important if your stamp is large. Rock the stamp back and forth from edge to edge without actually lifting the edges up.

STEP 3. If the stamp is small, lift it straight up and off the fabric. When working with larger stamps, lift one side first, as if it had a hinge, then lift the whole stamp up and off the fabric.

STEP 4. Set the fabric aside to dry completely. Heat-set (see page 22) if necessary.

A WORD ABOUT COMMERCIAL STAMPS

Commercial stamps are very tempting to use, but because they are designed for use on relatively small sheets of paper, the overall scale of the imagery is usually small. Also, the depth of a stamp intended for use on paper is much shallower then the ideal depth of a stamp meant for printing on fabric. Although commercial stamps are licensed for your personal use, it's possible that there could be copyright infringement if you were to sell an art piece that incorporates the use of these stamps.

EXPLORING THE POSSIBILITIES:
Homemade Stamps

For some of these experiments, you will need additional supplies, such as Velcro, materials that create texture, a brayer, hot-glue gun, yarn or string, weather stripping, Magic Stamps, disposable foam food trays, Fun Foam, craft foam, roller stamp, and linoleum block.

- **Erasers Ⓐ & Ⓑ.** Make a stamping block by gluing several erasers in a row to a sturdy base. Or, create a mix-and-match stamp block: Attach the loop side of self-adhesive Velcro to the underside of the erasers and a strip of the hook side to a piece of Plexiglas. You can then rearrange the erasers for different-patterned stamps.

- **Abstract texture Ⓒ.** Choose items you've collected to create texture (such as bubble wrap), use a brayer to apply paint directly to the material, then stamp it onto your fabric. If the area you are printing is large, rub your hands or a clean brayer over the stamping material.

- **Yarn and string Ⓓ.** Use a hot-glue gun or E-6000 glue to attach yarn or string, swirled or curled as you wish, to a piece of Plexiglas.

- **Weather stripping Ⓔ.** Cut pieces of weather stripping into different shapes, then apply to a sturdy base.

- **Foam brush Ⓕ.** Use a foam brush as a stamp. Here, I printed the side of the brush, which reminds me of a tall, narrow house.

73

EXPLORING THE POSSIBILITIES:
Homemade Stamps (cont'd)

- **Disposable foam food trays Ⓐ.** Cut the sides off the tray, then use a ballpoint pen or pencil to carve a design in the foam, taking care not to cut all the way through, or take a hard, flat object (such as a coin, as shown here) and press it into the foam. Roll paint onto it with a brayer, then stamp the image on your fabric. Scratch-Foam is a commercial product that does the same trick.

- **Fun Foam and craft foam Ⓑ.** Because you can cut shapes from these products with scissors, you can make fairly elaborate designs. Buy the kind with a self-adhesive backing. With a pencil or pen, draw your design directly on the foam. If your design is complex, use embroidery scissors to cut it out. Because the foam is thin, adhere your cutout to another piece of foam larger than your design, then cut around it to make a double-layer stamp. (The two pieces don't need to exactly match.) Fasten the stamp to a sturdy base.

- **Rolling stamp Ⓒ & Ⓓ.** Make a rolling stamp by cutting shapes from craft foam or weather stripping and gluing them to an old rolling pin, lint brush, brayer, or foam roller.

- **Linoleum blocks Ⓔ.** I printed with this abstract stamp four times, twice with a direct application of the paint and twice as "ghost" prints — a second print without renewing the paint.

- **Magic Stamps Ⓕ.** These moldable foam stamps manufactured by PenScore are great fun to work with. Heat a block with a hair dryer or heat gun, and then press a shape (such as a seashell or, as shown, a clothespin) into the soft foam. You'll be printing the negative space around the image, not the image itself. The stamps are reusable, so if you don't like what you made or you'd like to try something new, you can reheat the stamp and begin again. Just be careful not to melt the foam.

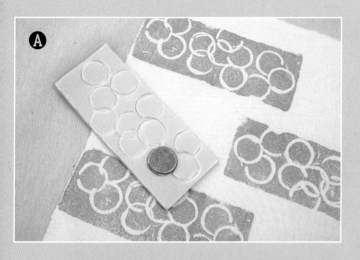

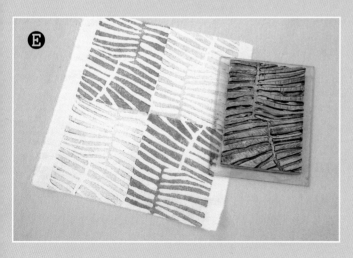

75

EXPLORING THE POSSIBILITIES:
Homemade Stamps (cont'd)

- **Smoother paint application Ⓐ & Ⓑ.** If you don't like your brush-strokes showing on the stamp, put some paint on a large foam brush and use it as a stamp pad. You can also use a stencil brush to dab the paint onto the stamp in a pouncing motion, or apply the paint to it with a brayer. (For more about using pouncing, and the use of a brayer, see page 51).

- **Glitter Ⓒ & Ⓓ.** Brush a bit of permanent, water-soluble white glue on the eraser. Stamp it on the fabric, then quickly sprinkle glitter on the glue. When the glue is dry, shake off the excess glitter. (Catch the glitter on a piece of wax paper so that you can put it back in the bottle and reuse it.)

- **Purposeful stamping Ⓔ.** Rather than take one stamp and stamp it randomly all over your fabric, try to be more purposeful about it. You might like the controlled look of a border. Even a partial border can rein in a piece that is a bit too wild visually.

- **Random energy Ⓕ.** Instead of purposeful stamping, maybe you'd like to go in the opposite direction: let some of the stamps go right off the fabric. This will give your piece the sense that it is larger than what you can actually see. It gives the piece energy.

- **Overprinting Ⓕ.** Use fabric you have already sprayed or direct painted.

- **Wet-and-dry technique Ⓕ.** Lightly brush water over the areas of the fabric where you plan to stamp, leaving parts dry. Place your stamp so it falls partially on a wet area and partially on dry. The paint will bleed a bit where the fabric is wet, but the image will be crisp on the dry fabric. It is a nice effect that easily adds a bit of dimension to your piece.

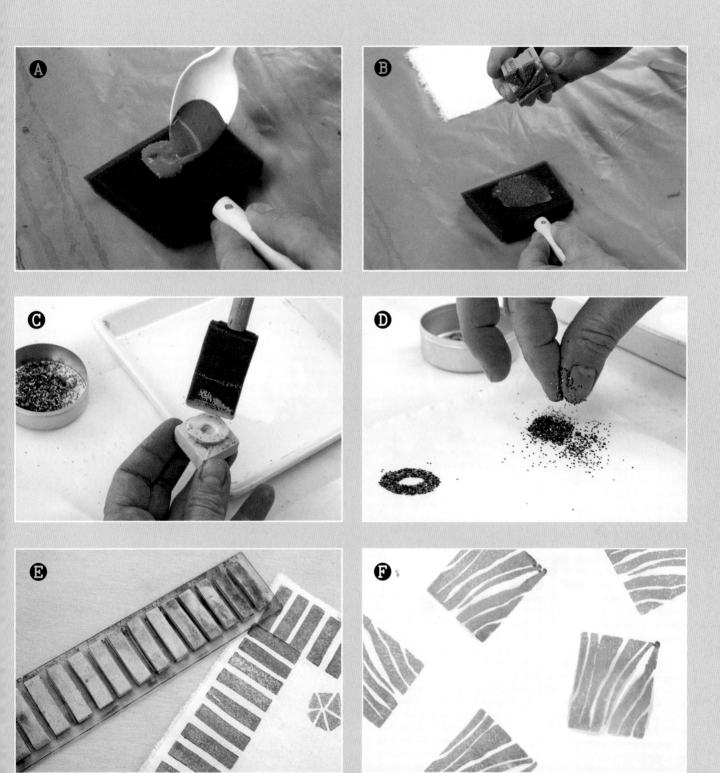

To create the fabric for this long vest, I stretched a length of silk chiffon, wet it, then used a foam brush to paint it with thin textile paints. After this base coat was thoroughly dry, I removed the fabric from the frame and stamped the peach-colored motifs on the garment after assembling it. I used two different stamps made from carved erasers. As a final embellishment, I added beads.

This vest uses two different fabrics: a brown cotton commercial batik (pre-printed with circles) and a pima cotton that I painted with thin textile paints (Dye-Na-Flow and Setasilk), some pieces in turquoise and some in a mustard color. I brushed the paint on wet fabric that was not stretched. The large leaves are stenciled, and the smaller shapes are printed with stamps carved from erasers.

CUSTOMIZING BOTH FABRICS AND GARMENT DESIGNS

When I'm planning my wearable art pieces, I often start with one, two, or even three different commercial patterns. I mix and match the different elements of each pattern until I like the result. For example, I might take the sleeve from one pattern, the collar from another, and perhaps the overall scale from yet another. To create the garment fabric, I begin by direct painting (or dyeing) a base fabric of the required yardage. At this stage, before applying any additional surface designs, I lay out and cut the pattern pieces. Then, taking into account the overall flow and drape of the finished garment, I compose and apply the different design elements directly on the cut pieces using techniques discussed throughout this book, such as stamping, stenciling, and screen printing.

CHAPTER 7

Stenciling Techniques

With stencils, you can print the same image as many times as you like. Among their many advantages, stencils have a wonderful way of simplifying an image by using both negative and positive spaces to their fullest. We usually think of something referred to as "negative" as being either nonexistent or undesirable. In the world of art and design, however, *negative space* refers to the space around an image, and often that space is just as interesting, if not more so, than the image itself. The Dutch graphic artist M. C. Escher was a master at negative and positive space deception! As you create your own designs, take advantage of this characteristic of stencils by paying close attention to both negative and positive space. Inspiration for cutting stencils is all around you. The potential for a new and exciting stencil is in every object you see. You don't even have to get out of your seat and open a book!

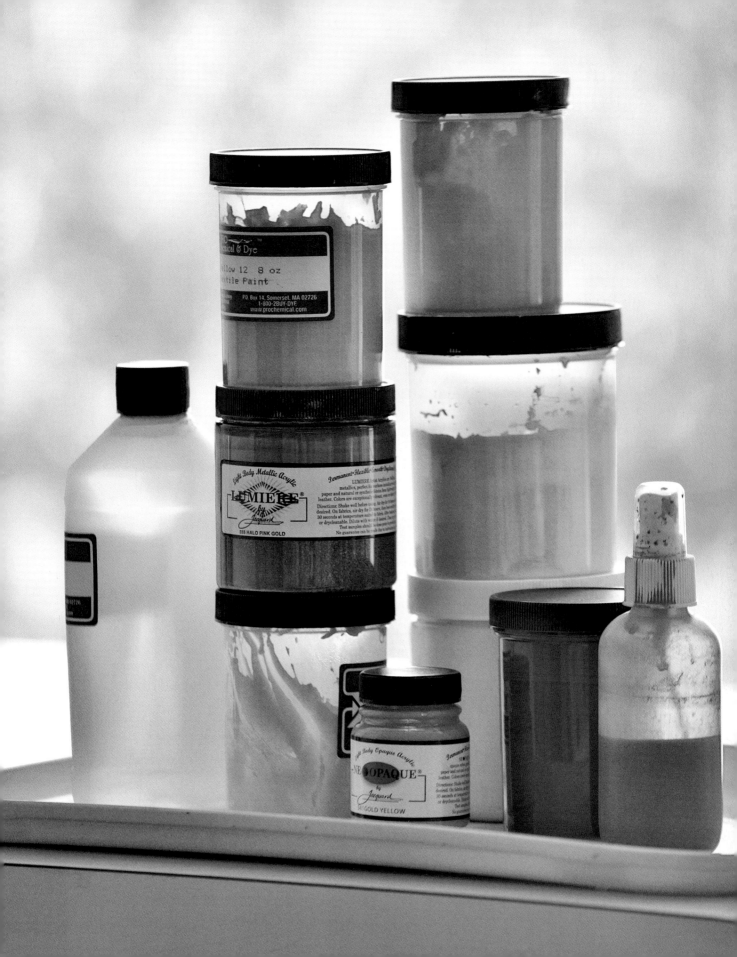

Stencil Material

The best material to cut stencils from is stencil film, which is available from a variety of suppliers. I like Grafix's Matte Stencil Film because it doesn't tear while you're cutting it, and it's very thin while still being durable. Grafix also makes Clear-Lay film that is very much like the plastic used for overlays. It is a breeze to cut, so it's worth trying when you're cutting a complex design, but it may tear if you aren't careful. I also like Wax-O stencil paper (by Scratch-Art) because, unlike Mylar and plastic films, its waxy surface is less likely to tear when you're cutting inside corners. These stencils don't last as long as acrylic ones, however. You can also cut stencils from overhead transparencies found at your local office-supply store and freezer paper from the grocery store.

DESIGNING IDEAS

- Don't throw away the part of your stencil you cut out! You can use it as a resist when you are spray painting.

Cutting Tools

You also have several choices for cutters. For cutting printing blocks (see page 68), I recommended an X-Acto knife with a size 11 blade and a #1 handle. That will work for cutting stencils as well, but you may also want to try an X-Acto with a swivel mechanism for the blade. This takes a bit of getting used to, but after your initial attempts, it makes cutting curves much, much easier! Electric stencil cutting tools are also available at craft-supply stores and online. These tools feature a hot tip that melts the plastic to make the cut. The tools are easy on your hands, but the melting plastic emits fumes, so it should be used only in a well-ventilated area or outside.

PROJECT: **Cutting a Stencil from Stencil Film**

SUPPLIES NEEDED

Drawing paper and pencil

Permanent marker

Blue painter's tape

Self-healing cutting mat or cutting board

Stencil film

X-Acto knife with a size 11 blade

STEP 1. Draw your design on a piece of paper, outline the design with your marker, and tape the paper to your cutting mat or board.

STEP 2. Place the stencil film over your drawing, tape it down, then use the permanent marker to trace over your drawing.

STEP 3. Remove the tape and your drawing, then carefully cut out your design along the marker lines using the X-Acto knife. When cutting curves and circles, it is sometimes easier to turn the stencil film as you cut, rather than moving the knife itself.

BUILDING BRIDGES

Designing and cutting your own stencils can be very rewarding. Start out simple; if you are basing your project on a complex design, you will have to simplify and make adjustments to the imagery to make it work as a stencil. Sometimes you'll need to join up the separate pieces with bridges, as in the case of this letter B stencil. Don't under-estimate the visual power of very simple shapes and forms!

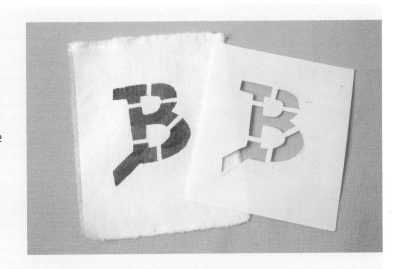

Using Your Stencils

Images made from stencils have a particular look. While many of the other techniques you use to apply images to your fabric, such as direct painting and spraying, may appear to recede into the background, stencils make images look as if they are sitting on the surface. This characteristic contributes greatly to a sense of depth and dimension in your design.

Paints

When you choose your paint, remember that medium-body and even some heavy-body paints are transparent, so the colors and images already on your fabric will show through the stenciled image. I prefer PROfab textile paints from PRO Chemical & Dye for most of my stenciling projects, but you can also use Jacquard Textile Color and Neopaque, as well as artist acrylic paints mixed with the appropriate textile medium (see page 19 for advice).

I usually pour or scoop out small amounts of two or three different colors on my palette, so that as I pick up paint with my brush, I can take more than one color at a time (a little of each), getting unplanned color variations on the fabric. This keeps the images from looking flat. If you use complementary colors (see page 294), don't let them mix too much, or you'll have brown or gray before you know it.

Applicators

Of the many kinds of stencil brushes that are available, I find the ones that work best on fabric are those made with a spongy material rather than with hair. Second best are those with very short and stumpy natural bristles. The synthetic, long-hair brushes are the least expensive, but they aren't worth a penny. Regardless of what you choose, you'll need a different brush for each color.

Work Surface

I like to stencil on a hard surface, especially if I'm using spongy brushes, so pull out some heavy cardboard or your cutting mat to put under your cloth before stenciling.

Fabric

Prewash your fabric in hot water using Synthrapol or heavy-duty laundry detergent without scent or fabric softener. If the fabric is lightweight and slippery, tape or pin it to your work surface, then tape the stencil to the fabric. Another way to prevent the fabric from shifting is to use a Teflon nonslip mat, such as Grip-n-Grip, between your work surface and the fabric. Or, you can use a removable spray adhesive, such as 505 or 404 Spray and Fix, or KK 2000 Temporary Spray Adhesive from Sulky. (See Resources for where to find these items.) Spray one of these on the back of your fabric so that it sticks temporarily to your work surface; any remaining adhesive can be removed with rubbing alcohol after you're finished stenciling.

PROJECT: Stenciling a Simple Design

SUPPLIES NEEDED

Work surface covered with heavy cardboard or a cutting mat and plastic sheeting or newspaper

Painter's tape or masking tape

Pushpins or straight pins (optional)

Prewashed fabric (see page 28)

Teflon nonslip mat or removable spray adhesive (optional)

Stencil

Medium- or heavy-body textile paints, two or three colors

Palette or other flat container for the paint

Stencil brushes

Damp cloth

STEP 1. Tape or pin slippery fabrics to your work surface, or use a nonslip mat or a removable spray to anchor it.

STEP 2. If your stencil is large (anything you can't comfortably hold down with just one hand) or if the fabric is slippery, tape the stencil to the fabric or use spray adhesive to hold it in place.

STEP 3. Spoon out two or three different-colored paints onto your palette.

STEP 4. Pick up paint with your stencil brush by dabbing it into the paint with an up-and-down pouncing motion. After some experience, you'll know how much paint is enough, so don't fret about your first attempts. In stenciling, however, the general rule of "less is more" definitely applies.

STEP 5. With your free hand (unless you've used tape or adhesive), hold down the stencil around the area you're painting. Apply paint to the stencil using the same up-down motion you used in step 4 to pick up the paint. Pay special attention to the edges to ensure that you have nice, clean outer lines. Avoid using the brush with a sweeping motion, as this can easily force paint under the edges.

STEP 6. Gently lift the stencil off the fabric with one hand, using your other hand to hold down the fabric if necessary.

STEP 7. Continue to print additional images as desired, always taking care to check the underside of your stencil *before* laying it down on a new spot. Often some paint seeps under the edges and attaches to the underside of the stencil, causing blobs the next time you lay it down. Keep a damp cloth nearby to clean off your fingers as you work.

STEP 8. After the paint has dried, heat-set the fabric (see page 22) if necessary.

EXPLORING THE POSSIBILITIES:
Stenciling

- **Supplies other than paint Ⓐ.** Use fabric crayons or paint sticks instead of paint (for advice, see Shiva Paintstiks on page 251)

- **Layering Ⓐ.** Use fabric you have already spray painted or printed on as your base.

- **Change stencil size Ⓑ.** Use your computer's printer to make copies of your design in several different sizes, then cut a stencil for each size and print them randomly over your fabric.

- **Highlighted images Ⓒ.** After the paint dries, use paint and a brush or paint sticks or other markers to highlight and enhance your image.

- **Use the negatives as a resist Ⓓ.** Instead of leaving the square outside edges of your stencil, cut them off, echoing the shape of the original design. Use that new outside edge as part of the finished stencil.

- **Overprinting Ⓔ.** Paint your stencil first with a dark color. Allow it to dry. Line the same stencil up slightly askew with the first printing, then print again with a lighter, or different, color. The first print will look like a shadow of the second, instantly adding depth to your piece.

- **Metallics Ⓕ.** This is a great time to get out some metallic paints. Jacquard Lumiere paints are particularly beautiful when used for stenciling.

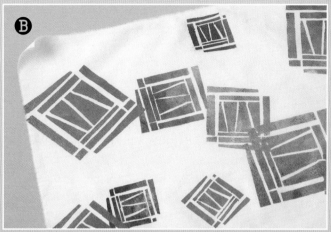

Freezer-Paper Stencils

Packaged in a large roll, freezer paper is sold in most grocery stores. One side of the paper is matte, and the other (the shiny side) is coated with a thin layer of plastic that can be ironed to your fabric. The beauty of freezer paper is that you can cut intricate designs using a pair of scissors rather than a knife, but the disadvantage is that the stencils are somewhat flimsy, and so you can usually use them only a few times.

You can create an original drawing or transfer an existing drawing with the use of graphite paper. Graphite paper is available in art-supply stores and online. Place it between the image you're copying and the freezer paper, then trace over the drawing: as with old-fashioned carbon paper, the pressure of the pencil transfers the drawing onto the freezer paper. To avoid marring the original drawing, cover it with a piece of tracing paper and draw over that.

PROJECT: **Stenciling with Freezer Paper**

SUPPLIES NEEDED

Freezer paper

Drawing pencil

Blue painter's tape

Tracing paper (optional)

Graphite paper (optional)

Paper scissors or an X-Acto knife with a size 11 blade

Prewashed fabric (see page 28)

Iron and ironing board

Work surface covered with plastic sheeting

Teflon nonslip mat or removable spray adhesive (optional)

Medium- or heavy-bodied textile paint or artist acrylic paint mixed with the appropriate medium

Foam stencil brush

STEP 1. Cut a piece of freezer paper big enough to hold your design, plus a border 1½" or more all around.

STEP 2. Draw your design on the matte side of the freezer paper. If you are transferring an existing drawing, you may want to tape down the papers to hold all the layers in place, with tracing paper on top and graphite paper sandwiched in between.

STEP 3. Cut out your design with scissors or a knife.

STEP 4. Position your fabric on your ironing board. Place the stencil, shiny-side down directly on the fabric (A). With your iron set on medium, iron the freezer paper to your fabric (B). Be gentle, keeping your pressure fairly light and checking the edges of the freezer paper every couple of minutes to see if it is sticking.

STEP 5. Place your fabric with the stencil on your prepared work surface. If the fabric is slippery, you may want to use a nonslip mat or removable adhesive to keep it from slipping as you paint.

STEP 6. Apply the paint with a foam stencil brush.

STEP 7. Allow the paint to begin to dry to a matte finish before carefully removing the freezer paper. It is important for the paint that is on the freezer paper to have completely dried so you don't accidentally drag it across your fabric when you are pulling it off. You may be able to use one freezer-paper stencil several times before throwing it away.

STEP 8. Heat-set the paint (see page 22) if necessary.

STEP 3

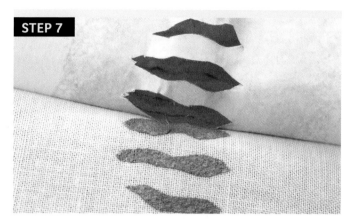

STEP 7

STEP 4A

STEP 4B

STEP 6

Caring for Your Hand-Cut Stencils

Don't leave dried paint on your stencils. Wet paint is easier to clean off than dry paint. Lay your paint-laden stencil down flat in your sink or in a washbasin. Gently wash it with a soft sponge, warm water, and some soap. Turn the stencil over and repeat the process on the other side.

I like to store my stencils lying flat in a drawer. I often put the smaller ones in the plastic sleeves designed for loose-leaf binders so their edges don't get caught up with some of the other larger stencils.

A Word about Commercial Stencils

The same precautions hold true for commercial stencils as I mentioned regarding commercial stamps (see page 71), with the exception of those with basic shapes like squares and circles, or perhaps a grid. These are difficult to cut by hand, and purchased precut ones are often useful.

89

I made this short, kimono-style jacket using a pattern from the Sewing Workshop collection called the Plaza Jacket (see Resources for information). To prepare the silk broadcloth, I scrunched the fabric and then spray painted it using thin textile paints diluted with water. The filled-in feathers and leaves are stencils, and the outlines of the leaves are silk screens.

To prepare the base for this jacket fabric, I stretched silk habotai on a frame, wet it, then sprayed it with pink textile paint. When the fabric was almost dry, I brushed on the yellow lines. Once the fabric was completely dry, I used a stencil to print the leafy vines and purple flowers.

90

Profile: April Sproule

April Sproule's up-cycled dress

I love **April Sproule's** up-cycled dress. It went from a frumpy, shapeless, long knit dress destined for the trash to a short, contemporary "little, black dress" with a distinctly Asian flare. April used Jacquard Lumiere and Neopaque textile paints with her own custom-cut stencils after recutting the dress using a commercial pattern. April finds that this particular way of working liberates her creativity.

April has been working with fabric for years. As a young child growing up in northern California, her grandmothers taught her a wealth of needlework skills, including sewing, quilting, knitting, lace making, and embroidery. April went on to study at the San Francisco School of Fashion Design. After graduation, she worked in the apparel and accessories industries in both the United States and Canada and is pleased now to be running her own business. She offers her stencil designs for sale through her website.
www.sproulestudios.com
www.sproulestudios.blogspot.com

CHAPTER 8

Nature
Printing

Printing from nature is indeed a straightforward, simple process. It harks back to our childhood days when the thrill of visual magic lurked behind something as mundane as a bottle of paint, a paintbrush, and a potato cut in half, or that a sunny spring day could produce X-ray-like images of feathers and leaves on a piece of painted cloth. However simplistic this process may seem to you, don't underestimate the high level of beauty, grace, and sophistication you can achieve from leaf printing, vegetable printing, and *gyotaku* printing, the Japanese art of fish prints.

Printing with Plants

Nature printing with leaves can be so rewarding. First, you collect those leaves, which may require a lovely walk in the park or a hike in the woods. Like collecting shells at the beach, collecting leaves can be a peaceful, meditative experience. You search, look, and observe — in other words, you're being attentive to your surroundings.

Bring your sketch pad and camera along on your walk. Besides finding leaves to print with, look for patterns to stencil and stamp, as well as all kinds of wonderful things to use for sun, collagraph, and gelatin printing (see pages 100, 112, 114). You might even want to pick up some small, flat pebbles to sew onto an art piece.

You can use nature prints as a way to identify the trees and other plants in your area, as well as exotic houseplants. Leaf prints also make lovely additions to other surface design techniques, as well as being complementary images to stylized designs. For example, I like to combine my hand-drawn, silk-screen images of leaves with prints from real leaves.

After collecting them, you can keep leaves green and fresh for quite a long time by putting them between sheets of dampened paper towels, then in a ziplock plastic bag. I have successfully stored them this way in my refrigerator for months at a time. You can also extend their life considerably by putting them in the freezer, but you need to defrost and dry them before using them to print.

Paints for Leaf Prints

Use medium- or heavy-body textile paints or artist acrylic paints mixed with textile medium and a drying agent for printing plant material on fabric. If you use PROfab textile paints, mix some of their PRO No Dri into it to prolong the time before the paint begins to dry. This makes it easier to wash off what may be a delicate leaf.

Applicators

If your goal is to print the whole leaf, apply paint to it with a brush, sponge, or dauber (see Homemade Dauber, left). If you want a more delicate look, with just the stem, veins, an outline of the leaf, and a faint image of the leaf as background, you may want to carefully apply the paint with a brayer, making sure to roll the paint out to the very edges of the leaf. If you don't want any brushstrokes from your method of paint application to show (you'll find that even a foam brush produces faint directional lines), see Homemade Dauber at left for instructions for making your own "grainless" applicator.

Other Supplies

Cut newspaper into 6- and 12-inch-squares, or whatever size will fit over your leaves while you are printing. (Pages from old telephone books work for this purpose, too.) You are going to use two sheets per leaf, so make yourself a nice pile before you start printing. You'll use these to protect the plant material as you imprint its image and to keep your hands clean of any excess paint.

HOMEMADE DAUBER

No brushstrokes ever show with this little homemade tool. All you need is a traditional round, doll-shaped wooden clothespin, a round cosmetic sponge, and a rubber band. Place the cosmetic sponge over the "head" of the clothespin, and use the rubber band to secure it in place.

PROJECT: **Making a Leaf Print**

SUPPLIES NEEDED

Work surface covered with plastic sheeting

Leaves of all shapes and sizes

Newspaper sheets, cut to size

Paint and paint palette

Foam brushes, cosmetic sponges, a brayer, and/ or a homemade dauber

Prewashed fabric (see page 28)

Sponge brayer for rubbing (optional)

Damp towel for wiping your hands (this can be a messy operation!)

STEP 1. On your plastic-covered work surface, place a leaf on a piece of newspaper, if desired, and apply paint to it with a brush, sponge, brayer, or dauber.

STEP 2. Carefully pick up the leaf and place it paint side down on your fabric, making sure that none of its edges roll under.

STEP 3. Put a piece of newspaper on top of the leaf, then rub on it with your hands or a soft sponge brayer to smooth the paint onto the fabric.

STEP 4. Carefully lift off the newspaper. (It will more than likely have paint on it, so be careful where you put it down. I usually crumple it up right away and throw it in the trash so I don't have any accidents.) Carefully lift off the leaf. I like to wipe it clean with a damp rag right away so I can use it again.

STEP 5. Use the same leaf to make additional prints. Most leaves will last through many printings.

STEP 6. Allow the paint to dry and then heat-set (see page 22), if necessary.

95

EXPLORING THE POSSIBILITIES:
Printing with Fruits, Vegetables, and Flowers

Remember potato printing in kindergarten? Well, it isn't just for kids. You can successfully use all sorts of fruits and vegetables for printing on fabric using medium- or heavy-body paints and artist acrylics mixed with textile medium. Some items I've found particularly successful are slices of rutabaga, carrots (crosswise or lengthwise, especially old floppy ones!), artichoke hearts, the butt end of iceberg lettuce, apples and pears, and star fruit.

- **Cabbage print Ⓐ & Ⓑ.** Cut a cabbage in half lengthwise, and use a brayer to apply paint to the exposed surface. Print directly onto your fabric.

- **Fruit prints Ⓒ & Ⓓ.** Cut an apple in half lengthwise and use a brayer to apply paint to the exposed area as you did for the cabbage. You may also like to cut the apple width-wise, for a different and equally interesting image. Star fruit makes an especially lovely print.

- **Flowers Ⓔ & Ⓕ.** Use a foam brush to apply paint to a flower. The flower stem makes a convenient handle to make the print. You can probably make several prints if you use sturdy plants, such as this daisy. When the paint dries, you may like to add stems and leaves to create a garden effect.

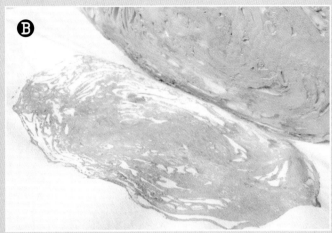

The Japanese Art of Gyotaku

This chapter wouldn't be complete if I didn't talk about a very different kind of nature printing: *gyotaku*, or the Japanese art of fish printing. *Gyo* means "fish," and *taku* means "impression" or "rubbing" in Japanese. The Japanese have been practicing gyotaku for more than 100 years. It was originally developed by fishermen to record the size of trophy catches. Later it was used for educational purposes in marine biology, but it also became an art form in its own right.

Image Maker

Prints are traditionally made from freshly caught, dead fish, but you can now buy rubber fish from art suppliers, such as Dick Blick, that work fairly well. If you decide to use a real fish, try to get a fairly flat kind, such as flounder or sole, for your first attempts. Traditionally, great care was taken to paint the fish in the same colors it displayed when alive, but you can paint it whatever colors you like. If you want to print more than one fish on your fabric, print them one at a time, waiting between each print for the previous one to dry completely.

PROJECT: **Gyotaku Printing**

SUPPLIES NEEDED

Work surface prepared with newspapers covered with plastic sheeting

A fish, real or rubber

Paper towels

Tissues (optional)

Cardboard or clay for propping up the fish

Foam brushes or a dauber

Palette for your paints

Medium- or heavy-body textile paints, such as Jacquard Textile Colors, Neopaque or Lumiere, PROfab, or Pébéo Setacolor, as well as any of the shimmer and metallic paints

Prewashed fabric (see page 28)

STEP 1. *For real fish:* Thoroughly wash and dry the fish with paper towels, paying close attention to any areas that may have mucus, which will stain your fabric. Plug up all orifices with paper towels or tissues; some people remove the eyes.

STEP 2. Set the fish on your covered work surface. To get a good print that includes the fins and tail, it helps to prop them up with cardboard or clay so they're level with the rest of the body.

STEP 3. Paint or daub the fish with an even but thin coat of paint. Lift the edges of the fish off the paper as you apply the paint, so that excess paint doesn't smear around the image when you print.

STEP 4. Lay your fabric on the fish. Using your hands, gently rub all around the fish, being very careful not to shift the fish's position.

STEP 5. Carefully remove the fabric.

STEP 6. Allow the paint to dry and then heat-set (see page 22), if necessary.

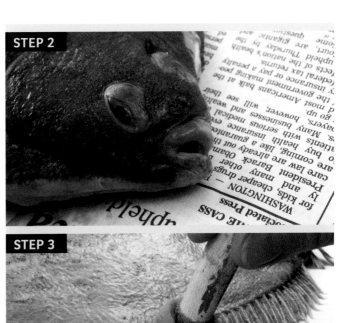

STEP 2

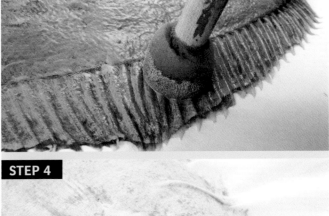

STEP 3

STEP 4

Sun Printing

Sun printing is a great project to do with the kids, but it can also bring some beautiful results for more sophisticated projects. The traditional sun-printing method is to place flat objects on freshly painted wet fabric, which you then set in the sun to dry. Areas under the objects dry lighter than the sun-exposed areas, where the paint is darker and brighter.

Image Makers

It's important to use only objects that will not curl or buckle from contact with the wet fabric. Typical items might be leaves, washers, feathers, plastic stencils, or shapes cut from craft foam or plastic stencil material. (Remember those pieces you saved from cutting stencils on page 82.) For fabric, a densely woven cotton works best.

Paints

You can successfully use any transparent textile paint for sun printing. Jacquard Dye-Na-Flow and Pébéo Setasilk and Setacolor Transparent, as well as PROfab textile paints, all work beautifully. The Setacolor Transparent should be diluted with water in a ratio of 2 parts water to 1 part paint; PROfab textile paints should be diluted with water in a ratio of 4 parts water to 1 part paint before use.

PROJECT: **Making a Sun Print**

SUPPLIES NEEDED

Plastic-covered board, foam core, a fabric-stretching system, or a large embroidery hoop (choose something that you can carry outdoors)

Painter's masking tape (or pushpins if you are using a board)

Paint, two or three colors, prepared as described above

Small containers or spray bottles, one for every paint color you use

Spray bottle for water

Prewashed fabric (see page 28)

Brushes and/or spray bottles

Flat objects to use as resists

Kosher, rock, starburst (see page 44), or table salt (optional)

Sunshine

STEP 1. Spritz water on your fabric from a spray bottle.

STEP 2. Using brushes and/or spray bottles, paint the fabric in a flowing, abstract way. Work quickly, keeping the fabric wet until it is placed in the sun.

STEP 3. Gently place a variety of selected objects on the wet fabric.

STEP 4. Sprinkle salt around the objects, if desired, to create a starburst effect as described on page 44.

STEP 5. Set the piece out in the sun to dry.

STEP 6. When the piece is thoroughly dry (this may take as long as 2 hours depending on the time of year and the strength of the sun), remove the objects and brush off the salt, if used.

STEP 7. Heat-set the fabric (see page 22), if necessary.

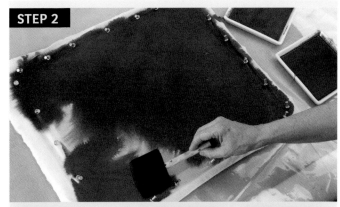

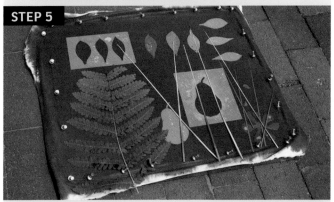

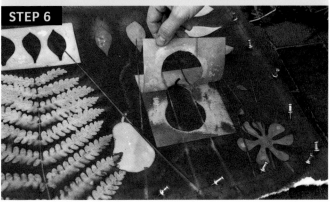

CHAPTER 9

Monotype, Collagraph, and Gelatin Prints

During the first 20 or so years of my art career, I was strictly a painter, even in my fiber work. I didn't have anything against other techniques; it was just that painting was my first love and the area in which I received my training. More recently, however, printmaking has taken center stage. It's no coincidence that I love monotype printing the best, of course, for it's the most painterly of them all. One might ask, "If it's so painterly, why not just paint?" My response is that as you work through this technique you will see there is a visual quality to monotype printing that direct painting just doesn't have. It seems to take the imagery one step further. I believe that this is because of the quality of light that resonates through the final printing, and there is always that element of surprise and serendipity.

Monotype Printing

You can prepare a plate for monotype printing by a "subtractive" method: completely cover the plate with paint, then remove bits of it with a rag, sponge, cotton swabs, your fingers, or drawing implements. This type of print is usually made only once, although sometimes a second, "ghost" image can be made with it as well. On the other hand, you can take an "additive" approach: purposefully paint colors and/or patterns directly on the plate and print from it. You can, of course, use both subtractive and additive methods on the same plate as well — my personal favorite way to monotype print!

Image Makers

For the printing plate, you'll need a flat, smooth surface, such as a sheet of Plexiglas measuring approximately 7 by 9 inches — longer if your design is an obvious horizontal or vertical. A 6- or 12-inch-square ceramic tile works nicely as well.

To create patterns on the printing surface, collect sponges, rags, pencils, paint scrapers, sticks, sponges, stencil brushes, cotton swabs, or any other implement that can be used to mark in the paint. Don't forget your fingers!

Paints

Use medium- and/or heavy-body textile paints for monotypes. My favorites are PRO Chemical & Dye's PROfab textile paints, although Jacquard's Textile Colors and Neopaque acrylics work well, too. Because textile paint dries much faster than ink, you might want to add PRO No Dri to these paints so you have more time to work with them before they start to dry. You can also use artist acrylic paints mixed with textile medium and an appropriate slow-drying medium. This is a great opportunity to use metallics as well!

Applicator

To ink (or paint) up your plate, you'll need a brayer. My favorite is a 4-inch-wide soft Rollrite Multi-Purpose foam brayer, model # 94B; it's available from Dick Blick (see Resources). For the palette, use another piece of Plexiglas or even a disposable foam food tray.

You might want to experiment with a foam brayer to create an interesting texture. I like Scratch-Art's 2½-inch Economy Foam Brayer (also available from Dick Blick) because you can cut abstract shapes out of the sponge roller with a pair of scissors. Inexpensive foam brayers with different shapes, such as dots and stripes, on them can often be found at the dollar store or in the kids' painting aisle of your favorite craft store. These foam rollers can be used to remove paint from your plate as well as putting paint on it.

Fabric

Good fabric choices are pieces of medium-weight cotton or silk broadcloth. Prewash fabric in hot water using Synthrapol or heavy-duty laundry detergent with no scent or fabric softener. Cut the fabric into several pieces that measure a couple of inches bigger than your printing plate.

GETTING VOCABULARY STRAIGHT

Many people confuse the terms *monotype printing* and *collagraph printing* with *monoprinting*. Although all three processes need a substrate or printing plate of some kind, the difference between monoprinting and monotype printing has to do with the printing plate itself.

- **Monoprinting.** An image of some kind is permanently etched into the surface of the plate, so that even though you change the ink or paint patterns, the etched image remains the same in every print made from that plate.

- **Monotype printing.** The plate itself is blank, and you develop the imagery by applying paint in various ways directly to the plate and then printing directly from the plate. The long vest shown above is made from a Tencel-and-silk blend. The filled-in circles are monotype prints done on a 6-by-6-inch ceramic tile with heavy-bodied textile paints. Because I was working on a large piece of fabric, I flipped the tile over to stamp the print on the fabric. I silk-screened the thin circles.

- **Collagraph printing.** A variety of textured elements are permanently glued to the plate. Paint is then applied, and a print is made with it. Every print created from this plate has the same imagery, but the prints can be done in different colors.

PROJECT: **Printing a Monotype**

SUPPLIES NEEDED

Work surface covered with plastic sheeting or newspaper

Textile or artist acrylic paints (two or three colors) mixed with textile medium or Golden's Silk-Screen Fabric Gel

Palette for your paints

Plastic spoons

Brayer

Printing plate (Plexiglas or ceramic tile)

Marking implements (see page 104)

Brayer

Prewashed fabric (see page 28), cut slightly larger than the printing plate

Clean foam brayer

Spray bottle with water (optional)

STEP 1. Dollop a few teaspoons of two or three colors of paint onto your palette.

STEP 2. Use the brayer to roll out the paint on your palette (see page 51 for advice on using a brayer).

STEP 3. Roll the paint out on your printing plate.

STEP 4. Using the implements you've collected for making marks, scratch through the paint on your printing plate to create line, texture, and pattern (A & B).

STEP 5. Lightly place a piece of fabric on the printing plate, then use a clean foam brayer to gently burnish it. Don't try to really saturate the cloth with paint: apply just enough pressure simply to print the image. It may take a few tries before you get the knack of how much pressure to use.

STEP 6. Remove the fabric from the plate.

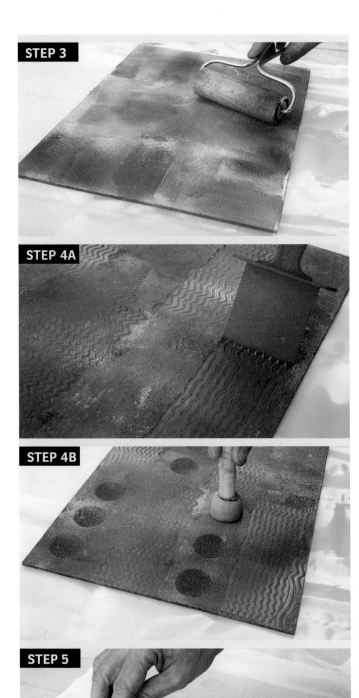

STEP 3

STEP 4A

STEP 4B

STEP 5

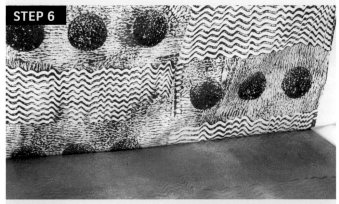

STEP 6

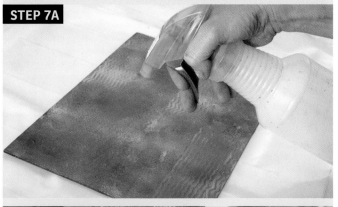

STEP 7A

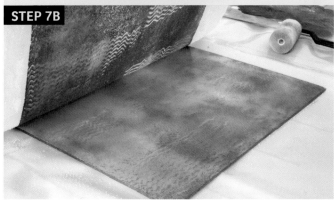

STEP 7B

STEP 7. Sometimes you can get a second ghost image by lightly spritzing the plate with water (A), then printing on a new piece of fabric or again on the same piece (B).

STEP 8. Allow the paint to dry and heat-set (see page 22), if necessary.

OVERSIZE FABRIC

When you use larger pieces of cloth, you'll need to flip your paint-laden printing plate over the fabric, instead of placing the fabric on the plate. Press firmly on the back of the plate and rock gently back and forth so you get a complete image. Be sure to use a padded work surface (see page 8).

EXPLORING THE POSSIBILITIES:
Monotype Printing

- **Linear motifs Ⓐ.** Arrange string and/or yarn in various ways to create wonderful linear patterns in your monotype prints.

- **Multiple prints Ⓑ.** Lay some of the flat items you collected on the paint-laden plate, then lay a piece of fabric over them and print. Apply more paint around the items or over them and print again. To achieve depth and dimension in your work, print on the same piece of fabric multiple times with multiple images.

- **Playing with negatives Ⓒ.** Use your stamps or a sponge (see page 38) to remove paint as well as to lay it on the printing plate.

- **Plastic wrap for texture Ⓓ.** Plastic wrap has great potential for making interesting textural and linear patterns on your fabric. Use a brayer to apply paint (several colors, if you wish) to the printing plate. Crumple a piece of plastic wrap, stamp it on the paint-laden plate to remove some paint, and then print. Alternatively, place a piece of plastic wrap across the paint-covered plate, stretching it out as you lay it down, so that lines, or narrow folds, appear in the plastic. Press the plastic down into the paint a bit with your fingers, then remove it. Lay your fabric on the plate, press over it with clean foam brayer or your hands, and then remove the fabric.

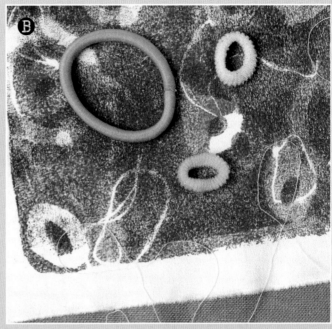

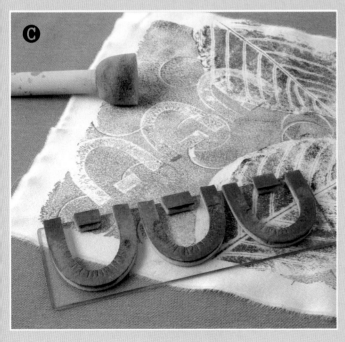

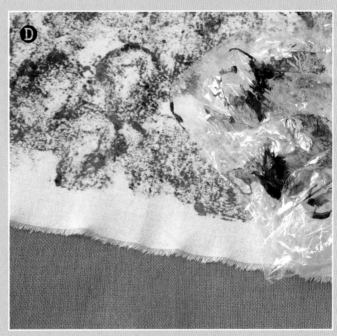

EXPLORING THE POSSIBILITIES:
Monotype Printing (cont'd)

• **Applicators make a difference.** Discover the different effects you get by applying paint to the plate with a variety of applicators, such as a kitchen basting brush **Ⓐ**, sponge brushes **Ⓑ**, and rags **Ⓒ**.

• **Wet and dry effects Ⓓ.** Get a watercolor effect by spritzing one side of the fabric with water before printing.

• **Layering.** Try layering prints on the same piece of fabric, using simple designs for each layer. If you want the individual prints to line up, make a small, light pencil mark on the fabric at the printing plate's top two corners when you are making the first print.

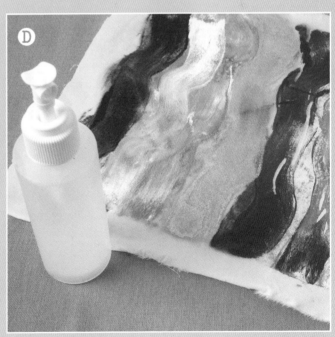

Collagraphs

Because you attach directly to the printing plate the items you are printing, choose a material, such as heavy cardboard or foam core, that is sturdy enough to serve as a base. A piece about 7 by 9 inches is a good size. Consider a wide variety of items you might use to create the images. Although they should be relatively flat, some possibilities include yarn, wire, cording, uncooked pasta, beans and seeds, sand, washers, rice, textured fabric, and small pieces of corrugated cardboard. Let your eyes — and your imagination — discover the surprising potential that's all around you!

Paints

Use medium- or heavy-body textile paints, such as PRO Chemical & Dye's PROfab textile paints, or Jacquard's Textile Colors or Neopaque. Mix in PRO Chemical & Dye PRO No Dri to lengthen the time you have to work before the paint begins to dry. You can also use artist acrylic paints mixed with the appropriate textile medium or Golden Silk-Screen Fabric Gel and a slow-drying agent. (See pages 16–17 for information about paint.)

Fabric

Prewash your fabric in hot water using Synthrapol or heavy-duty laundry detergent without scent or fabric softener, then cut pieces a few inches larger than the printing plate.

PROJECT: **Printing a Collagraph**

SUPPLIES NEEDED

Work surface prepared with plastic sheeting or newspaper

Brushes

Acrylic gloss medium or matte medium (any brand; even inexpensive ones work just fine)

Cardboard or foam core for the printing plate

Hot glue gun or white glue that is permanent when dried

Flat items to affix to the plate (see Image Makers, page 104, for suggestions)

Textile or artist acrylic paint and a paint palette

Prewashed fabric (see page 28)

Items to provide texture, such as rice, aluminum foil, plastic netting, lentils, pasta, and sand

Textile or artist acrylic paint and a paint palette

Sponge brushes to apply paint and a mason's brush (or any hard-bristle brush) to print to fabric

STEP 1. Brush an even coat of acrylic medium on both sides of your printing plate to make it water resistant. Let it dry completely.

STEP 2. Draw a simple design on your printing plate.

STEP 3. Glue textural items to the printing plate, following the design you drew in step 2. Let the glue dry. Check to make sure everything is tightly glued down.

STEP 4. To make everything water resistant, brush another coat of acrylic medium over the printing plate and the glued-on objects. Let it dry.

STEP 5. Brush several colors of paint on the printing plate. (You can accent the design by using different colors for each section.)

STEP 2

STEP 3

STEP 4

STEP 5

STEP 6

STEP 7A

STEP 7B

STEP 6. Lay your fabric over the printing plate. Use your fingers and/or a mason's brush to push the fabric into all the crevices created by the objects. Remove the fabric.

STEP 7. Lightly spritz water on the printing plate (A) and make a second ghost print, if desired (B). Allow paints to dry, and heat-set (see page 22).

113

Gelatin Printing

Gelatin printing is so much fun! The concept is very much like monotype printing, except that your printing plate is unflavored gelatin — the same gelatin that you buy in the grocery store, mixed up in much the same way as if you were making flavored gelatin dessert. The beauty of this printing plate is that it holds an incredible amount of detail when you apply paint to it. You can then transfer this detail to your fabric, yielding rich and interesting results. In addition to this characteristic, because it is soft and flexible, it's easy to make prints using just your hands. It's a bit of a sensory experience, so kids really like it. Because gelatin is a food product, it has a shelf life of about two weeks when stored in the refrigerator, but during that time it can be reused over and over again. You'll know it's time to toss it out when it starts to break down, smells funny, or acquires a fuzzy, green coating!

You might also want to try one of the commercial gelatins designed for artists. Since 2009, Gelatin Innovations, a company that specializes in custom gelatin products, has manufactured MonoPrint Gelatin, formulated specifically for artists. More durable then the grocery-store variety, it includes an anti-foaming agent, making it easier to prepare the gelatin plate. Gelli Arts makes Gel Printing Plates, a synthetic gelatin plate consisting of plastic and mineral oil. Gel Printing Plate handles in much the same way as natural gelatin, but it has the convenience of always being ready for use.

Gelatin plates are fun and easy to make. You prepare the mixture as described on these pages, and then pour it into a flat cookie sheet. To ensure a perfectly flat surface, you might want to purchase a new cookie sheet specifically for this purpose. You might also want a butter knife to remove the gelatin from the cookie sheet, but you can also use the gelatin while it's still in the pan.

PROJECT: **Making a Gelatin Plate**

SUPPLIES NEEDED

Work surface prepared with plastic sheeting

3 cups cold water

Mixing bowl

6 tablespoons ordinary food-grade gelatin or 6 tablespoons MonoPrint Gelatin

Medium-size saucepan

Fork, for mixing

Nonstick cookie sheet with sides

Newspaper, torn in 2-inch-wide strips about as long as the width of the cookie sheet

Butter knife or small spatula (optional)

Clean paper, glass, or Plexiglas, the same size as, or a bit larger than, the cookie sheet

STEP 1. Pour 1½ cups cold water into the mixing bowl. Sprinkle 6 tablespoons of dry gelatin granules evenly over the water.

STEP 2. Pour the remaining 1½ cups water into the saucepan and bring to a boil. Pour the boiling water into the mixing bowl, stirring gently with a fork until the gelatin is completely dissolved.

STEP 3. Pour mixture very gently onto the nonstick cookie sheet, trying not to create foam and air bubbles (A). Drag the torn edge of a piece of newspaper across the top of the gelatin to remove any air bubbles or foam that may appear (B). You may have to do this several times.

STEP 4. Allow the gelatin to firm up a bit, then put it in the refrigerator for several hours or overnight. The gelatin should be firm, without any liquid.

TEASING THE PLATE OFF THE SHEET

- If your cookie sheet is not nonstick, use a little spray oil or line it with plastic wrap to make it easier to remove the gelatin once it has set.

- If you have trouble removing the gelatin, lay the pan flat on your work surface, right side up. Lift one corner of the gelatin plate off the sheet with your knife, then get your fingers underneath it and slowly walk them down the length of the pan until you have the entire gelatin plate in your hands, free of the sheet, then gently lay it down on clean paper, glass, or Plexiglas.

EXPLORING THE POSSIBILITIES: Gelatin Printing

- **Different-size and different-shaped gelatin plates.** Use a variety of baking trays or containers to vary the size and shape of your gelatin plates. Each plate should be ¾- to 1-inch thick. To determine how much gelatin mixture to prepare, pour plain water in the container of your choice until it reaches this level, then measure the amount of water you used. Make your gelatin mixture following the basic formula of 2 tablespoons gelatin to 1 cup water.

- **Free-form gelatin plates.** Instead of making your gelatin plate in a square, rectangular, or circular container, you can create your own free-form shapes. Roll a piece of modeling or polymer clay into a long snake, shape it however you like, and affix it to a piece of glass or Plexiglas to serve as the "wall" for your gelatin plate. Pour in the gelatin mixture, allow it to dry, and after it has set, cut away the clay with an X-Acto knife.

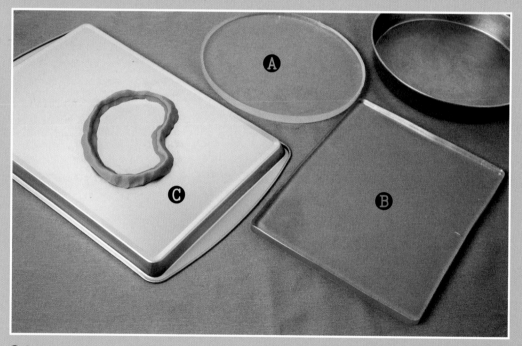

Ⓐ Gelatin plate made in a round cake pan

Ⓑ Synthetic gelatin plate

Ⓒ Free-form plate framed with modeling clay

Using Your Plate

As with all forms of surface design, don't forget that you can print on the same piece of cloth several times to achieve depth and richness. Allow yourself plenty of time for gelatin printing. Let any inhibitions or predetermined expectations fall away. This is a technique you can easily get lost in — time will fly by, and life will be still.

Paints

Use medium- and/or heavy-body textile paints, mixed with a painting medium that slows the drying process. You can also use artist acrylic paints mixed with the appropriate textile medium and an appropriate slow-drying agent. For your paint palette, use a piece of Plexiglas, an old plate, or a disposable foam food tray.

Some useful image makers for gelatin prints

Image Makers

You'll need a variety of tools and objects to make marks in the paint without scraping into the gelatin. Here are some suggestions:

- Sponges
- Rags
- Sponge brushes
- Your fingers
- Cotton swabs
- Rubber-pointed tool (like a paintbrush, but with a rubber point instead of hair)
- Stamps
- Jar covers
- Berry-basket bottoms
- Cardboard (use the edge)
- Cork
- Potato masher
- Tray packaged with frozen parsley and basil (available in grocery store frozen-food sections)
- Cardboard coffee cups (especially if you love circles!)

For use as resists, add to this collection relatively flat items, such as any of the following:

- String
- Yarn
- Cardboard or foam cutouts
- Sticks
- Leaves and grass
- Plastic fencing material
- Plastic mesh bags

Fabric

Medium-weight fabrics, such as cotton, rayon challis, or silk broadcloth, work nicely for this technique. Prewash your fabric in hot water using Synthrapol or heavy-duty laundry detergent without scent or fabric softener, then cut it into pieces a couple of inches bigger than your printing plate. Some artists like to stabilize their fabric with a paper backing before printing on it. This is particularly helpful with a fabric, such as rayon, that tends to be floppy. If you think this would make your work easier, simply iron your fabric to a piece of freezer paper before printing.

PROJECT: **Making a Gelatin Print**

SUPPLIES NEEDED

Work surface prepared with plastic sheeting

Gelatin plate

Clean paper

Piece of glass or Plexiglas (see Making a Gelatin Plate, page 114)

Foam tray or old plate to use as a palette

Brayer, for inking the plate

Textile or artist acrylic paint, one or two colors, mixed with textile medium

Implements for making marks in the paint (see Image Makers, page 117)

Flat items to use as resists

Prewashed fabric (see page 28), cut into pieces larger than the gelatin plate

Freezer paper, if necessary, for stabilizing the fabric (optional)

Clean brayer, for printing (optional)

Newspaper

STEP 1. Remove the gelatin plate from the cookie sheet by running a butter knife around the edges and then inverting the sheet or by sliding your fingers under the gelatin and gently lifting it off the cookie sheet (A). Lay the gelatin on a piece of clean paper, glass, or Plexiglas (B).

STEP 2. With the brayer, roll out one or two colors of paint on your palette until the brayer is fully loaded with paint (A), then roll the paint onto the gelatin plate (B). If this is the first time you are using the plate, you will need to condition it by taking a few passes with the brayer before the paint adheres.

STEP 3. Make some marks on the plate by lifting off some of the paint, using any of the tools suggested (A–E). Even your fingers will do nicely!

STEP 4. Choose several of the flat items and place them onto the plate in a pleasing design to act as a resist.

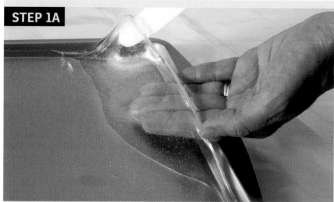
STEP 1A

STEP 1B

STEP 2A

STEP 2B

STEP 3A

STEP 3B

STEP 3C

STEP 3D

STEP 3E

STEP 4

STEP 5. Lay a piece of fabric over the plate, and rub it with your hands or another brayer to print (A). Remove the fabric (B).

STEP 6. Clean your plate by printing whatever paint is left on the plate onto a piece of newspaper. You can also use a bit a sanitizing gel, especially around the edges if need be.

STEP 7. Allow the paint to dry and heat-set (see page 22), if necessary.

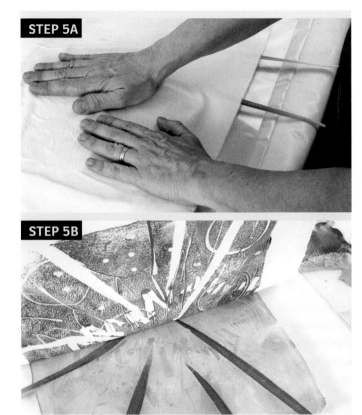

STEP 5A

STEP 5B

EXPLORING THE POSSIBILITIES:
Gelatin Printing (cont'd)

When you've completed the printing process through step 5 at left, you can consider the piece done, or proceed with these options:

- **Remove the flat items Ⓐ** from the plate and then make a second "ghost print" with your plate on a new piece of fabric.

- **While the paint is still wet Ⓑ** on the resist items, use them to make further prints on your fabric.

Profile: Jane LaFazio

Jane LaFazio's work is alive with spontaneity and joy. Her use of everyday images, bold color, simple shapes, and stitched outlines give her work an ethnic quality that I find particularly compelling. Jane's work has appeared in numerous magazine articles. She teaches extensively throughout the United States and has become quite well known not only for her mixed-media art quilts but for her narrative sketchbook work as well.

Her website and blog are a wealth of information about Jane, her whereabouts, and her classes and workshops, as well as what is on her personal bookshelf, information on her prayer-flag project, and some free, mini tutorials.

www.janelafazio.com
www.janelafazio.blogspot.com

Jane LaFazio's *Four Seasons* (above; 9" × 9½") and *Poe* (right; 5" × 10")

Profile: Rayna Gillman

Rayna Gillman is an award-winning, internationally renowned fiber artist, author, and teacher whose work has appeared in galleries and museums across the United States. She works spontaneously in mixed media, using printmaking techniques to add texture to her hand-printed cloth. *Blue Plate Special* and *Broken Dreams* are wonderful examples of her pioneering work with gelatin printing. In *Blue Plate Special*, she expertly uses the natural properties of the medium to print texture and pattern using clear, bright colors that are unmuddied. Machine quilting further adds to the success of this wonderful piece, (left, top). In *Broken Dreams*, she has added screen printing on top of the gelatin print to add text, scratch marks, and additional pattern. One does not even have to read the text to feel the pain and struggle of broken dreams.

Rayna's best-selling book, *Create Your Own Hand-Printed Cloth* (C&T, 2008), was nominated for two book awards, and *Create Your Own Free-Form Quilts* (C&T, 2011) has been a best seller, as well.
www.studio78.net
www.studio78notes.blogspot

Rayna Gilman's *Blue Plate Special* (top; 12" × 12") and *Broken Dreams* (bottom; 31" × 38")

CHAPTER 10

Silk-Screen Printing

A silk screen is best described as a sophisticated stencil technique. Instead of cutting your image out of the stencil material, however, you cover a frame with a fine-mesh fabric and then use various mediums to cover the areas you don't want to print, leaving your image exposed. Using the mesh fabric as a carrier for the blocking agent means that you don't need "bridges" to stabilize the stencil. (With stencils, bridges help define areas of the design that would merge, or disappear, if not supported and/or defined by these connectors.) To create the printed image, you push ink, paint, or glue through the areas you left exposed onto a substrate. This indispensable technique enables artists to make multiple identical prints of an image.

This is a particularly useful technique for textile artists, because it allows you to print on even the most delicate textiles, while changing the hand (or feel) of the fabric only slightly, if at all.

At one time, I found this technique overwhelming or simply unapproachable, and I think it's not unusual to have misgivings about it. But because of the incredibly inventive mind of fiber artist Jane Dunnewold, I've learned that screen prints can easily be a fun, exciting, and inexpensive tool for the fiber artist. We'll begin by building the silk-screen frame and covering it with fabric. Next, I describe some of the most basic and innovative ways Dunnewold has invented for blocking out areas of the screen, then progress to the more complicated methods, such as photo emulsion. Finally, with the screens or resists prepared, we'll describe how to apply color to your fabric.

A LONG HISTORY

Screen printing dates back as far as the Song dynasty in China (960–1279 CE). Japan and other Asian countries used the technique as well. The earliest screens were made by gluing simple stencils to a wooden frame that was woven with stretched human hair. Screens were later made with silk. The Japanese are known for combining screen printing with their elaborate block printing to achieve gorgeous imagery on paper, fabric, and wallpaper.

Screen printing was introduced to western Europe in the late eighteenth century, and in 1907 Samuel Simon patented the technique in England. Shortly after, the invention of a chemical solution in the United States enabled the use of photographic imagery on silk, revolutionizing commercial screen printing for the textile industry, and making possible, for instance, the widespread production of flags and banners during World War I. In the 1930s, a group of artists coined the term *serigraphy*, to make a distinction between commercial and fine art uses of screen printing. However, it was Andy Warhol, who, in the 1960s, popularized the technique as an art form with his iconic screened images of celebrities like Marilyn Monroe (shown here) and Jackie Kennedy.

Constructing and Preparing Your Silk-Screen Frame

You can purchase ready-made wood or metal silk screens with the mesh fabric already stretched onto them: all you have to do to get started is to tape off your "well" (more on that in a minute). I don't recommend metal-framed screens, however, for the simple fact that should you want to replace the mesh fabric yourself in the future, you wouldn't be able to.

You can also make your own wood-frame screen from wood strips or (my favorite) the artist stretcher bars that are designed for making canvases. These bars are inexpensive, easily available from both online and brick-and-mortar art-supply stores, and a snap to assemble.

A screen measuring about 18 by 20 inches is a good size to start with. If you are using artist stretcher bars, buy two 18-inch and two 20-inch bars, and fit the grooved corners together. Your stretcher bars may have a raised lip on one side, which is designed to keep the canvas from touching the wood strips; make sure these lips are all on the same side. You will probably need to tap on the corners with a hammer to get the frame square; they should fit snugly. Position the screen with the raised lip facing down on your work surface. Put a couple of staples across all four corner joints to give them added stability.

Planning for Your Image

To give yourself room to spread your paint smoothly with your squeegee, you should plan your image so that you have a 2- to 3-inch margin all around it inside the frame. This will leave you enough room for a "well," the area where you spoon your paint before you pull it through the mesh. You can get away with a lot less, but it's easier to work with a wider margin. This means that for an 18-by-20-inch frame, where the frame itself measures 1¼-inch wide, your image should not be larger than approximately 11½ by 13½ inches. If your image turns out to be smaller than that, you can always mask off the unwanted area with blue painter's tape or masking tape.

Fabric Mesh

Nowadays, polyester or nylon is used for the screen rather than silk. This can be purchased from online art-supply stores or stores that cater specifically to silk-screening. Many fiber artists have great success using synthetic, sheer curtain fabric for simpler screen-printing techniques. Because this is a very economical way to go, I'll let you know which techniques you can use with this fabric as we go along.

The polyester mesh manufactured for silk screening comes in two forms: monofilament and multifilament. Because the monofilament fabric is woven of smooth, single threads, it is especially useful when you want exact detail and registration of your prints, although these fabrics don't accept emulsion or other blocking mediums very easily. This fabric is easy to clean and holds up well for production usages. Multifilament fabric is woven with polyester threads made up of many fine threads that have been spun together. This fabric has a slight texture or roughness that enables it to hold onto water-based paints and inks better than the monofilament fabric. It has a slightly flexible quality that makes it easier to print on textured fabrics and curved surfaces, but it doesn't hold up well for mass production purposes.

When you purchase mesh fabric, look for the number that indicates the thread count (number of threads per inch in the weave). Monofilaments have three-digit numbers, whereas multifilaments have a single- or double-digit number. The higher the number, the more threads there are per inch of fabric. Multifilaments also show a series of x's after the number. These refer to the thickness of the multifilament threads, and the smaller the number, the looser the weave. Both monofilament and multifilament fabrics come in different widths; they are usually sold by the yard.

I recommend using a 10xx or 12xx multifilament mesh, which is available at online art-supply stores such as Dick Blick and silk-screen specialty shops. Cut the fabric about 1 inch larger in both height and width than the screen dimensions.

You need a staple gun to attach the mesh to the screen, so treat yourself to one of the new, lightweight ones. These small plastic guns can be easily operated with one hand, even if your hand is not very big or you're not very strong. You'll need the other hand to stretch the fabric. Don't forget to buy the appropriate-size staples, too.

It's helpful to prepare several silk-screen frames before you are actually working on a project, so they're ready to go when inspiration strikes.

PROJECT: **Constructing a Silk-Screen Frame**

SUPPLIES NEEDED

Work surface covered with plastic sheeting

18" × 20" frame made of four artist stretcher bars or wooden strips

19" × 21" piece of multifilament mesh or sheer curtain fabric

Staple gun and staples

X-Acto knife

Waterproof duct tape, 3M Scotch High Performance Masking Tape, or tape made for silk-screening

Kitchen cleanser, such as Bon Ami or Comet

A household sponge with a nonscratch scrubber on one side

STEP 1. After assembling the frame (see page 127), place it on your work surface with the lip side down and one of the long sides nearest you. Lay the fabric on the frame and center it. Begin attaching the fabric to the frame by using the staple gun to put three staples, slightly angled and about 1¼" apart, at the center of the long side nearest you.

STEP 2. Turn the frame and do the same on the opposite side, stretching the fabric taut.

STEP 3. Rotate the frame so one of the shorter sides is closest to you. Put three staples in the center of that side, then rotate again to staple the final side in the same manner, pulling the fabric taut.

STEP 4. Continue to place staples on each side in turn, working from the center out toward the corners. The goal is to stretch the fabric tight enough to eliminate any ridges, but not so tight as to warp the frame.

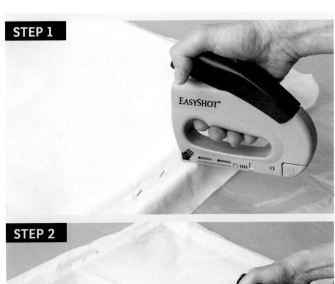

STEP 1

STEP 2

STEP 4

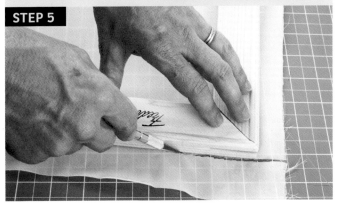

STEP 5

STEP 5. When each side is completely stapled down, trim the fabric flush with the frame. It's easier to do this if you place the frame on a cutting mat and trim the excess material away with an X-Acto knife.

STEP 6. To protect the frame from water, it must be completely covered with tape. This taping also creates the area where you will place your image, along with the well for your paint. With the frame flat on your work surface, mesh side up, run a piece of tape 1½"–2" in from the inside edge of the frame over the mesh from one end all the way to the opposite end and down the edge a bit (A). (For very large frames, cover a wider area with tape — up to 3".) Tape all four sides in the same way (B).

STEP 7. Trim a piece of tape slightly longer than the inside edge. Turn the frame over so the mesh lies on the work surface. Run tape exactly over the areas taped on the other side, sandwiching the mesh between the two layers of tape. Tape all four sides.

STEP 8. Overlap a piece of tape on the bottom edge of the tape you just laid, then continue up the inside edge of the frame, so paint and water cannot creep into the space between the mesh and the frame. Do this on all four sides. (If your screen is small, the tape you applied in step 5 will run up the inside of the frame, and this step won't be necessary.)

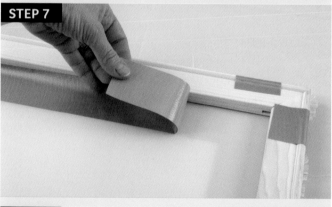

STEP 9. Cover any other exposed areas of the frame with tape, overlapping edges, so that no bare wood shows. As you cover the corners, trim as shown, so the tape lies flat.

STEP 10. The inside corners are the trickiest part to tape! Cut a piece of tape a little bit longer than it is wide. Cut a slit halfway up the middle of one side so that it resembles a pair of pants (A). With the "pants' legs" facing up, fold the tape in half, then push the fold into the corner. Unfold the tape. Pull the "legs" up and over the inside edge of the frame, making sure to totally cover the exposed wood (B).

STEP 11. Let the tape cure for 24 hours. Don't be impatient. If you don't wait, the tape will come up the first time you wash the frame.

STEP 12. After the tape has cured, clean the mesh with a bit of cleanser and the scrubber on your sponge. You don't have to scrub really hard, just enough to remove any grease or oils that might be lurking on the surface. Hold the screen upright in your sink as you scrub, then rinse thoroughly. Let dry.

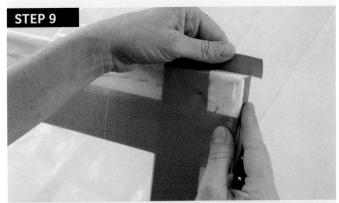

STEP 9

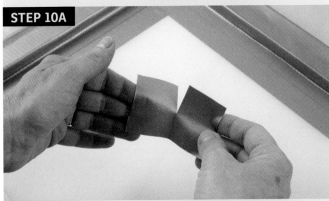

STEP 10A

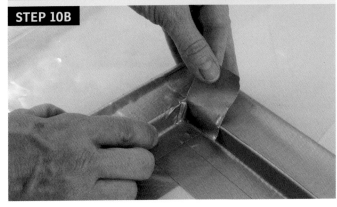

STEP 10B

PROJECT: **Preparing a Tape Mask for Your Silk Screen**

Don't underestimate what this very simple printing medium can accomplish! With this method, wherever you place tape will be the unpainted areas: you are printing the space around the taped shapes. You can use the straight edge of the tape to create a geometric design or tear the edges to create areas that are more organic. You should be able to get quite a few prints before the tape starts to come unglued.

SUPPLIES NEEDED

Work surface covered with plastic sheeting

Blue painter's tape or masking tape

Silk screen with either multifilament mesh or sheer curtain fabric that has been taped and washed (see instructions on pages 129–31)

STEP 1. With the back (flat) side of the screen facing up, apply tape to the mesh, masking off areas of the screen where you don't want paint.

STEP 2. Print on prewashed fabric following the directions on page 153.

STEP 1

FINISHED

PROJECT: **Preparing a Newspaper Mask for Your Silk Screen**

When you tear newspaper, you'll notice that if you tear in one direction you get a relatively straight edge, but if you tear in the other direction you get a curved edge. You can take advantage of these characteristics as you develop your design. After your first print, the newspaper pieces will stick to the screen, enabling you to print many times before they start to fall off. Consider printing even after they do start to fall off. Your prints won't be exactly the same, but the variation could be interesting.

SUPPLIES NEEDED

Work surface covered with plastic sheeting

Newspaper, torn or cut in desired strips or shapes

Prewashed fabric (see page 28)

Silk screen with either multifilament mesh or sheer curtain fabric that has been washed and taped (see instructions on pages 129–31)

STEP 1. Lay the pieces of newspaper down on the fabric you are planning to print on. Take care to stay within the area that your screen covers.

STEP 2. Place your screen over the newspaper pattern.

STEP 3. Print following the directions on page 153. After your first print, the newspaper will adhere to the back of the screen, enabling you to make several more prints before the newspaper starts to fall off.

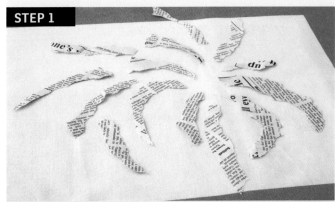

STEP 1

STEP 2

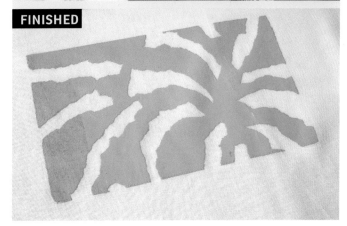

FINISHED

133

PROJECT: **Preparing a Freezer-Paper Mask for Your Silk Screen**

The material for this technique is ordinary freezer paper, available in the aisle with plastic and paper products in most grocery stores. You can cut individual shapes, or prepare a stencil following the procedure for cutting freezer paper stencils described on page 88. If you find that you really like your results, I recommend dedicating one of your silk screens to just this technique.

SUPPLIES NEEDED

Hard work surface, such as a drawing board or piece of wood larger than your frame, or a tabletop protected with a couple of layers of muslin

Silk screen with either multifilament mesh or sheer curtain fabric that has been washed and taped (see instructions on pages 129–31)

Iron

Freezer paper (precut into shapes or a stencil)

Baking parchment paper (optional)

STEP 1. With the back (flat) side of the screen facing up, iron the freezer-paper stencil or shapes to the screen. Sometimes it helps to turn the screen over so that you can iron from the other side. (You may want to place a piece of baking parchment paper over the screen mesh both to protect your iron and to prevent the tape from melting if you inadvertently touch it with your hot iron.) It helps to have your screen on a hard surface rather than on an ironing board.

STEP 2. Print on prewashed fabric by following the directions on page 153.

STEP 1

FINISHED

TIPS FOR CLEANING FREEZER PAPER OFF SCREENS

It takes a little experience (and a few ruined screens!) to know how much to iron the paper before it becomes permanent on a silk screen. When you are done printing, you should be able to remove the freezer paper with soap and warm water or with a spritz of citrus cleaner, such as Citra Solv.

PROJECT: Preparing a Contact-Paper Mask for Your Silk Screen

This method uses contact paper or shelf-lining paper that is available in most hardware stores or in the home section of department stores. Make sure to get the kind that has adhesive on the back.

SUPPLIES NEEDED

Work surface covered with plastic sheeting

X-Acto knife or scissors for cutting paper

Adhesive contact paper or shelf-lining paper

Silk screen with either multifilament mesh or sheer curtain fabric that has been washed and taped (see instructions on page 129–31)

STEP 1. Cut out a design from contact paper to a size that will fit your screen.

STEP 2. Remove the paper backing and adhere your template to the back (flat) side of your screen.

STEP 3. Print on prewashed fabric by following the directions on page 153.

STEP 2

FINISHED

PROJECT: **Silk-Screening with Stencils**

You might be wondering why not just use stencils as stencils, right? If done correctly, screening with a stencil changes the hand of the fabric only slightly, compared with stenciling with a brush. This makes screening a better choice for fabric that may be sewn into a garment. It also gives more printing options, as you will see. Any flat material that behaves like a stencil can be used for this method. For instance, portable plastic construction fencing, deer fencing, snow fencing, or similar materials all work beautifully.

Prepare a stencil on thin plastic or transparency material as described on page 83.

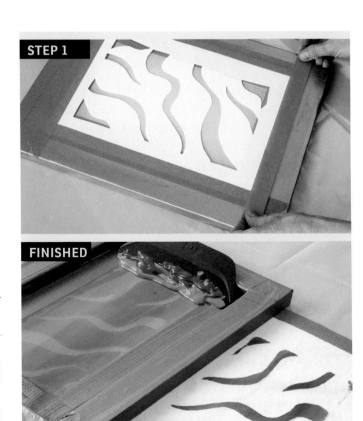

SUPPLIES NEEDED

Work surface covered with plastic sheeting

Masking tape or blue painter's tape

Prepared stencil

Silk screen with either multifilament mesh or sheer curtain fabric that has been washed and taped (see instructions on pages 129-31)

STEP 1. Tape the stencil to the back or flat side of your screen, making sure to cover all of the exposed mesh that is not part of your image with either the stencil or tape.

STEP 2. Print on prewashed fabric by following the directions on page 28.

EXPLORING THE POSSIBILITIES:

Silk-Screening with Stencils

- After removing the stencil from your screen, notice that it now has a layer of paint on it in the areas you didn't screen (the negative spaces). Place the stencil over on your fabric and use a brayer or your hands to print the negative spaces. (See photo, below.)

- If it looks as if there's too much paint on your fabric, lay another piece of cloth on top of the print, and use your brayer to transfer the excess paint onto the top layer of fabric.

- The screen itself probably still has a layer of paint in it too, so go ahead and print that as well, creating a "ghost" image.

PROJECT: Silk-Screening with Interfacing

This is, without a doubt, my favorite of all the screening techniques I offer you in this book. It was invented by fiber artist Jane Dunnewold, and there are both controlled and serendipitous aspects to it.

I use a medium-weight Pellon interfacing (*not* fusible). Cut it to the size of your screen or smaller. For the paint, I like heavy-body transparent or opaque textile paints, but you can also use artist acrylic paints mixed with the appropriate textile medium.

After you cut your design out of the interfacing, if the piece fits your screen nicely or you don't mind borders of paint, you do not need to tape the interfacing. After the first pull of paint with the squeegee, it will stick to the screen without tape.

SUPPLIES NEEDED

Work surface covered with plastic sheeting

X-Acto knife or scissors

Medium-weight interfacing

Blue painter's tape or masking tape

Silk screen with either multifilament mesh or sheer curtain fabric that has been washed and taped (see instructions on pages 129–31)

Paper or scrap fabric

Plastic spoons

Heavy-body transparent or opaque textile paints, or artist acrylic paint mixed with Golden Silk Screen Fabric Gel

Squeegee

Prewashed fabric (see page 28), five or six pieces or a long continuous strip

EXPLORING THE POSSIBILITIES:
Silk-Screening with Interfacing

- **Using acrylic paint** (leftover house paint will do just fine) or acrylic medium, paint a design, small pattern, or shapes on the interfacing around your cutout design. Once dry, these painted areas will act as a resist, blocking the printing paint from penetrating that part of the interfacing.

STEP 1. Use an X-Acto knife or scissors to cut a simple design into the interfacing.

STEP 2. Tape the cutout design to the back (flat) side of your screen, taking care that areas of the exposed mesh are covered with either the interfacing or tape.

STEP 3. Place your screen on a piece of paper or scrap fabric with the front of the screen flat on the paper. Spoon one color into the well of the screen, then use the squeegee to pull the paint through several times to flood the screen. As you start to run out of paint, add another color or two.

STEP 4. Set out five or six pieces of fabric to print on, or a continuous strip of fabric. After a few prints the interfacing will begin to absorb the paint. Once saturated, your prints will show both the stenciled design and the area around the design. The colors will mix and blend on their own with each print you make.

STEP 5. Allow the paint to dry and heat-set (see page 22) if necessary.

PROJECT: **Using School Glue Gel for Your Silk Screen**

This simple, inexpensive medium can produce very exciting results. It is particularly great for achieving textural surfaces as opposed to images with fine detail. I use Elmer's Washable School Glue Gel. (Traditional white school glue does not work for this method.)

For more control and finer lines, use an applicator bottle with a fine tip, such as PRO Chem's Tapered Gold Tip Bottle.

Because the glue is water soluble, it will start to break down after several pulls. Use that to your advantage, especially if you have created an abstract textural design.

When you have finished printing this particular image, remove the glue from your screen with soap and warm water. Because you may not be able to get all the glue out, I recommend dedicating one of your silk screens to just this technique if you find that you really like the results you get with school glue gel.

SUPPLIES NEEDED

Work surface covered with plastic sheeting

Elmer's Washable School Glue Gel

Silk screen with either multifilament mesh or sheer curtain fabric that has been washed and taped (see instructions on pages 129–31)

STEP 1. Apply the glue to the back (flat) side of your screen in any design you desire. Wait for the glue to dry thoroughly before printing.

STEP 2. Print on prewashed fabric by following the directions on page 153.

PROJECT: **Preparing a Silk Screen with Screen Filler**

Perhaps the most basic and straightforward way to create imagery on your silk screen is with screen filler, a product designed specifically for silk screens. (For suppliers, see Resources.) It can be either directly applied with a brush or applied after drawing fluid has been used.

Screen filler is not water soluble, so you can wash out the printing paint with soap and water without destroying your design. If you want to use the screen for something different, you will need to reclaim it by washing it with Greased Lightning, Mr. Clean, or any cleaning agent that is a degreaser. If the screen will fit, lay it down flat in the sink with the back or flat side facing down and spray it with the degreaser. Let it sit for a few minutes before washing it. You might need to scrub a bit with a nonscratch scrubber.

SUPPLIES NEEDED

Work surface covered with plastic sheeting

Paper

Soft pencil

Black permanent marker

Blank silk screen with multifilament mesh (see pages 129–31)

Screen filler

Several fine watercolor brushes

Four small cups or containers

Fan or hair dryer (optional)

STEP 1. Draw your design on a piece of paper the size of your screen. Go over the pencil lines with a black marker.

STEP 2. Place the back (flat) side of the screen down on top of your drawing. Trace the design onto the screen with a soft pencil.

STEP 3. With the back (flat) side of the screen facing up toward you, use an appropriate-size brush (such as a watercolor brush) to paint screen filler in all the areas that surround the image, leaving the image open. Periodically hold the screen up to the light to check for any pinholes or areas of the mesh that did not get filled in. Pay close attention to the areas of the mesh that are closest to the tape.

141

STEP 4. Prop up the four corners of the screen on cups or other containers so it's horizontal, and allow the filler to dry. You can speed up the drying process by placing the screen in front of a fan or by using a hair dryer.

STEP 5. Print following the directions on page 153.

STEP 4

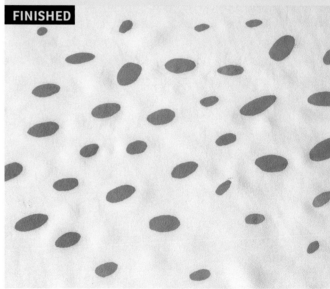

FINISHED

PROJECT: **Preparing a Tushe Resist with Drawing Fluid for Your Silk Screen**

With this method of preparing your screen, you fill in the areas of the actual image with drawing fluid. (For suppliers of drawing fluid, see Resources.) After applying the drawing fluid and allowing it to dry, you fill the rest of the screen with screen filler, allow it to dry, and then wash off the drawing fluid so that you can print.

It's important to use enough screen filler so that you can cover the entire screen with it with one pull of the squeegee. If you have to do more than one pull, the drawing fluid is likely to start dissolving, thus spoiling your design. Alternatively, instead of using the squeegee to spread the filler over the screen, you can paint it over the back side of the screen using a foam brush, but you have to be very careful not to dissolve the drawing fluid at the same time.

SUPPLIES NEEDED

Work surface covered with plastic sheeting

Paper, the same size as your screen

Soft pencil

Black permanent marker

Blank silk screen with multifilament mesh (see pages 129–31)

Drawing fluid

Several fine watercolor brushes

Fan or hair dryer (optional)

Screen filler

Plastic spoon

Squeegee (for advice about squeegees, see page 151)

Four small cups or containers

Foam or soft brush (optional)

Dish-washing sponge (optional)

STEP 3

STEP 4

STEP 1. Draw your design on a piece of paper the size of your screen. Go over the drawn lines with a black marker.

STEP 2. Place the back (flat) side of the screen facedown on your drawing. Use a soft pencil to trace it onto the screen.

STEP 3. Turn the screen over, and use drawing fluid and a watercolor brush to fill in your image on the front (inside) of your screen, covering the area that you want to print. Allow to dry. You can speed up the drying process by placing the screen in front of a fan or by using a hair dryer.

STEP 4. Stir the screen filler well before using, ensuring that it is thoroughly mixed and smooth in texture. On the same side you painted the drawing fluid, pour a line of screen filler on the far end of the taped area of your screen, going from one side to the other.

STEP 5. Place the blade of the squeegee between the frame of your screen and the line or "bead" of screen filler. With an even, slow motion, pull the squeegee across the frame toward your body. Spoon the excess screen filler back into the bottle for future use.

STEP 6. Prop up the four corners of the screen on cups or other containers so it's horizontal (see step 4, page 142) and allow the filler to dry. You can speed up the drying process by placing the screen in front of a fan or by using a hair dryer.

STEP 7. Hold the screen up to the light to make sure there are no pinholes where the screen filler is missing. Pay close attention to the areas where the screen filler meets the tape. If need be, apply more screen filler with a foam or soft brush and again allow to dry.

STEP 8. Hold the screen upright in your sink and spray cold water over it to dissolve and wash out the drawing fluid. It should come out pretty easily, but if it needs a little help, use the soft side of a sponge. Do not use warm or hot water at this time.

STEP 9. Print by following the directions on page 153. The print will be the same as shown on page 142.

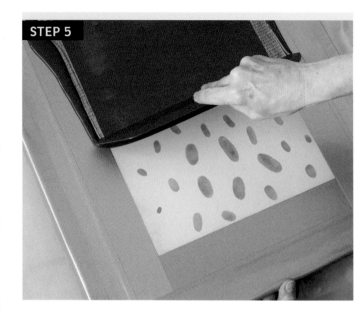

SILK-SCREENING WITH SOY WAX

Soy wax is another option to use as a resist on a silk screen. All of the techniques covered on pages 140–45 can be applied on screens. Even though soy wax will wash or iron out of your screen, I recommend having a dedicated screen for soy-wax resist.

PROJECT: **Preparing a House-Paint Resist for Your Silk Screen**

This is an easy and inexpensive way to put permanent imagery on your screen. If you decide to reclaim or reuse the screen for another project and you're feeling lazy, you can simply take a utility knife and cut the screen out, then staple and tape a new piece of mesh to the screen. If you want to reclaim the screen a second time, however, you'll need to remove all of the tape and staples before stretching and taping a new piece of mesh.

SUPPLIES NEEDED

Work surface covered with plastic sheeting

Paper, the same size as your screen

Soft pencil

Black permanent marker

Silk screen with either multifilament mesh or sheer curtain fabric that has been washed and taped (see instructions on pages 129–31)

Acrylic house paint (leftovers are fine)

Watercolor brushes

Four small cups or containers of the same size or height

Fan or hair dryer (optional)

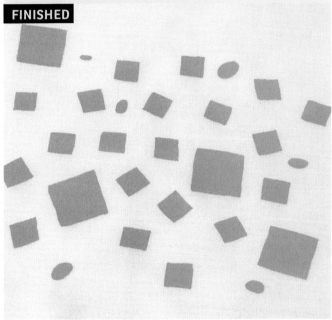

STEP 1. Draw your design on a piece of paper the size of your screen. Go over the drawn lines with a black marker.

STEP 2. Place the front of the screen over your drawing, and use a soft pencil to trace it onto the screen.

STEP 3. Turn your screen to the back (flat) side, and paint the areas around your image (in other words, the areas that you do not want to print).

STEP 4. Prop up the four corners of the screen on cups or other containers so it's horizontal (see step 4, page 142), and allow the filler to dry. You can speed up the drying process by placing the screen in front of a fan or by using a hair dryer.

STEP 5. Print on prewashed fabric by following the directions on page 153.

For ways to use acrylic sprays with silk screens, see page 160.

Silk Screening with a Photo Emulsion

Photo emulsion is the best technique for getting sharp, detailed imagery onto your silk screen, and it's not at all difficult to accomplish. You first coat your screen with photo emulsion, and allow it to dry in a completely dark room. When the emulsion is dry, place a transparency on which you have drawn or printed your image over the silk screen and expose it to a light source for a specific amount of time. During this time, the emulsion dissolves wherever there are marks on the transparency. You then wash the screen to get rid of any emulsion remaining in those areas, dry the screen, and then print through it. I recommend purchasing a Speedball Diazo Photo Emulsion Screen Printing Kit when you first work with this technique. The kit includes bottles of photo emulsion, light sensitizer, and photo-emulsion remover.

I have always thought of photo emulsion as being a permanent way to burn images to your silk screen. The truth is, however, that as long as you haven't left the emulsion on the screen for too long after printing, you can remove it with specially formulated photo-emulsion remover. Follow the manufacturer's directions carefully for washing out the emulsion.

Preparing Your Image on a Transparency

The first step in making a photo emulsion is to prepare your artwork on a sheet of transparency film. You can either draw directly on the film with a black marker, or print black clip art or an original black image. Regardless of which technique you choose to create an image on the transparency and your screen, remember that cannot have any gray tones. Here are several ways to prepare a computer-generated image.

Make a tracing. Make a pencil drawing on paper, then trace over your image with black marker and scan it or take a digital photograph of it.

Use drawing software. Drawing programs such as Adobe Illustrator, CorelDRAW, SmartDraw, or EazyDraw (for Mac) allow you to create images directly on your computer.

Use the Stamp feature. If you have Adobe Photoshop or Adobe Photoshop Elements, you can prepare a black computer-generated image using the Stamp feature. This works well for portraits. Open an original drawing or a photograph in Photoshop. On the toolbar with the drawing and painting tools you'll see two overlapping color squares; the top should be white and the bottom, black. If not, use the color picker to select these colors. This sets your background and foreground default colors to black and white. Next, click on Filter on the drop-down menu, then Sketch, and then Stamp. This changes your image into a simple negative and positive: black and white.

Now, find the slider options, Light/Dark Balance and Smoothness. Experiment with those to determine how much detail you want. If you want to switch the black-and-white sections, go back to the two squares you used to select these colors and click on the curved arrow to reverse the colors on your image. Ultimately, the black areas are what will print.

Use a photograph. Your artwork must have high contrast in black and white, so even though it's possible to use a black-and-white photograph, the halftones (gray areas) of the photo must first be converted to dots, a process that once had to be done professionally with special equipment but can now be accomplished using Adobe Photoshop. Simply put, the dots will be much closer together in dark areas and farther apart in light areas. Open a photo in Photoshop or Photoshop Elements. On the menu bar, click on Image, then click on Grayscale. In the pop-up window where you are asked if you want to discard the color information, click Discard, then again click on Image on the menu bar. Click on Bitmap. In the new pop-up window, under Frequency, enter 20 line/inch; under Angle, enter 45; under Shape, choose round. Click Okay.

If your photo is big to start with, you may not get a sense of the effect of what you have done unless you zoom into the picture. Do this by holding down the Option key (or the Command key on Macs) while at the same time clicking on the plus-sign key. Keep in mind that you can play around with any of these numbers in order to change the overall size and look of the details in the photo.

There is a wrong and a right side to the transparency film. Hold the film up to the light at a slight angle and you will see that one side is dull and the other shiny. You may be able to tell the difference by feeling it: the dull side has a slight texture or tooth to it. You want to print on the dull side. Most printers are set by default to a color setting, so be sure to click Black under Print Settings when you're ready to print.

Preparing the Emulsion and Coating the Silk Screen

Mix the Speedball Diazio Photo Emulsion with Sensitizer following the directions on the container, partially cover, and let the mixture sit for a couple of hours to allow any air bubbles that might have formed in the mixing process to be released. You can store the mixture in the refrigerator for up to four months. Make sure you write the date on the container before storing it. I promise that you won't remember when it was mixed otherwise!

It's important that you apply the photo emulsion mixture in a way that completely covers the silk screen, with no breaks. You might want to purchase a relatively inexpensive screen coater for this purpose. It comes in many widths and makes the chore of evenly coating the screen much easier. If you're using a large screen, it is almost essential. You can prop your screen against a wall, and then use two hands to draw the emulsion across the screen from the bottom edge up to the top.

Setting up the Light Source and Timing the Exposure

You must set up a place to dry your silk screen that can be totally darkened. To help you navigate in the darkened room, you may want to use a darkroom safe light. This small, red-coated, 7.5-watt lightbulb can be screwed into a regular lightbulb socket in any household lamp. It can be purchased online from photo-supply houses. When you're ready to expose the screen to light, you'll need a light source, which is easy to make with a few readily available, inexpensive supplies. You need a standard ceramic light socket with an electrical cord attached or a metal clip-on light with a ceramic socket. Hardware stores

Estimated Distances and Exposure Times		
Screen Size	**Distance from Light**	**Exposure Time**
10" × 14"	12"	10 minutes
12" × 18"	15"	16 minutes
16" × 20"	17"	20 minutes
18" × 20"	17"	20 minutes

and home-improvement centers carry both. If you aren't using a clip light, you'll also need a disposable aluminum pie plate to use as a reflector. For the bulb, purchase a 250-watt photoflood lightbulb at a photography-supply store or website.

If you're using a pie plate as a reflector, cut a hole in its center no bigger than the diameter of the socket. Run the electrical plug and cord through the hole so that the pie plate fits around the socket, then screw in the bulb. You can also expose your screen in sunlight or under a fluorescent lamp or tube. I use an ordinary grow light designed for plants to expose my smaller screens.

The distance between your silk screen and light source depends on the size of the screen: the larger your screen, the farther away your light source must be and the longer the exposure time. For instance, for a 10-by-14-inch silk screen, the light source should be about 12 inches from the screen. You can tape or clamp the light to an old floor lamp to get the right distance, or you may want to tape the light to the underside of a table and place your screen on the floor directly underneath, assuming it is the correct distance for the size of your screen. A 10-by-14-inch silk screen needs an exposure time of about 10 minutes.

The chart on page 147 offers an estimated range of distances and times according to screen size, but you may have to play around with these numbers in order to get it right. If you underexpose the screen, the emulsion will wash off; if overexposed, the emulsion will dry evenly throughout the screen, preventing your image from being washed out.

PROJECT: Preparing a Silk Screen with Photo Emulsion

SUPPLIES NEEDED

Work surface covered with plastic sheeting

Artwork on a transparency (see page 146)

Blank screen with monofilament mesh that has been washed and taped (see instructions on pages 129–31)

Speedball Diazo Photo Emulsion Screen Printing Kit

Squeegee or screen coater

Four small cups or containers of the same size or height to prop up screen while it dries

Fan (optional)

Black paper or black felt, several inches larger than your screen

Sheet of glass or Plexiglas that fits into your screen and covers your artwork

Darkroom safelight (see page 147)

Light-safe bulb (optional)

STEP 1. Prepare your image, following the instructions on page 146.

STEP 2. Hold your screen at a slight angle, and pour a bead of the photo emulsion mixture across the top edge of the back side of the screen. Using your squeegee or screen coater, pull the solution down to the bottom of the screen in one even, continuous stroke (A). Repeat on the bottom edge of the inside of the screen (B).

STEP 3. Set your screen in the darkened room propped up on cups in a horizontal position with the inside facing up. Check to be sure the containers are not touching the emulsion. If you want to speed the drying time, set a fan close to the screen. Once the screen is dry, it must remain in the darkened room until you are ready to expose it to the light.

STEP 4. To expose your image, lay the black felt or paper on the work surface under the light source. Lay your screen back (flat) side down

STEP 2A

STEP 3

STEP 2B

STEP 4

STEP 6

and centered on the felt. Place your artwork in the center of the screen, then lay the sheet of glass or Plexiglas on top of the artwork. Refer to the chart on page 147 for an estimate of how far to place the light source from the screen.

STEP 5. Time the exposure following the estimates in the chart on page 147.

STEP 6. When your screen is dry, take it to your sink or outside and spray it with cold or body-temperature water; do not use hot water. Once the image is clear, let it dry raised on cups in a horizontal position.

STEP 7. Print on prewashed fabric by following the directions on page 153. (See this print used on fabric on page 161.)

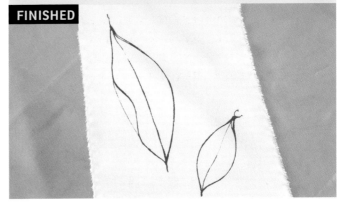

FINISHED

Printing a Silk Screen

No matter what kind of mask or resist you've used to prepare your silk screen, the printing method itself is pretty much the same. It's possible to print the same image several times on the same piece of fabric, but you must avoid placing the screen on paint that is still wet from a previous print. Otherwise, you'll pick up paint on the underside of your frame, which will smear and print the next time you put the frame down on the fabric. You can simply wait between printings for the paint to dry, use a hair dryer to speed things along, scatter the prints far enough apart on the fabric that the screen won't touch them, or put a piece of protective paper or fabric on each previous print. It is always helpful to keep a damp rag or towel handy for quick cleanup.

Off Contact

Another important factor in screen printing is something called off contact. This refers to the distance between the mesh of your screen and the fabric you're printing on. Ideally, the screen should not rest flat on the surface of the fabric, but be just enough above the fabric that the screen bounces off just after you've made a pass with the squeegee. If the screen rests on the fabric, you are likely to lift paint off the fabric when you remove the screen, with the result that the stenciled surface will be rough or textured rather than smooth. If the off contact is too high, on the other hand, you must use added pressure on the squeegee as you pull, making it difficult to print. Generally speaking, an off contact that is $1/16$ to $1/8$ inch works very nicely. Sometimes just the thickness of your emulsion, stencil, house paint, or

Fabrics Suitable for Screen Printing			
Fabric Type	Densely Woven	Loosely Woven	Textured
Silk habotai	x	x	
Silk crêpe de Chine	x		
Silk charmeuse	x		
Silk chiffon		x	
Silk organza		x	
Silk broadcloth	x		
Kona cotton	x		
Cotton sheeting	x		
Cotton knit	x	x	
Cotton broadcloth	x		
Cotton organdy		x	
Bamboo	x	x	
Bamboo knit	x		
Linen	x	x	x
Burlap		x	x

Creating off contact

screen filler is enough to allow good prints, or you may want to tape a penny or piece of cardboard to the corners of the silk screen closest to your body to raise it above the fabric.

Work Surface

Prepare a work surface that is firm with a slight give to it. Several layers of craft felt, fleece, or newspaper on top of an ordinary table that is covered with a sheet of plastic will do just fine. I find that a layer of muslin or newspaper placed over the plastic and under the fabric I am going to print on helps absorb any paint that may seep through the cloth to the back side. This prevents it from sticking to the plastic and removes the possibility of any smearing that may occur on the back side if you've used too much paint or your fabric is loosely woven. Be sure to pin or tape the muslin or newspaper down.

Fabric

The fabric you choose to print on will make a difference in what your print looks like. Generally speaking, a fine, tightly woven fabric gives the best results with the cleanest, sharpest edges to the lines. That said, however, screen printing on a textured fabric can yield some pretty interesting effects as well. You can also print on sheer or knit fabrics.

Paint

Heavy-body textile paints, with the consistency of pudding or yogurt, as well as artist acrylic paints work the best. PROfab textile paints from PRO Chemical & Dye are my personal favorites for silk-screening. Thinner paints tend to bleed or run under the image. Try not to use paint with large pieces of glitter in it, as these will prevent the paint from passing easily through the mesh. If you use PROfab paints, adding a bit of PRO No Dri will help to lengthen the time you have to work before the paints begin to dry. Artist acrylic paints tend to leave a hand to the fabric, but if you use Golden Silk-Screen Fabric Gel with Golden acrylics, this problem will be significantly alleviated.

Squeegee

The traditional wood-handled squeegee with a square blade is recommended for printing on paper. Speedball makes a squeegee specifically designed for printing on textiles that has a lightweight plastic handle and a neoprene blade that comes to a rounded point. These come in a variety of lengths. Ideally, your squeegee should be about 2 inches narrower than the width of your screen, so you can cover your entire design in one pass. If your squeegee is smaller, however, you'll just have to go over the screen a couple of times. Also,

Squeegees come with both rounded and square edges.

if you already have one with a wood handle and a squared edge, you can use it, but try to hold the blade at a 45-degree angle so you're using the squared edge to spread the paint. Another option is to use a one-piece plastic squeegee, which is available in several sizes (see Resources). For small screens, an old credit card does the trick very nicely.

Applying a Bead of Paint

When you prepared your screen, you created a taped-off area at the top against the frame (see page 127). This is known as the "well," and it's where you spoon paint so that you can draw it down across the screen, pushing it through the mesh in order to print the image. The spooned paint is called a "bead." Experience will tell you how much paint you need. With screen printing, it's better to err by placing too much paint rather than not enough, so you can pull a nice smooth stroke of paint over the screen. You can always scoop any excess paint back into its jar. That said, if you end up not having enough paint, just add more and print again.

Sometimes the difference between a print with sharp, crisp edges and a blurry print is determined by the angle at which you hold your squeegee and the way you pull it through. Try to hold the squeegee at an 80- to 85-degree angle and always pull toward your body. As you pull the squeegee toward you, concentrate on putting pressure on the screen and on the fabric, not on how hard you are pulling. Ideally, you need only one pass with the squeegee to totally clear the screen of paint.

It's important to have a tray of some sort, or even paper towels or newspaper, where you can lay your paint-laden squeegee when you finish printing but before you lift your screen. Paper can be problematic, as it can stick to your squeegee, making cleanup just a little bit harder. I also find the tray easier to see from the corner of my eye, so I'm less apt to put the squeegee down in the wrong place! Experienced screen printers rest the squeegee inside the screen against one of the sides of the frame.

PROJECT: **Making a Silk Screen Print**

SUPPLIES NEEDED

Work surface covered with plastic sheeting and topped with a layer of craft felt, fleece, muslin, or newspaper

Blue painter's tape, masking tape, or dressmaker's pins

Prewashed fabric (see page 28)

Prepared silk screen (see pages 129–31)

Plastic spoons (one for every color you use)

Heavy-body textile paints or artist acrylic paints mixed with Golden Silk-Screen Fabric Gel and the appropriate slow-drying agent for the paint you are using

Small containers with covers for mixing colors

Squeegee

A tray or plate for your wet squeegee between printings

STEP 1. Pin or tape the fabric you are printing onto your work surface. If you plan to make several prints in succession, tape several pieces of fabric to the work surface.

STEP 2. Lay your screen with the back (flat) side down on the fabric.

STEP 3. Spoon some paint into the screen's well on the far side away from you.

STEP 4. Holding your squeegee at a slight angle (about 80 to 85 degrees), place the blade between the frame and the bead of paint (A). With a steady hand, use a nice even stroke to pull the squeegee toward you, pushing the paint through the screen as you go; hold down the frame with your free hand (B). When

STEP 2

STEP 3

STEP 4A

STEP 4B

153

you get to the opposite edge, tilt the blade up so you can scoop up any unused paint and transfer it back to the well (C). Repeat once or twice more, as needed. (If your fabric is highly textured, you may need to go over it again.)

STEP 5. Remove the screen by pulling it up on the side closest to you, as if it had a hinge on the opposite far side, then lift the whole thing up and off your fabric.

STEP 6. Allow the paint to dry thoroughly and heat-set (see page 22), if necessary.

FLOODING THE SCREEN TO PREPARE FOR ADDITIONAL PRINTS

If you're going to make another print with the same paint or without washing out the existing color, you may want to flood the screen after the first print to prevent the paint from drying. After printing, and returning the unused paint to the well, lift the edge of the screen that is closest to you as if the opposite side is on hinges. While the screen if lifted, flood the screen by pulling the paint through it as if you were creating another print in the air. Some screen printers like to flood the screen before the first print as well as a way of conditioning it with paint, so they aren't pulling the first print through a dry screen.

- When your first print is dry, reposition the same screen and use a different color to print again. Use multiple colors, as shown here, if desired.

- Spoon more than one color in the well, then watch the colors mix and blend together as you print.

- Do not wash the frame out between colors.

- Compose a design that has multiple layers, with a different screen prepared for each layer. If you want to print the different layers in exactly the same spot, you must register your screen by marking the fabric lightly with pencil where the four corners of your screen should be placed for each print. For greater control, you can use hinge clamps on the upper side of each screen that are then screwed to a board. Speedball makes a deluxe hinge clamp with a thumbscrew so you don't have to use a screwdriver to screw and unscrew every time you want to change a screen.

Water-Soluble Crayons

I absolutely love the results you can get from this inventive technique. I use the Caran d'Ache Neocolor II water-soluble crayons (sometime referred to as water-soluble wax pastels). They are more expensive than some similar products, but they perform beautifully and consistently. I recommend using Jacquard Textile Color Colorless Extender for the medium, as it leaves the least amount of hand to your finished piece.

Choose a densely woven, smooth fabric, such as cotton, rayon, or silk broadcloth. You can work on thinner fabric as well, but the medium will leave more of a stiff hand to it. Prewash the fabric in hot water using Synthrapol or heavy-duty laundry detergent without scent or fabric softener.

With this technique, you "crayon" your design on the screen, completely filling it with color, and then squeegee medium through the mesh, taking your color design with it. You can draw a little landscape, a simple still life, or an abstract design — whatever you desire. In order to provide a hard surface when you're drawing your image on the screen, you'll need a book about the overall size and height of your screen.

You must get a fair amount of color on the screen, but keep in mind that the more color you have, the harder it will be to push the medium through the mesh. As the crayon starts to build up on the screen, it fills in the holes of the weave and then acts as a resist until it is really saturated with medium. Experience will guide you to the correct amount of color to use for the look you want.

A hard plastic squeegee makes this technique a little easier to pull off. If your screen or image is small, you can use an old credit card as a squeegee. You'll need to squeegee across the surface four or five times before getting a good print. It all depends on how much crayon you have on your screen and how hard you

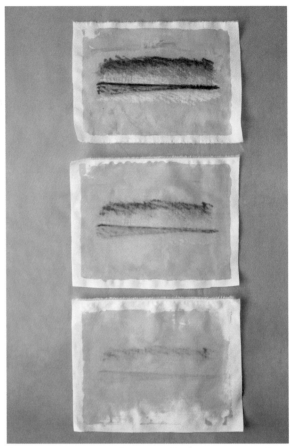

These are the results of a series of silk screen prints done using the process shown on the facing page.

press. You should be able to get several prints from one screen, with each print being somewhat lighter than the one before, but again, it depends on your own personal technique. It may take you a few tries to get the knack of this technique. But it is worth the trouble.

Don't be alarmed if you start to see color in the medium. The water in the medium starts to liquefy the crayon almost right away. It is in the nature of this technique to have some of the color smear, depending on how many pulls you make and how much medium you use. This technique is easier if you use a relatively small screen (approximately 4 by 6 inches). If you don't have a small screen, you can mask off a small area with painter's tape on the back side of a larger screen as shown.

PROJECT: Silk-Screening Water-Soluble Crayons

SUPPLIES NEEDED

Work surface covered with plastic sheeting

Hardcover book or other flat object about the size and height of your screen, not including the frame, so that the screen can sit flat on it when you draw

Some newspaper to cushion and protect the work surface and book

Silk screen with either multifilament mesh or sheer curtain fabric that has been washed and taped (see instructions on page 128)

Water-soluble crayons

Acrylic textile, gloss, or matte medium

Prewashed fabric (see page 28)

Hard plastic squeegee, or credit card for small designs

Masking tape or blue painter's tape to mask off a small area of a big screen (optional)

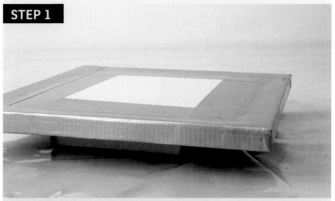
STEP 1

STEP 1. Cover the book with a few pieces of newspaper, then place the silk screen over it with the back (flat) side of the screen facing up and resting on the book.

STEP 2

STEP 2. Draw your design right on the mesh with the crayons, completely covering the screen if you desire.

STEP 3

STEP 3. Pour a line of medium across the top edge of the inside of your screen or where your well is. Lightly squeegee the medium across the screen. Then let it sit for 20 seconds or so, if desired. Waiting makes the printing easier, but it's also more than likely to smear the color. This is not necessarily a bad thing, so just go with it!

STEP 4

STEP 4. Use the squeegee to pull the medium through the screen, pulling and scraping the screen in all directions. Don't be afraid to use some elbow grease.

STEP 5. Allow the paint to dry and heat-set (see page 22) if necessary.

EXPLORING THE POSSIBILITIES:
Using Water-Soluble Crayons

- Using the side of a crayon to apply the color, place a rubbing plate under the screen as you fill in the desired areas.

- Start rubbing with one color, then keep adding colors as you move around the screen. Move the rubbing plate around between colors as well to achieve a great textural piece.

- For a wonderful watercolor effect, use Golden GAC 900 fabric/textile medium.

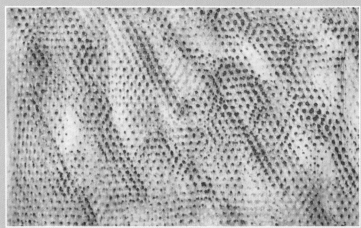

158

CLEANING UP AFTER SILK-SCREENING

Use soap and warm water to wash your frame out as soon as you are done printing, then dry it with a towel. The mesh of the screen will undoubtedly be stained from the paint, so hold it up to the light to make sure none of the holes in the mesh fabric are clogged with paint or medium. It may look like the holes are clogged with medium, when in fact it is just water, so do take time to dry it with a towel first. If you left the screen with paint on it a bit too long before washing, try spraying it with a citrus-based cleaner, such as Citra Solv, and let it sit for a bit before washing again. If you left the paint on your screen so long that you can't wash it out, you can reclaim the screen by replacing the mesh fabric. We all do it at least once!

EXPLORING THE POSSIBILITIES:
Acrylic Spray Resists

- **Using acrylic spray Ⓐ** (the type formulated to paint on plastic; available at hardware stores), paint a misty, abstract image onto the screen so that the screen is only partially filled in. This creates a lovely textural screen that you may find yourself using again and again.

- **Tape a piece of portable plastic construction fencing Ⓑ & Ⓒ**, deer fencing, snow fencing, or similar material to the back (flat) side of your screen. Spray the screen with acrylic paint. Carefully remove the taped material from the screen, then allow the paint to dry.

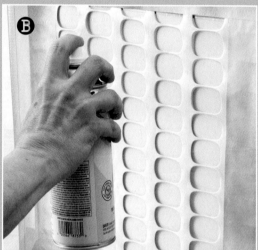

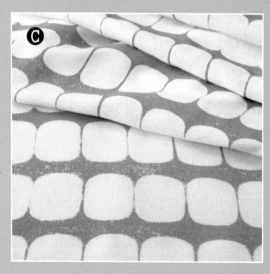

Designing with Original Fabric

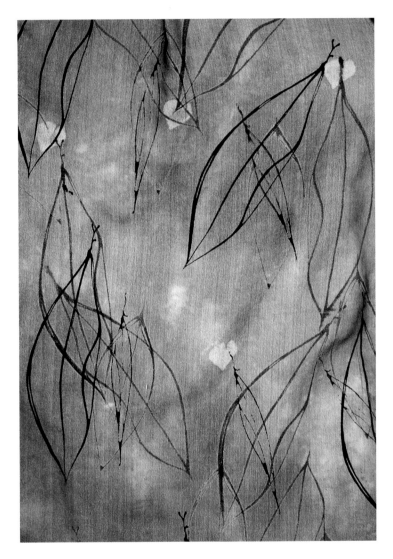

To create a lovely blending of colors, I wet and then sprayed this piece of silk habotai with thin textile paints (Dye-Na-Flow and Setasilk), using a different spray bottle for each color. When this base was dry, I stamped the small white leaves and hearts on it and then added silk screens of the leaf outlines.

Profile: Jane Dunnewold

Jane Dunnewold's two pieces shown here exemplify the beautiful and visually complex results one can attain using her multicolored printing process. Jane always begins with a piece of white fabric. Working with layers of colors and patterns, she is able to fashion fiber art that is rich with texture, mood, and nuance.

Jane is an internationally known artist, teacher, and author. She coined the widely and commonly used expressions "complex cloth" and "art cloth." Her books *Complex Cloth* and *Finding Your Own Visual Language*, as well as her artistic concepts and visions, have set the stage for contemporary fiber art around the world.

Currently the president of the international Surface Design Association, Jane maintains Art Cloth Studios in San Antonio, Texas. Her most recent book is *Art Cloth: A Guide to Surface Design for Fabric* (Interweave, 2010).
www.complexcloth.com
www.existentialneighborhoodblogspot.com
www.artclothstudios.com

Jane Dunnewold's *Block Party* (left; 44" × 48") and untitled (38" × 47")

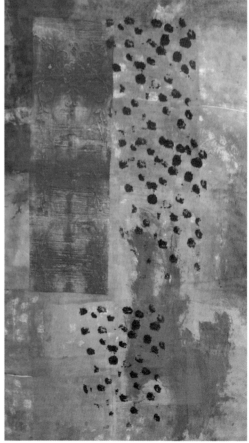

Profile: Monique Plunkett

I discovered **Monique Plunkett** of Elkhorn Design through Etsy, and fell in love with her fresh designs silk-screened on eco-friendly hemp, cotton, and linen pillows, table runners, and tea towels. With their quiet detail and clean, simple lines printed in a limited palette, her feather screen prints are my favorites among her images. Monique's design process can start with ideas that have their roots in old photos, magazines, and found objects from the beach. She works in her sketchbook until the design starts to materialize, and from there, cuts out stencils of the design before having them made into silk-screens. This allows her to hold them in her hand and see how they'll look on fabric before making the screen. She creates the final design on her computer.

Based in Melbourne, Australia, Monique precuts all her fabrics to the size of the project before printing, so that she can hand place and individually compose each element rather then randomly cutting from a large piece of printed cloth. The resulting work could easily grace any home or table setting.

www.elkhorndesign.blogspot.com; www.etsy.com/shop/elkhorndesign

Monique Plunkett's *Feather* table runner (top; 17" × 59–71") and *Orange Grove Patch* cushion (below, 18" × 18")

163

CHAPTER 11

Working with Resists

A resist is anything that blocks the penetration of paint or dye to the fabric. Technically speaking, even a stencil or a silk screen is a resist. For the purposes of this chapter, however, I'm referring to liquid products such as soy wax, water-soluble *gutta*, and school glue gel that can be applied to cloth as resists before adding paint.

Products That Can Be Used as Resists

Brand and Description	Uses	Comments
Jacquard Colorless Water-Based Resist: gutta-like resist, available in various sizes	Serti technique Brushwork Screen prints Air pen	• Very economical • Flows easily and consistently through both squeeze bottles and from a brush • Can be tinted with paint • Must be dry before painting • Washes out easily with warm water after paint has been heat-set
Jacquard Permanent Metallics and Black Water-Based Resist: gutta-like resist, available in small jars	Serti technique Brushwork Screen prints Air pen	• Once applied and heat-set, these resists are permanent • Available in 7 beautiful metallic colors and black • Makes lovely, fine, crisp lines that do not spread or bleed • Leaves a hand on the fabric even after washing • Must be dry before painting
Silkpaint! Resist (water-soluble); gutta-like resist, available in various sizes	Serti technique Brushwork Screen prints Stamping Air pen Stop-flow	• A bit more expensive but more versatile than some others • Can be used as a stop-flow when thinned with water (see No More Bleeding, page 167.) • Fabric can be painted while resist is still wet • Washes out easily with warm water
Pébéo Water-Based Gutta: gutta-like resist, comes in tubes	Serti technique	• Ready to use straight out of the tube • Available in 6 colors plus clear; I find them hard to handle, making it difficult to create consistent, even lines, but the convenience is great for classroom settings and working with children • Must be heat-set
Dupont Colored Gutta: gutta-like resist, comes in tubes	Serti technique	• Ready to use straight out of the tube • Available in 11 colors • Rather pricey • I find these hard to handle, making it difficult to create consistent, even line • Must be heat-set
Presist: thicker than gutta, comes in jars	Textural imagery Fine lines, stamping, stenciling, screen printing, and sponge printing on silk and other lightweight fabrics	• I love this resist, especially for creating texture over a large area of heavier fabric • Resist must be dry before painting • Washes out easily with warm water
Flour paste, oatmeal, instant mashed potato buds	An allover application results in a crackle effect similar to batik and interesting textural designs	• Fun, playful, and very unexacting resist • Useful with artist acrylic paints mixed with painting medium, acrylic inks, or india ink
Elmer's Washable School Glue Gel: comes in applicator bottle	Use direct from bottle Brushwork	• Inexpensive • Readily accessible • Great for certain projects where fine line and detail are not required

Products That Can Be Used as Resists

Brand and Description	Uses	Comments
Soy wax flakes	Batik	• An economical, safe alternative to traditional beeswax/paraffin batik
Liquid soy wax pen: comes in applicator bottle	Easy to use direct from bottle Serti-like and batik-like effects	• Designed for decorating candles, but it's excellent for simple batik • Produces consistent lines • Also may be used to achieve a soft, batik crackle effect • Applicator opening may clog, but that hasn't been my experience • Dries in 24 hours or less and washes out easily with hot water after paint has been heat-set

Fabrics Suitable for Resist Printing

Fabrics for Gutta-like Resists (with applicator bottles)

- China silk or habotai
- Silk crêpe de Chine
- Cotton voile
- Cotton lawn
- Cotton challis

Fabrics for Painting, Stenciling, and Stamping Resists

- All of the fabrics suitable for gutta-like resists
- Heavier weights, such as lightweight linen and rayon

Fabrics for Silk-Screen Resists

- Lightweight fabric
- Experiment! (Note that the resist has to penetrate through the fabric to the reverse side.)

Fabrics for Soy Wax Batik

- Any fabric is worth a try. Note that the tighter the weave and the heaver the fabric, the more difficult it will be for the soy wax to penetrate to the reverse side. On the other hand, the lighter the fabric, the harder it is to get imagery that doesn't bleed out. For your first experiments, use a medium-weight cotton like Kona cotton, cotton broadcloth, or a rayon challis.

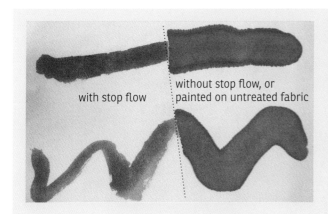

with stop flow

without stop flow, or painted on untreated fabric

NO MORE BLEEDING

Silkpaint! Resist can be used as a stop flow. This enables you to paint directly on silk without your brushstrokes bleeding out into the unpainted areas. Mix 1 part resist with 3 parts water. Brush the diluted mixture on stretched fabric. Allow to dry, then paint directly on the stop-flow to achieve brushstrokes that do not bleed out. Layer colors as desired. Heat-set the paint (see page 22, then wash out the resist following the manufacturer's instructions.

Serti Technique

Serti silk painting traditionally uses a rubber product called *gutta* to outline a design on silk fabric. Because the traditional, rubber-based gutta requires the use of solvents and dry cleaning, it's not a technique that I personally choose to use, but you can use water-soluble, gutta-like resists as fairly decent substitutes. Although you'll never achieve the clear, crisp lines of a traditional gutta, you can come pretty darn close.

Water-soluble, gutta-like resists are available in clear, metallic, and colored forms. The clear resists are meant to be washed out after you've finished painting. The metallic and colored versions are permanent. Note that the metallic and colored versions change the hand (feel) of the fabric, even after it has been washed.

Real gutta is applied using a handheld plastic applicator bottle outfitted with a metal tip. Tips come in a variety of sizes, allowing various line widths. You can use the traditional bottles and tips to apply water-based resists, outlining your design and then painting in the spaces between the drawn lines once the resist has dried. These supplies are available at silk-painting supply houses, including PRO Chemical & Dye and Dharma Trading (see resources, page 306).

Most serti painting artists use a predrawn design, but you don't have to. If you are really a free-form kind of artist, you can design as you "draw" with the resist — in other words, just go for it! If you prefer to transfer your design to the stretched fabric rather than drawing freehand directly on the fabric, see Creating Your Design on page 171.

Fabric

Fabric should be lightweight so the resist can penetrate to the reverse side, and, for the crispest lines possible, it should also be densely woven. A piece of white silk, such as 8 mm, 10mm, or 12 mm silk habotai or 12 mm crêpe de Chine, about 14 to 17 inches square is a good choice for your first attempt. Prewash it in hot water using Synthrapol or a laundry detergent that is free of scent and fabric softener. Water-based resists should be applied only to dry fabric. If you try to use them on wet fabric, they won't fully suffuse the fibers. It may be helpful to stretch a small piece of fabric to use as a sample where you can try out the different tips, gutta-like resists, the dilutant, and painting techniques before working on your design.

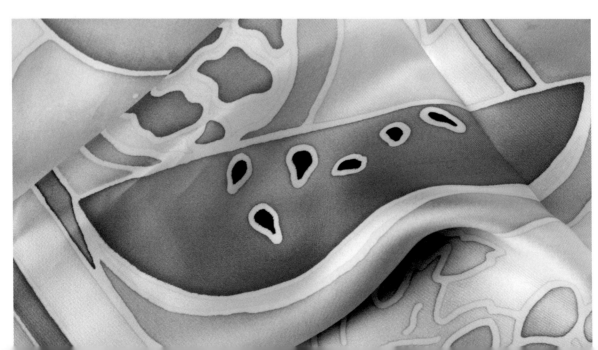

Resists and Resist Applicators

Gutta-dispensing plastic bottles and assorted metal tips found at silk-painting supply houses, such as PRO Chemical & Dye and Dharma Trading, come in a variety of shapes and sizes. I prefer the small, round plastic bottles from Jacquard. These bottles are very soft, which makes them much easier on your hands when you have to squeeze them for an extended time. They come with tips that can be easily screwed onto the plastic stem of the bottle, as well as with screw-on caps, so you can store the resist in the bottle for future use. Oval squeeze bottles are also available, and some artists prefer them. You may want to experiment to see which is best for you.

Use a water-soluble, gutta-like resist such as Jacquard's water-based colorless or permanent metallic (or black) resists, or Silkpaint! Resist for your first attempts. Fill the bottle three-quarters full with the resist. (If you fill it more than that, there won't be enough air for the resist to flow evenly.) When you choose your applicator, select the metal tip size appropriate for your design, and follow the

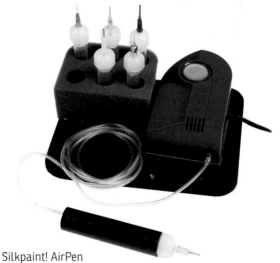

Silkpaint! AirPen

manufacturer's directions on how to put the tip on the dispensing bottle.

Squeezing these little plastic bottles can be very hard on your hands and wrists, especially if you suffer from arthritis or carpal tunnel syndrome. The Silkpaint! AirPen is a great remedy for this. It's fairly inexpensive, easy to use, and comes with a variety of tips. It takes a relatively small effort to learn how to use it, but if you really love the look of serti painting, it

can change your project from drudgery to joy. You can use the pen with heavy-body textile paints in other projects, as well — a great trick if you enjoy writing on your fabrics. Just remember to wash out the tips as soon as you are finished using them.

Paints and Brushes

Use thin textile paints, such as Jacquard Dye-Na-Flow or Pébéo Setasilk. Experiment with various brushes: both round and flat watercolor brushes, Japanese *sumi* brushes (see photo on page 169), and sponge brushes for filling in larger areas all work well. Small, round watercolor and sumi brushes are great for filling in small areas. If you find you love this technique, you can switch to more expensive natural-bristle brushes, such as squirrel-hair quill brushes, which can hold large quantities of paint while still coming to a very fine point.

Prepare a dilutant in a small container by mixing 2 parts 70% isopropyl alcohol (ordinary household rubbing alcohol) to 1 part water. If you wish, you can brush this mixture on the fabric just before applying paint. This dilutant increases the time it takes for the paint to spread to the resist lines, thus giving you more time to achieve blended, watercolor-like effects. It also tends to soften the color.

Creating Your Design

Use a soft pencil, washable marker, erasable fabric pencil, or a vanishing fabric marker (available at fabric stores) to draw a design free-hand on your fabric; you can also trace your design. (Please note that pencil is often difficult to wash out, so select your drawing implement wisely.) You may want to do this before stretching your fabric, but I find silk-painting artist Susan Louise Moyer's method to be much easier, because it keeps the fabric from shifting around as you work. Draw or trace your design on a piece of paper, then go over the design with a black sharp-tip, permanent marker. Stretch your fabric as described on pages 31 or 32. Tape your drawing to the underside of your fabric; place a book that is approximately the same thickness as the stretcher frame under the stretched fabric and drawing, then trace your design onto the fabric.

When you're planning your design, keep in mind that large areas of even color are hard to achieve. You might want to consider breaking up large open areas of your design with patterning details such as stripes, circles, or simple organic shapes like leaves.

Application Technique

Before you begin to apply the resist, plan ahead so that you don't face the problem of having your hand and arm dragging through the wet resist. If you're right-handed, start at the upper left-hand corner of your design, and work your way down a few inches before moving across the top edge of the fabric. Go back and pick up the design on the left-hand side again, then work your way across to the right-hand side. Continue in this manner until you have completed your design. If you're left-handed, start at the upper right-hand corner and reverse this approach.

To achieve even distribution of the resist, squeeze the bottle with a consistent amount of pressure. The rate at which you move your hand greatly determines the thickness of your line, regardless of the tip size you are using. The gutta lines will be thick if you move slowly, and thin if you move quickly, so adjust your movements accordingly.

When you're done, carefully look over your design to make sure all points where lines intersect are fully connected. Hold the fabric up to the light and carefully inspect the back side. If any of the gutta lines didn't completely penetrate the fabric, apply more resist to the back side.

PROJECT: **Serti Technique**

SUPPLIES NEEDED

Work surface covered with plastic sheeting

Newspaper to protect your work surface

Prewashed fabric (see page 28)

Stretching system (see page 29)

A design

Water-soluble, gutta-like resist

Gutta-dispensing bottles and assorted metal tips

Assorted watercolor paintbrushes

Dilutant (2 parts 70% isopropyl alcohol and
1 part water)

Thin textile paints, acrylic ink, or Tsukineko inks

Small containers for color mixing

Iron and ironing board

Pieces of cotton cloth or baking parchment paper,
for heat-setting

Dryer or fan (optional)

STEP 2

STEP 3

STEP 4

STEP 1. Prepare your work surface with either
newspaper or plastic sheeting, and stretch your
fabric.

STEP 2. Transfer your design as described on
page 171.

STEP 3. To apply the resist, fill the gutta-
dispensing bottles three-fourths full and
lightly touch the tip of your applicator bottle to
the surface of your stretched fabric and trace
over the outline of your design.

STEP 4. Check to be sure all points of intersecting lines are fully connected. Check also
to be sure the resist has penetrated to the
reverse side, and if not, apply more resist on
the reverse.

OTHER USES FOR GUTTA

- Apply gutta to a stamp and print the stamp on
fabric. After the gutta has dried, paint the area,
heat-set the paint, and then rinse out the gutta.
This is similar to the technique for using school
glue on a stamp, described on page 190.

- Apply gutta through a silk screen or stencil, and
allow it to dry. Paint the area around the print,
heat-set the paint, and then rinse out the gutta.

STEP 5. Wait for the resist to dry (unless you are using Silkpaint! Resist); you can use a hair dryer or fan to shorten the drying period. This is very important. If you find yourself getting impatient, go do something else!

STEP 6. Dip a round brush into the alcohol/water dilutant and touch it to the center of an area you are going to paint. The amount of dilutant to use depends on the size of the area: the idea is to have enough so that it spreads on its own just to the edges of the resist line, but you will more than likely have to coax it along with more dilutant unless the space you are painting is very small. Take care not to use too much. Since the resist is water soluble, too much dilutant or paint could easily break through the resist line. Also try painting without using the dilutant. (See Extra Credit: Playing with Paints and Dilutants, page 176.)

STEP 7. Working quickly so the dilutant doesn't have time to dry, dip your brush into the paint, then touch it to the center of the area where you used the dilutant, using just enough paint to fill the space. Move your brush out to the edges of the shape if you need to, but take care not to get too much liquid against the resist. Be sure to clean your brush when you change colors.

STEP 8. Fill in all the spaces of your design, then allow the piece to dry.

STEP 9. Heat-set the paint according to the manufacturer's recommendations and the appropriate temperature for your fabric. Protect your ironing board and your iron by sandwiching your fabric between pieces of cotton cloth or parchment paper.

STEP 10. Follow the manufacturer's directions to wash out the resist.

173

EXPLORING THE POSSIBILITIES:
Serti Silk Painting

- **Purposefully leave some areas Ⓐ** of your gutta design lines disconnected.

- **Create accents Ⓑ** by painting with a dry brush or painting with heavy-body, opaque textile paint, artist acrylic paints, or acrylic ink on top of the finished design after the first layer of paint has been set and the resist washed out.

- **Create a textured effect** by letting droplets of the alcohol/water dilutant drop from the tip of your brush or a dropper onto the wet or almost-dried paint.

- **Sprinkle salt** on the wet paint for another type of textural effect. (See page 44 for more details about using salt.)

- **Restretch the finished piece** then brush on more, tinting some or all of the resist lines with paint.

- **Use a liquid soy wax pen** to block out areas of your fabric before painting. These pens were designed for candlemakers, but work beautifully on fabric as well. They are available at Dharma Trading and from candlemaking-supply houses. Make sure to heat-set the fabric before washing out the wax.

TIPS FOR SUCCESSFUL RESISTS

- Use a different brush for each color, or make sure you rinse your brush well before changing colors. A light swish in a jar of water isn't sufficient. When you use a dirty brush, your colors lose their vibrancy and become gray or brown.

- Clean your rinse water often. I find it helpful to have two containers of water, one for the first rinse, and one for the final rinse before changing colors.

- Return any unused resist to its original jar unless your applicator bottles come with screw-on caps. Wash out the applicator bottle, then wash out the metal tip by filling the applicator bottle with hot water and squeezing the water through the tip several times.

Extra Credit: Playing with Paints and Dilutants

If you're interested in exploring the way paints and dilutants interact before plunging into a project, you may like to try this exercise. As you fill each square, note how quickly the color spreads to the edges of the resist and also how much paint or, in some cases, dilutant you use. Take care to rinse your brush each time you change colors or use the dilutant. (Instead of turquoise, you can use blue paint.)

PROJECT: Playing with Paints and Dilutants

SUPPLIES NEEDED

Work surface covered with plastic sheeting

Resist in a squeeze bottle

Prewashed fabric (see page 28), cut to a size that will fit your stretcher frame and that will accommodate a row of nine 2-inch squares, stretched on a frame

Small round brush

Thin textile paints, or medium-body paints thinned with water to the consistency of a dye

Red, brown, turquoise, and yellow paints

Dilutant (2 parts 70% isopropyl alcohol and 1 part water)

Small container of clean, plain water

Containers of water for cleaning brushes

SETUP. Stretch your fabric on your frame. Using the resist, make a column of nine 2" squares on the fabric. Allow to dry unless you are using Silkpaint! Resist.

STEP 1. Fill the brush with red paint, and touch the tip of it in the center of square 1. (Remember to rinse your brush each time you change colors.)

STEP 2. Fill the brush with dilutant, and touch the tip of it in the center of square 2. Before the dilutant dries, touch the square with red paint.

STEP 3. Wet square 3 with a bit of clean, plain water. When the water has spread to the edge of the resist, add a drop of red paint. Compare squares 1, 2, and 3.

STEP 4. Rinse your brush, then fill it with brown paint, and touch the tip of it in the center of square 4. When the paint begins to dry, add a bit of clean, plain water to the center of the square. Notice how the color lightens in the middle and how the water actually pushes the paint out toward the resist, causing a dark brown line to form right next to the resist.

STEP 5. Wet square 5 with a bit of clean, plain water. Add a drop of brown paint. Compare squares 4 and 5.

STEP 6. Put a drop of turquoise paint in the center of square 6. When the paint spreads to the resist, add a drop of yellow paint to the center of the square.

STEP 7. Put a drop of yellow paint in the center of square 7. When the paint spreads to the resist, add a drop of the turquoise paint. Compare squares 6 and 7.

STEPS 8 AND 9. Put a drop of dilutant in the centers of squares 8 and 9, then repeat steps 6 and 7.

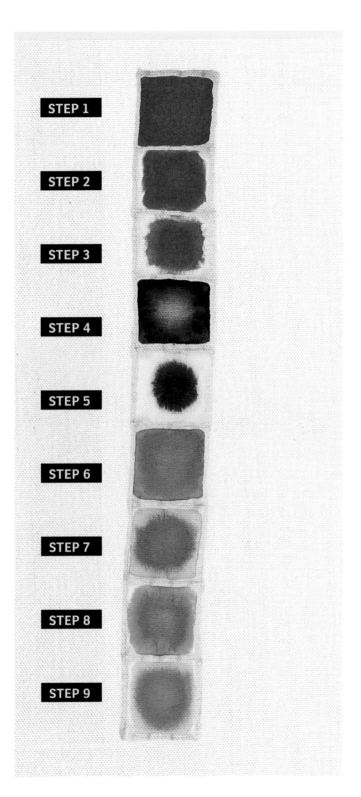

STEP 1
STEP 2
STEP 3
STEP 4
STEP 5
STEP 6
STEP 7
STEP 8
STEP 9

Profile: Colleen Ansbaugh

Colleen Ansbaugh's soy wax batik *Trees* is very expressionistic. I love its playful nature and the silhouettes of the white tree trunks against a colorful backdrop, which give it the illusion of a dense forest or a grouping of trees. The simple, tiny hand stitchery adds movement and rhythm, as if the leaves of the trees are blowing in a breeze.

Colleen likes to do a light drawing with pencil on the fabric before batiking. She also works with the fabric flat on a piece of Plexiglas. Colleen actively photographs nature to use as inspiration for her art quilts. Her work has been published in Ray Hemachandra's and Karey Bresenha's *500 Art Quilts* (Lark, 2010) and has been exhibited in galleries throughout Wisconsin.

Colleen Ansbaugh's *Trees* (8" × 10")

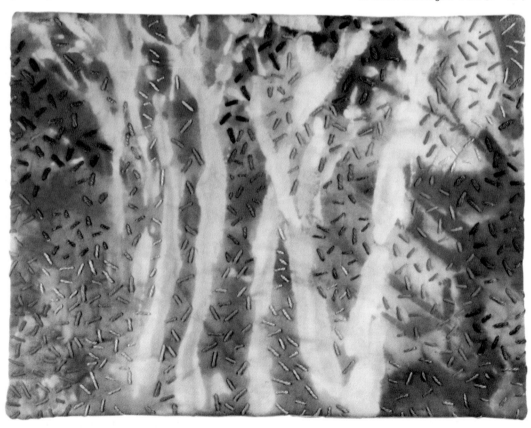

Creating Batik Fabrics

Wax resist on fabric has a long history, dating back to 4 BCE in Egypt, where it was used to wrap mummies; in Indonesia it even predates written records. The elaborate patterning in traditional batiked fabrics continues to identify royalty to this day, and it carries ethnic and spiritual meaning, even for the artist creating it.

Batik work can be extremely precise, realistic, and detailed, but it can also be spontaneous and experimental. If this is your first batik, it's a good idea to simply stretch a small piece of fabric and play with the tools and paint. Think of this as your batik sample. Understanding the process before working with an elaborate design will greatly increase your chances of success. You also might find that you prefer, as I do, to use this technique with a more playful style.

The Resist

Traditional batik is made using a combination of beeswax and paraffin wax heated to melting point, which is then used to block out areas of the fabric before applying dye. There are great drawbacks, however, to this combination of materials. For instance, the melting point of paraffin and beeswax is quite high, making it a fire hazard. Also, when it's melting, the fumes are quite toxic, and the wax can be removed only by dry cleaners who use a highly toxic chemical. (Many dry-cleaning facilities are phasing out these chemicals in favor of more environmentally safe alternatives.)

In the early 1990s, Michael Richards developed soy wax for candle makers. When Dorothy Bunny Bowen, a contemporary batik artist, ran across information about soy wax, she became very intrigued, and after extensive research, delivered a paper on its possibilities at the 2005 Kuala Lumpur International Batik Convention. Fiber artist Rayna Gillman was so interested in the "fabulous, non-toxic, and accessible" qualities of soy wax that she began teaching about it. For many artists and for many reasons, soy wax is now the batik medium of choice.

The melting point of soy wax is much lower, making it less dangerous, and it doesn't produce toxic fumes. This eliminates the need for an elaborate ventilation system, although soy wax does have a strong odor that some people find objectionable. Simply working by an open window alleviates this problem. Another advantage of soy wax is that it is water soluble, making it much easier to remove the wax once the piece is finished.

Artists with years of experience using the traditional beeswax and paraffin mix will find soy wax very frustrating for a variety of reasons. If you're just starting out, however, I think soy wax is definitely the way to go, especially because it lends itself to the direct application of textile paints instead of immersion and vat dyeing, which would cause the soy wax to dissolve.

You'll more than likely find soy wax marketed for candle making at your local craft store. Look for pillar wax or the pillar/votive wax blend, which is harder than the soy wax blends meant for container candles. To ensure you're getting the right wax, however, I recommend that you order soy wax flakes from a company that specializes in soy wax for batik. (Both PRO Chemical & Dye and Dharma Trading carry it; see Resources.)

Melting the Wax

You can use a special melting pot to melt the wax, but an electric skillet works just fine. Do not, however, use your favorite skillet for flipping pancakes for this purpose. Either buy a new skillet and dedicate it to soy-wax use, or buy yourself a new skillet for cooking and use the old one for batiking; you may also be able to find a used one at a yard sale or thrift shop.

In an electric skillet measuring about 11 inches square, you'll need about 1 pound of soy wax flakes to get the melted wax at a level where you can easily fill the bowl of a *tjanting* tool (at right), if you're using one. Your metal tools need to be kept hot as well, so you must keep them in the melted wax while you're working. Wrap the ends of the handles of your brushes and tjanting tools with rubber bands so they don't slip completely into the wax.

For your first experiments, note the color and transparency of the melted wax. The wax is hot enough to use when it is transparent and clear of color. Also take note of the temperature setting of your pot or skillet. Make some test stamps: If the wax doesn't penetrate thin fabric, you may need to increase the temperature of the wax a bit. If your fabric is thick, you may have to apply the wax to the reverse side as well.

Some artists have success melting their soy wax in a microwave oven. I personally find it difficult to control the temperature of the wax with this method, but you should give it a whirl if you find the idea intriguing. Keep in mind that if the wax is too cool, it will not penetrate the fabric. If the wax is not completely transparent when you apply it to the fabric, it's not hot enough. (See steps 2 and 3, page 183, for tips on how to assess whether the wax is hot enough.) Experience will help you get a feel for the correct temperature and what the printed fabric should look like.

Applicators: Tjantings

Tjantings are the traditional batik tool for drawing lines and delicate designs. They come with spouts in a variety of thicknesses, with different size bowls and in different metals. Copper is the most expensive, but only by a little, and it's worth the additional cost. Copper bowls and spouts retain the heat longer than other metals, keeping the wax at a more consistent temperature for a longer period of time. Electric tjantings are also available.

Stamping Tools

Copper and wooden stamps called *tjaps* are available from some batik-supply houses, as well as specialty auctions and flea markets.

SAFETY FIRST

- Never leave a pot of hot wax unattended.

- Keep the temperature control somewhere between 200°F and 225°F, or set it for medium heat if your skillet doesn't have numbers. Never heat the soy wax to the point of smoking. If it smokes, the temperature is too hot. Not every skillet or melting pot is the same, so you may need to adjust the control to get the right temperature.

- Metal handles may get hot as well. Use a cloth or pot holder, or clamps and clothespins attached to metal holders, if necessary, to protect your hands.

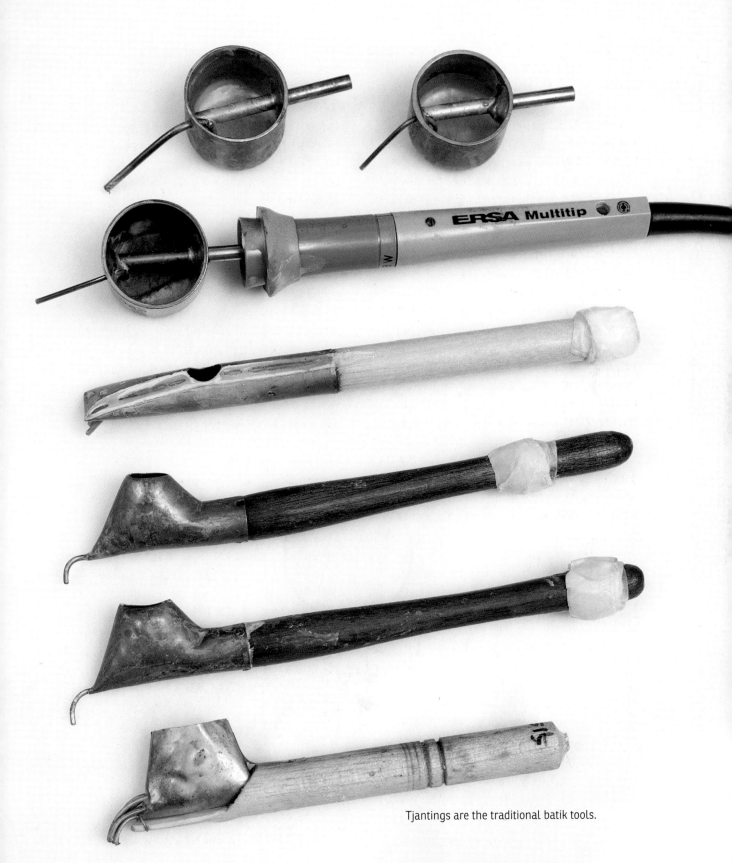

Tjantings are the traditional batik tools.

They range from very simple to very elaborate designs. Many household items work beautifully for batik as well. In fact, anything that won't melt is a possibility. Look around your garage and kitchen, or at a thrift store, for such metal and wood items as old potato mashers, mesh screens, wooden blocks, and cookie cutters. Plastic products made of resin work well, too, because they don't melt when placed in the hot wax. Rather than allowing them to sit in the wax like the metal items, simply hold them in the wax for a few minutes just before using them to stamp on the fabric. For metal tools, always use something, such as a wooden or plastic clip or clothespin, as a handle if you're going to immerse the implement in the hot, melted wax. As a reminder, as tempting as it can be, never use kitchen implements to handle food after you've used them for any art project.

For this project, we'll experiment using a fork as a stamping tool.

Fabric

Although many of us think of cotton as the fabric of choice for batik, really any fabric will do. Tightly woven, medium-weight fabrics yield the most traditional results, but don't let that stop you from trying less traditional materials. Keep in mind that the thicker your fabric is, the harder it will be for the hot wax to penetrate completely. You can get around this by turning the fabric over before you print and waxing it from the back side wherever it hasn't permeated.

Most people find that working on stretched fabric is the way to go, but several of my students have had satisfying results simply laying the fabric on a pile of newspapers. This works best if your fabric isn't too thick, as turning it over to wax the back side wouldn't be an option if it's not stretched. For first-time batiking, however, I recommend stretching your fabric.

Working with Color

What makes batik stand out from gutta and other resists is that you work in stages, layering wax and paint as you go along, thus producing more complex imagery. Understanding color mixing helps considerably (see pages 298–299 for advice). With batik, you apply wax wherever you don't want paint. You then paint certain areas, allow the paint to dry, and again apply wax wherever you want to block the next layer of paint. (Don't forget to wax over the areas you just painted.) You can cover the entire piece, or apply wax only in specific areas. You continue applying alternate layers of wax and paint until there are no longer any areas not covered with wax. Once the paint is dry, you begin to remove the wax by placing blank newsprint over the piece and ironing it, replacing the newsprint as needed until all but a hint of the wax has been removed. This ironing process will also heat-set the paint. The piece can now be washed to remove the last of the wax.

You'll get the best results if you put down light colors first, and then move to darker colors for subsequent layers. If you begin with dark colors, you won't be able to create the desired depth of color, because light transparent colors can't be painted over dark ones. You can, however, use a more opaque, heavy-body paint for your last layer, if you like. If you take this approach, the hand of your fabric will be a bit stiffer, but that's not necessarily a bad thing.

PROJECT: Using Soy Wax for Batik

SUPPLIES NEEDED

Work surface protected with newspapers or a piece of plastic

Prewashed fabric (see page 28), such as a 17" × 17" piece of lightweight cotton or silk

Stretching system (see pages 29–32)

Melting pot or an electric skillet

Soy wax flakes manufactured for batik, 1 pound

A fork, or other metal and/or resin tools for stamping

Thin textile paints or medium-body paints thinned with water to the consistency of dyes

Brushes, spray bottles, and/or sponges for applying the paint

Hair dryer (optional)

Natural-bristle brushes (synthetic brushes melt), tjanting tool (optional), or other implements for applying hot wax

Blank newsprint

Iron and ironing board

Container of hot water, large enough to hold your fabric

STEP 1. Stretch your fabric on a frame (see page 32).

STEP 2. Set your skillet or melting pot to 225°F (or just below Medium, if your appliance doesn't have numbers), and pour in the soy wax flakes. Bring the wax up to temperature; when it's completely transparent, it should be the right temperature to work with. Place a fork in the melted wax.

STEP 3. Take the wax-coated fork out of the skillet and press the tines into your fabric. Check the back side of the fabric to see if the wax has penetrated it. If not, increase the skillet's temperature a bit. Apply wax in the same manner with other implements.

STEP 4. Brush, spray, or sponge one of your light colors in areas of your cloth, leaving some spaces unpainted; you'll be painting over these areas with another color either at this stage or on a subsequent layer. If I'm working with white fabric, I often like to leave some small areas unpainted even to the very end, because I like the little sparks, or highlights, these white areas add to the finished piece. Wait for the paint to dry.

STEP 5. With a brush, apply spots of color and pattern in an all-over design. Wait for the paint to dry. You can hit it with a hair dryer to help set the paint as you continue to add layers. (Alternatively, you can use wax as your first layer, and apply it directly to the unpainted fabric.)

STEP 6. Use a brush, implement, or tjanting tool to apply hot wax to areas of the fabric. Try out different tools and techniques. Wait for the wax to dry.

STEP 7. Spray, brush, or sponge another layer of paint in selected areas.

STEP 8. Add more wax. Continue to layer wax and paint in this manner until the fabric is completely covered in wax (or until you are happy with what you see).

STEP 9. Heat-set the paint by placing your piece between two layers of blank newsprint (A), then ironing it (B). This step removes much of the wax as well; replace the newsprint as it becomes saturated with wax.

STEP 10. When most of the wax has been removed, immerse the fabric in hot water to remove the last remaining bits. If your fabric is washable, you may want to wash it clean in your washing machine.

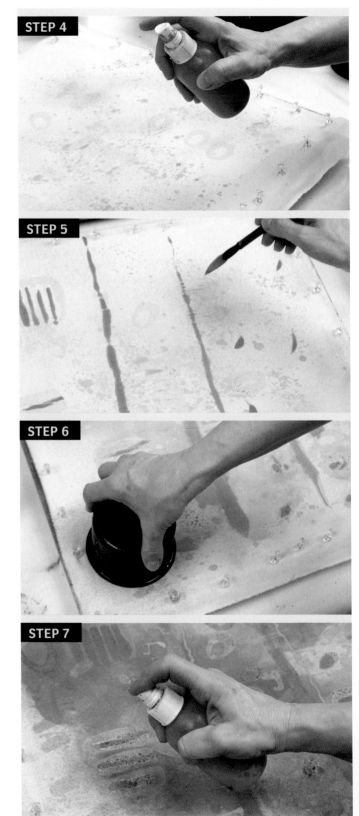

STEP 8

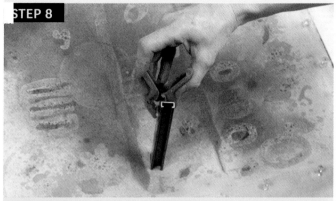

STEP 8

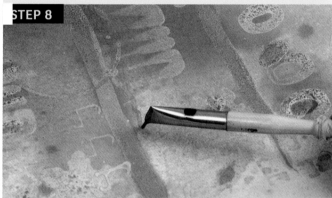

STEP 9A

STEP 9B

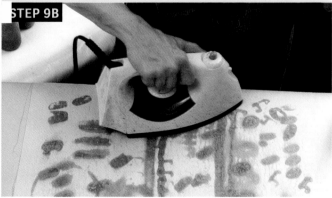

THE CRACKLE EFFECT

To achieve the traditional batik crackle, remove the wax-laden fabric from your stretching frame after the last application of wax and paint. Crunch the fabric up with your hands as much or as little as you want. Lay it out flat on your work surface, then paint over the entire surface with a thin or medium-body dark-colored textile paint that has been thinned with water. (You can also use india ink, acrylic inks, or artist acrylic paints that have been thinned with textile medium for this step.)

Some artists get great results by putting the finished piece in the freezer before crunching. This gives it a stronger crackle, as the frozen, hard wax tends to crack with sharper lines.

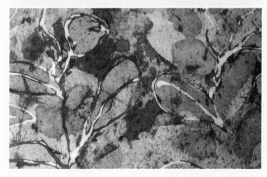

185

Flour as a Resist

Using flour paste as a resist is another method that has been around for a very long time. In recent years, many contemporary fiber artists have given it a new twist that can yield spectacular results, quite similar to the crackle effect of traditional batik. This is a messy project, so working outdoors is a great option!

Most artists use dyes, rather than paint, for this technique, because you have to submerge the piece in water to remove the flour and you can't heat-set the paint before doing so. You can get around this, however, by adding Jacquard Versatex No Heat Fixative to thin textile paint, or medium-body textile paints that are thinned with water. This fixer sets the paint without heat, allowing you to safely submerge the piece in water. Another choice is india ink, acrylic ink, or artist acrylic paints that have been thinned with textile painting medium.

Fabric

I worked the technique I describe here on white fabric, but you can use painted or dyed fabric as well. Use a light- to medium-weight fabric that measures approximately the size of a fat quarter (one-fourth of a yard, about 18 by 22 inches). You can, of course, work with much larger pieces of cloth, but this is a good size to start with. Another option is to lay out several smaller pieces of cloth so you can try drawing a variety of marks into the drying flour paste. Paint the entire piece using a direct painting method (see chapter 4) with relatively dark colors.

PROJECT: Creating a Flour-Paste Resist

SUPPLIES NEEDED

Work surface covered with plastic sheeting

Light- to medium-weight fabric, about 18" × 22"

Straight pins, T pins, or pushpins

All-purpose white flour (about 1¼ cups, depending on the size of your fabric)

1 cup water (approximately)

Mixing bowl and large mixing spoon

Squeegee, brayer, or plastic paint scraper

Hair dryer (optional)

Drawing implement (your finger, a stick, pen, paint scraper, etc.)

Thin textile paints, OR medium-bodied textile paints that have been thinned with water and Jacquard Versatex No Heat Fixative, india ink, OR acrylic ink OR artist acrylic paints that have been thinned with textile medium (Note: These paints should be much darker in color if you are using dyed or painted fabric.)

Fairly wide foam paintbrushes

Bucket of warm water for rinsing the fabric

STEP 1. Lay your fabric out flat on your work surface. Pin down all four edges of the fabric.

STEP 2. Mix flour and water together to achieve the consistency of a very thick pancake batter.

STEP 3. Pour or spoon the mixture onto your fabric, then use the squeegee or the back of a wooden spoon to spread a thin coat over the entire piece.

STEP 4. Wait for the flour to begin to dry. Depending on how thick the flour paste is, this could take as long as 8–10 hours. (The edges will begin to curl as this happens, and you may need to change the position of your pins.) You can use a hair dryer or set the piece out in the sun to speed the process.)

STEP 5. When the flour is partially dry, if you wish, you can draw into it with your finger, a stick, a closed pen, a paint scraper, or anything else that scores through the flour to the fabric.

STEP 6. When the flour is completely dry, crunch it with your hands, handling it as little or as much as you want. Be careful — dry flour particles will go flying! Wherever the flour flakes off, the now-exposed fabric will take on the paint/ink you apply in the next step. Sometimes the crackle lines are very faint, so don't worry if you don't see any.

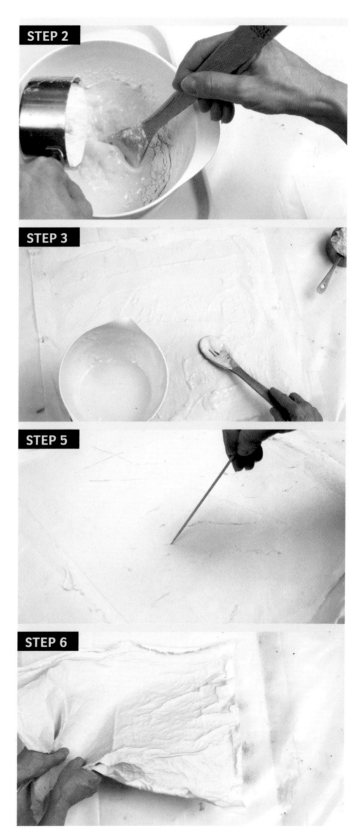

STEP 7. Flatten the fabric and pin it down as best you can. Paint the india ink, acrylic ink, Versatex-treated textile paints, or diluted artist acrylic paint over the flour. Let it dry (you can hit it with a hair dryer again).

STEP 8. Dunk the fabric in a bucket of warm water to rinse out as much of the flour as possible. You may need to use your fingers to help the process along. Dump the bucket water outside so that the flour paste doesn't clog your drain. Run the fabric through the washing machine for a final cleaning. (No heat-setting is necessary.)

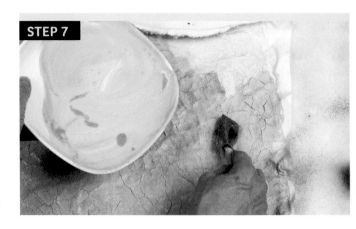

STEP 7

EXPLORING THE POSSIBILITIES:
Flour-Paste Resist

- Apply the flour paste only to certain areas of the cloth.

- Use several colors of paint on top of the flour paste.

- Use instant mashed potato buds and steel-cut oatmeal instead of flour for a variation in texture.

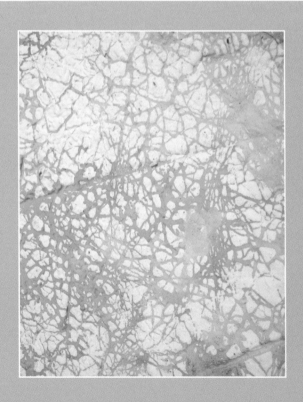

School Glue Gel as a Resist

I have no idea who first discovered this neat trick, but I know for certain that many artists are grateful. For this technique, the school glue is essentially a substitute for a gutta-like manufactured resist. The difference is that the glue is kind of gooey and much more viscous, so it can spread and ooze, producing wonderful lines and organic textures. You can work from a predetermined design if you wish, but this medium really lends itself to a bit of freewheeling activity! Don't try this with traditional white school glue: it won't work.

Mix Jacquard Versatex No Heat Fixative into textile paints to eliminate the need for heat-setting. Stretching the fabric on a frame is optional, but it does make the application of the glue a lot easier.

PROJECT: Using Washable School Glue Gel

SUPPLIES NEEDED

Work surface prepared with plastic sheeting or newspaper

Light- to medium-weight fabric, approximately 17" × 17"

Stretching system (see pages 29–32)

Design (optional)

Elmer's Washable School Glue Gel

A plastic squeeze bottle with a fine tip (optional)

An assortment of different-size brushes or spray bottles for the paint

Thin textile paints, medium-body textile paints thinned with water, acrylic inks, or acrylic artist paints thinned with textile medium (Mixing Jacquard Versatex with the textile paints would be an asset, but it is not necessary.)

A brush designated for the glue

EXPLORING THE POSSIBILITIES:
Washable School Glue Gel

- Apply glue with a paintbrush or stamps.

- Be inconsistent about how well the glue permeates the fabric, allowing some paint to pass through the glue resist.

- Use a piece of fabric that already has paint or imagery on it.

STEP 1. Stretch the fabric (see pages 31–32).

STEP 2. Transfer your design, if you are using one (see page 171).

STEP 3. Squeeze the glue directly out of the bottle onto the fabric (A), or transfer it to a squeeze bottle with a finer tip, or use a small paintbrush to apply the glue (B). Alternatively, you can brush the glue onto a stamp and stamp it onto the fabric (C). Make sure the glue has penetrated to the reverse side of the fabric. Wait for it to dry.

STEP 4. Brush or spray the paint or ink onto the fabric, taking care not to saturate the fabric too much, as the glue is water soluble. That said, however, you can get a great, organic look if you allow some glue to dissolve before washing. Wait for it to dry.

STEP 5. Heat-set the paint, if necessary, following the manufacturer's directions and at the temperature appropriate for your fabric. If you heat-set by ironing, protect your iron by laying a piece of parchment paper over the fabric.

STEP 6. Remove the glue by washing in warm or hot water. It helps to do this first by hand, as you might have to rub with your fingers in order to remove the glue.

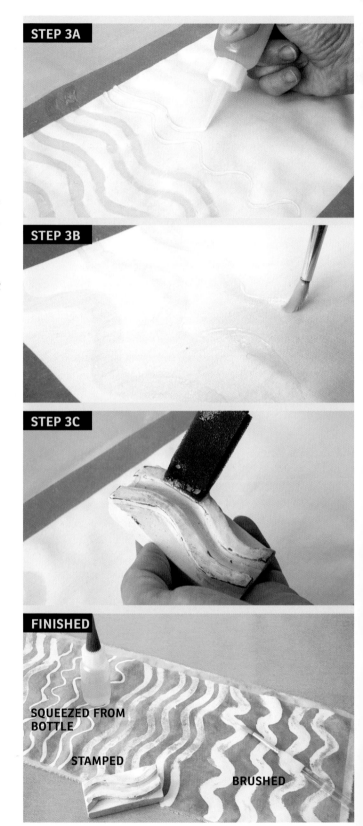

STEP 3A

STEP 3B

STEP 3C

FINISHED

SQUEEZED FROM BOTTLE

STAMPED

BRUSHED

Profile: Jeanne Sisson

Jeanne Sisson's acuity in combining realistic and expressionistic imagery, using soy wax batik and paint, is exemplified in these two lovely pieces. Her passion for working from the female figure is beautifully captured in *Janushka,* while *Wild Wood* shows a relaxed sensibility, leaving room for a more personal interpretation. *Janushka* is refined and calculated; *Wild Wood* resembles the rough cut of a woodblock print.

Jeanne starts her batik paintings with a light drawing directly on the fabric. After painting in the outlines of various objects with a brush, she then carefully covers the outlines with soy wax. Layers of wax and gradating colors follow until the piece is completely covered with wax.

In 2009, Jeanne completed an Art Cloth Mastery Program with Jane Dunnewold. Since then, her work has been juried into the Art Cloth Network and into various other shows throughout the country.

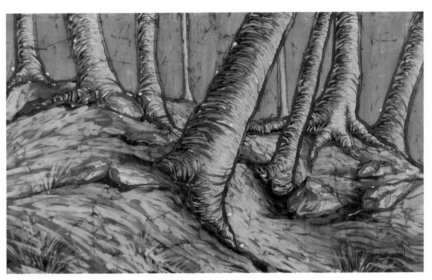

Jeanne Sisson's *Wild Wood*
(above, 30" × 21") and
Janushka (left, 16" × 16")

Profile: Daniel Jean-Baptiste

Daniel Jean-Baptiste grew up on the island of Saint Lucia in the Caribbean. During childhood, he spent his spare time fishing off his village's long wooden jetty. As an adult, Daniel moved to Canada where he was introduced to painting on silk with water-based paints and resist. Captivated by the medium, he found that his boyhood memories of the colorful plants and animals he saw while fishing dominated as the subject matter for his silk paintings.

One day while he was working on a painting, his daughter accidentally spilled some water on the wet silk. Daniel was so intrigued with the result that he coined it "the shimmering light water technique," a technique he continues to use on purpose to this day.
www.jean-baptiste.com

Daniel Jean-Baptiste's *St. Lucia Bird of Paradise* (top, 30" × 40"); *Under the Bahamian Sea* (bottom, 60" × 50")

Profile: Carol Dunn

Carol Dunn is an award-winning printmaker and photographer who specializes in using alternative processes for creating her artwork. Like many artists, she loves to mix several techniques in one art piece. While I was writing this book, Carol took a batik class with me where we used soy wax and textile paints. Although she had never used the technique before, it was clear early on that she already had an affinity with art materials and the art-making process. She simply transferred what she knew from printmaking and photography to create these two wonderful pieces. *Order in Chaos* is my favorite and it was her very first batik. She created *Kinetic Energy* by simply cutting up a batik, then laying out the pieces on black fabric out of order.

Dunn's work is in private collections throughout the United States, as well as in Ireland, France, and Australia.

www.caroldunnart.com

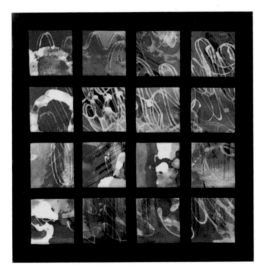

Carol Dunn's *Kinetic Energy* (above, 12" × 12") and *Order in Chaos* (right, 13½" × 21")

CHAPTER 12

Image Transfer

A computer opens up new possibilities for printing quite detailed and sometimes realistic photographs onto cloth, using a process known as image transfer. It's a lot easier than you might think and is great fun to play with.

You can transfer photographic images onto cloth using many different processes, such as:

- Print onto an iron-on transfer sheet with either an inkjet or laser printer.

- Print directly on the fabric itself with an inkjet printer.

- Use paint and acrylic medium to lift a photographic image printed on plain paper with a laser printer, an image printed with an inkjet printer on transparency film, or an image from a magazine.

- Use a wonderful product called Sheer Heaven.

- Use digital precoats, such as inkAID and Golden Digital Grounds.

If you are planning to try these techniques on your home computer and desktop printer, you need certain kinds of equipment and some basic skills in order to be successful with digital image transfer. Here are some considerations:

- Note whether your printer is inkjet or laser.

- You'll need access to image-altering software, such as Adobe Photoshop, Adobe Photoshop Elements, Corel PaintShop Pro, or ArcSoft PhotoStudio. Most computer operating systems come with some kind of photo-viewing software, but not all have photo-editing options. Check to see what's possible with your computer before you buy something expensive that you can't return. Online photo editing resources include some free software options, such as Photoscape, GNU Image Manipulation Program (GIMP), Photo Pos Pro Photo Editor, Pixlr, and Aviary. Know which operating system your computer needs before downloading.

- Be familiar with how to change the size or resolution of an image as well as how to alter the color saturation, color balance, or contrast of an image.

Generally speaking, you have to be able to work on your images in something other than JPEG format. JPEGs are small and fast to load and thus easier to work with, but these conveniences come at a cost. Because JPEGs are compressed image files, every time you work on and save a particular JPEG file it gets compressed again, resulting in loss of detail and loss of overall image quality. For this reason, it would be better to use software that allows you to work in another format. TIFF is the most universal, but different software programs may have their own proprietary formats, such as Adobe Photoshop's PSD. These image file formats are larger and slower, but well worth the occasional aggravation.

Iron-on Transfer Sheets

This is definitely the easiest method of photo transferring images. The end result, however, is always a bit stiff on your fabric — some brands more so than others.

You'll find iron-on transfer sheets at office-supply stores, fabric stores, and online. Each sheet is backed with paper so it can be fed through the printer. Before you buy, check on whether you have an inkjet or laser printer so that you choose the appropriate iron-on sheets. You also have the option of transfer sheets designed to be used on light or dark fabric.

Note that whatever you print will be a mirror image of the original picture. If that's undesirable (if you have lettering, for instance), you must use your computer software to flip the image before printing. In Adobe Photoshop and Adobe Photoshop Elements, go to the drop-down menu at the top of your screen. Click on Image, then Image Rotation. Choose either Flip the Canvas Horizontally or Flip the Canvas Vertically, whichever works for your image.

PROJECT: **Using Iron-On Transfer Sheets**

SUPPLIES NEEDED

Image downloaded to your computer

Laser or inkjet printer

Iron-on transfer sheets appropriate for your printer style

Prewashed fabric (see page 28)

Iron and ironing board

Photo-editing software (optional)

STEP 1. Select your image, and make sure it's the proper size for the iron-on sheets. For instance, if you're using Adobe Photoshop or Photoshop Elements, go to the drop-down menu at the top of your screen and click on Image, then Image Size. Change the width and length of the Document Size, if necessary. While you have this window open, check the resolution as well: it should be between 200 and 300 ppi (pixels per inch).

STEP 2. Load the iron-on transfer sheet into your printer, taking care to place the correct side down, and print. If you are unsure as to what side of the paper will get printed on, see step 4, page 200. Print the image.

STEP 3. Place the print onto your fabric, image side down. Iron according to the manufacturer's directions. Compare result below with prints of the same image on different fabrics on pages 200 and 202.

Image transfer printed using Epson Iron-on Inkjet Transfer Paper.

Digital Image Transfer

Printing images directly onto your fabric is a bit more complicated and can be a very extensive process. For the purposes of this book, I am going to talk about the basics, which should get you started. If you want more extensive information, however, check out one of the books mentioned in the resources section (see page 307).

To accomplish digital image transfer on fabric, you need a computer and an inkjet printer. (A laser printer is not suitable for this technique.) The quality of your final print is dependent on many factors, including image resolution, your inkjet printer, the ink in your inkjet printer, and your fabric, including whether it's pretreated.

TRANSFER ARTIST PAPER

Transfer Artist Paper (TAP) is a fantastic, iron-on image transfer paper developed by a paper company, with the help of art quilter Lesley Riley, an aptly self-described Queen of Transfers. (For information about purchasing TAP and related materials, see Resources.) There are many reasons why this particular transfer paper is so amazing:

- Once your image is transferred and the fabric is washed, the original hand of the fabric will return.

- The image can be ironed without the use of a protective sheet.

- Most exciting, you can draw directly on the paper prior to transferring, which means you can use pencils and pastels as design elements for your piece.

Printer Requirements

Any inkjet-printer brand works, but results vary. A printer with a straight-line paper feed is easier to use than one where the paper has to work its way around a roller inside the printer. Inkjet printers use either a dye-based or a pigmented ink. Pigmented ink is preferred, as it is water- and UV-resistant. Check your owner's manual, the ink cartridge package, or call the manufacturer to find out what kind of ink your printer uses. If you see UltraChrome or DURABrite ink named on the packaging, you're good to go. If your printer uses dye-based ink, you must pretreat your fabric with Bubble Jet Set 2000 (see below) before printing, or purchase pretreated fabric.

Fabric

Fabric selection is important. If you want clean, sharp images, choose a densely woven, smooth cotton or silk. A variety of companies offer pretreated fabric that makes the print water-resistant and permanent but not UV resistant. Pretreated fabric comes already backed with paper. The Jacquard, C. Jenkins, and Color Plus Fabrics brands of pretreated fabrics all work very nicely (see resources, page 306).

If your printer uses dye-based ink, you can pretreat your fabric with Bubble Jet Set 2000, a product developed by C. Jenkins Company, or use the pretreated fabric mentioned above. Your fiber should be 100 percent natural if you use Bubble Jet Set. Although the manufacturer recommends cotton or silk, I have tried linen and rayon with successful results. (For advice on using Bubble Jet Set, see page 202.)

If you use untreated fabric, you must stabilize it in some way so it can feed smoothly through the printer. One great way to do this is to iron it onto freezer paper. The C. Jenkins Company makes a freezer paper specifically for this purpose. It's heavier than the grocery-store variety, so it doesn't curl and adheres better to fabric. It's also been conveniently cut to fit a standard-size printer. If you use Bubble Jet Set 2000, you should use this particular freezer paper as well. If you're working with untreated fabric, another option is to use temporary spray adhesive to mount the fabric on a piece of heavy paper stock. Another alternative is to remove the labels from a sheet of self-adhesive labels (available in office-supply stores) and mount the fabric on the blank sheet.

Print Quality

Fabric is much more absorbent than paper. Because of this, your print more than likely will be less vivid than it appears on your computer screen or on paper. Learn to adjust the color saturation, color balance, and contrast options in your software as needed. You may discover you have to push these to such an extent that the image no longer looks right on your monitor. That's okay. What counts is how it ends up looking on the fabric. After a while you'll come to understand the nuances of your particular printer and software program, and you'll be making great prints in no time at all.

Keep in mind, too, that because the inks are not opaque, you can get interesting results by printing on colored fabric, your own painted fabric, or even on preprinted commercial fabrics.

TIPS FOR FABRIC BACKING

- If you're using freezer paper, take care to align the edge of it with the straight edge of the fabric.

- Use a rotary cutter and a ruler to cut loose threads and uneven, raggedy edges.

- Use a lint roller or a piece of masking tape to remove any stray threads or pet hair from the fabric: otherwise, these will act as a resist.

- To pretreat your fabric with Bubble Jet Set 2000, see instructions on page 202.

- Fold a length of masking tape over the leading edge of the paper-backed fabric (the edge that will feed through the printer first). Adhere the tape to the fabric side first **Ⓐ**, then fold it over onto the paper side **Ⓑ**. This will help the rollers in your printer grab the edges of the fabric so it feeds through evenly.

PROJECT: **Creating a Digital Image Transfer**

SUPPLIES NEEDED

Image downloaded to your computer

Computer with photo-editing software

Inkjet printer (laser printers do not work for this process)

Prewashed fabric treated with Bubble Jet Set 2000 and freezer paper, if using dye-based inks, OR plain fabric ironed to freezer paper or pretreated fabric

Plain copy paper

Lint roller or masking tape (optional)

STEP 1. Select your image, and follow step 1 under Iron-on Transfer Sheets (page 197).

STEP 2. If you're using untreated fabric, iron it to a sheet of freezer paper cut to fit your printer. (See Tips for Fabric Backing, page 199.)

STEP 3. Make a test print on a plain piece of paper. Set the printer for low or draft quality so you don't waste ink.

STEP 4. Set the prepared fabric in the printer tray. To ensure proper feed, put in only one piece at a time. Take care to line the fabric up straight and with the proper side up, so you print on the fabric and not on the paper. Most printers have an icon on the plastic tray that indicates which side will print. If yours doesn't, use a test sheet marked with an *X* and make note of which side prints.

STEP 5. Allow your fabric to completely dry before removing the paper backing. I generally wait about 24 hours before handling, but some artists feel that the fabric needs a week before fully curing. (If you're using Bubble Jet Set 2000, see instructions on page 202.) Compare the print below, done on silk, with the one done with an iron-on transfer sheet shown on page 197 and the one on pretreated fabric on page 202.

STEP 6. Heat-setting is not necessary, but I always do it anyway: It never hurts!

Image transfer printed using Jacquard paper-backed silk Inkjet Fabric Sheet.

EXPLORING THE POSSIBILITIES:
Digital Image Transfer

- **Print on sheer fabric Ⓐ.** Here, I made one print of a close-up shot of leaves on cotton fabric, and another print of the same image on sheer organza. When the sheer is laid over the other, but not aligned, a new, even more interesting graphic design appears.

- **Scan actual objects Ⓑ & Ⓒ.** If your printer is an all-in-one model, place actual objects on the scanner. Scan them in, manipulate the image in your software, and then print. For an interesting background, if your objects are not flat, simply place a piece of cloth over them before scanning, or use a black cloth if you don't want any background.

- If your printer accommodates long lengths of paper, buy pretreated fabric that has been cut and hemmed for printing banners, neckties, and scarves.

- If you're planning to use fusible webbing to adhere your print to fabric afterward, and the fabric you're using is untreated, you can fuse it to one side of the fusible webbing's paper backing as the stabilizer for printing.

Bubble Jet Set 2000 and Bubble Jet Rinse

Please read the instructions and safety precautions on the Bubble Jet Set bottles before you begin. Steps 1–4 provide instruction on how to use this product to pretreat fabric; steps 5–8 describe the rinse procedure.

PROJECT: **Using Bubble Jet Set 2000**

SUPPLIES NEEDED

Densely woven, all-natural 100 percent silk or cotton fabric

Synthrapol or unscented, heavy-duty laundry detergent without fabric softener

Scissors

Rubber gloves

Bubble Jet Set 2000

Container large enough to hold the fabric

Towels

Bubble Jet Rinse

Freezer paper

Hair dryer or clothes dryer (optional)

STEP 1. Prewash your fabric in hot water using Synthrapol or heavy-duty laundry detergent without scent or fabric softener, then cut it slightly larger than the print you're making.

STEP 2. Wearing rubber gloves, pour enough Bubble Jet Set 2000 in the container to cover the bottom. Set the fabric in the container and then add more Bubble Jet Set to cover. Soak for 5 minutes. If you want to soak more than one piece of cloth at a time, simply continue to alternate between fabric and additional Bubble Jet Set until all the fabric is fully saturated.

STEP 3. Remove the fabric pieces and lay them out on a towel to dry. I usually transfer the pieces to a clothesline or rack when the towel has absorbed most of the excess solution, but the fabric must be kept out of the sun when drying.

Image transfer printed on pima cotton prepared with Bubble Jet Set

STEP 4. Once the fabric is completely dry, iron it to the shiny side of freezer paper, and use immediately. Some artists have had success storing treated fabric for several months before use, but the manufacturer does suggest using it immediately. Some experimentation will tell you what works for your particular environment. The treated fabric reacts with oxygen, however, so you should store it in an airtight container.

STEP 5. Follow steps 1–4 of Digital Image Transfer on page 200. Allow the fabric to dry for 30 minutes, then remove the paper backing.

STEP 6. Pour 1 gallon of cool water in a container or washbasin. Add 4 capfuls of Bubble Jet Rinse to the water. Using rubber gloves, swish the mixture to combine.

STEP 7. Lay only one piece of fabric at a time in the solution. Take two opposite corners of the fabric in your hands and then gently pull it back and forth through the solution for approximately 2 minutes. Don't lift it up and down out of the solution, and don't be alarmed if you see some loose particles of color or dye coming off. That's why we're rinsing!

STEP 8. Lay the wet fabric on towels to dry. You can transfer them to a clothesline or rack once the excess solution has drained out. You can use a hair dryer to hasten the drying process along, and some artists put them in the clothes dryer as well. I worry, however, that the friction of the pieces rubbing up against each other or the drum of the machine would compromise the print. Compare the result (left) with prints of the same image on pages 197 and 200.

STEP 9. Heat setting is not necessary, but I always do it anyway.

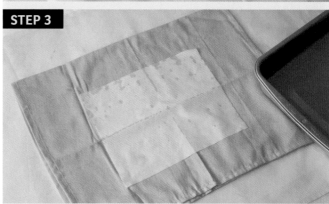

BE CONSCIENTIOUS ABOUT COPYRIGHT

Be respectful of copyright if you use images from a magazine. You may want to use only partial, unrecognizable images or random text, rather than full-blown photos, to avoid infringement.

Image Transfer with Paint or Medium

This fun technique almost always holds a few surprises at the end. You begin with an image taken from a magazine or a photograph that is printed on plain paper with a laser or toner-based photocopier or printer, or printed on transparency film with an inkjet printer. You then paint a medium of some kind on your fabric, and place the image facedown on the wet medium. After the medium dries, you rub off the paper to expose the transferred image. It's not an exacting technique, but it can glean some wonderful results that often have an antique, old-world feel to them, especially if you work in black-and-white or sepia tones. Use your computer software to make these kinds of changes on your own photographs, digital images of artwork you have done in the past, or old family photos that you have scanned into your computer.

You can use literally any acrylic gloss or matte medium for this technique, although different mediums give a different hand to the finished product, and some just work better than others. I will describe my particular favorites, along with the results I get from them. All of them do leave at least a slight hand on your fabric. Much depends on the weight of your fabric: lighter-weight fabrics will have a heavier hand when you are finished. All of them can be sewn through, however, and none has a plastic look.

PROJECT: Using Acrylic Mediums

These include Jacquard Neopaque Flowable Extender, Golden Regular Gel Medium (Matte), and Golden Fluid Matte Medium.

- **Jacquard Neopaque Flowable Extender.** Images can be faded if you rub too hard, but this may not be a bad thing. It leaves the least hand of them all and does not discolor the fabric in the areas beyond the image.

- **Golden Regular Gel Medium (Matte) or Golden Fluid Matte Medium.** Images adhere beautifully. The hand on cotton is similar to what you'd get with heavy starching, and the medium may leave a slightly white cast beyond the image area on colored or dark fabrics.

With all of these, use a densely woven, smooth cloth that has been prewashed in hot water using Synthrapol or heavy-duty laundry detergent without scent or fabric softener.

USING CITRA SOLV FOR IMAGE TRANSFER

Lay an image printed on a toner-based (laser) printer facedown on your fabric. Saturate a cotton ball or piece of paper towel or tissue with Citra Solv Natural Cleaner & Degreaser Concentrate. Rub over the back of the printed image until you can clearly see the image through the paper. Burnish the area with a bone folder, the edge of a coin, or the back of a spoon. Check to make sure the image is transferring by pulling up a corner and taking a peek. Continue rubbing until the image has transferred. It's a good idea to tape down both your fabric and the paper with the image on it, so that nothing slides around and smears while you're burnishing.

SUPPLIES NEEDED FOR USING JACQUARD NEOPAQUE FLOWABLE EXTENDER

Work surface with a hard mat, or your original tabletop

Jacquard Neopaque Flowable Extender

Paintbrush

Pencil (optional)

Prewashed fabric (see page 28)

Image that has been printed on ordinary paper from a laser or toner-based printer and cut down to size

Hard plastic squeegee, bone folder, or brayer

Spray bottle filled with water

Paper towels (optional)

Small piece of fine-grade sandpaper (optional)

Iron (optional)

Pressing cloth or baking parchment paper, for ironing (optional)

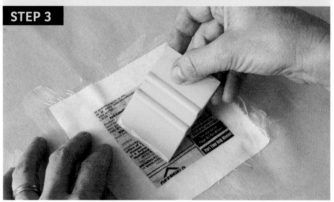

STEP 1. Apply the Jacquard medium to an area of your fabric slightly larger than the image you are transferring, or make register marks with a pencil on the fabric prior to painting on the medium. The fabric should be fully saturated and quite wet to the touch.

STEP 2. Paint a coating of medium over your image.

STEP 3. Lay your image facedown on the medium-coated fabric. Starting from the center and working your way out to the edges, use a brayer, squeegee, or your fingers to push out any air bubbles and to make sure the image is fully attached.

STEP 4. Let the fabric dry completely. This may take several hours or longer, depending on your fabric and the amount of medium you used. Patience pays here!

STEP 5. Spritz the back of the image (the paper side) with water.

STEP 6. Gently rub with your fingers or a paper towel to remove the paper. Continue rubbing and spraying with water as necessary until all the paper has come off. You can spritz stubborn bits with more water or rub gently with fine sandpaper. Be careful; you can easily rub the entire image off.

STEP 7. Air-dry or iron dry with a press cloth or piece of parchment paper placed over the fabric.

STEP 8. Apply a thin coat of Jacquard Neopaque Flowable Extender on top of the image. Allow to dry then heat-set according to manufacturer's instructions.

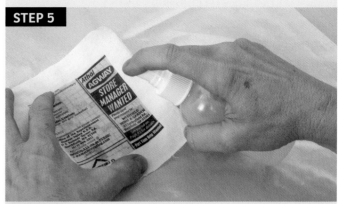

STEP 5

STEP 6

USING PAINT AS THE MEDIUM

Using paint to make a colored background for your image can yield some exciting results. Simply mix any artist acrylic paint with the Golden mediums (mentioned on page 204) prior to painting on your cloth. Add equal parts of any textile paint to equal parts of medium, then follow the directions above.

PROJECT: **Using Sheer Heaven**

Developed by Cre8it, Sheer Heaven is a unique synthetic art sheet with many wonderful properties, including the ability to transfer inkjet prints onto fabric. (See Resources for buying information.) One of the beauties of Sheer Heaven is the watercolor-like effect you can achieve with it. You can print over another image once it's dry, and it doesn't leave any detectable hand to the fabric, unless the fabric is very thin and sheer. Choose a densely woven fabric that has been prewashed in hot water using Synthrapol or heavy-duty laundry detergent without scent or fabric softener. The folks at Cre8it have discovered that the rough side of Ultrasuede works fabulously well, too! The product is available directly only from Cre8it. com. The print does not have to be freshly made for this technique to work.

I suggest using a bone folder for burnishing. A bone folder is a tool generally used for book arts. It's a very handy tool to have around, but you can also use the heel of your hand for this purpose.

At step 3 on the next page, you have several options for how to proceed, depending largely on your fabric selection, as well as your personal preference. Try out all the methods I describe to find which you prefer. No matter which transfer method you use, if the image will not transfer, your copy was not printed with the correct printer.

SUPPLIES NEEDED

Work surface prepared with plastic sheeting or newspaper

Sheer Heaven

Image of your choice

Inkjet printer, with either dye-based inks or pigment inks

Spray bottle filled with 70% isopropyl alcohol (rubbing alcohol)

Prewashed fabric (see page 28)

Bone folder, spoon, or coin for burnishing (optional)

Cloth, for covering the fabric (optional)

Books, for weight (optional)

STEP 1. Insert one sheet of Sheer Heaven into your printer. You must print on the rough (suedelike) side, so make certain you load it correctly. Print your image.

STEP 2. Lay the print flat on your work surface. Spray it generously with rubbing alcohol. The surface of Sheer Heaven should have an even, glossy sheen. Don't spray so much that the alcohol pools, but do make sure not to leave any dry spots. Check by tipping the piece up to the light as you inspect its surface.

STEP 3, OPTION A. Flip the wet Sheer Heaven onto your fabric. Burnish it with a bone folder, the side of a coin, or the back of a spoon, working from the center out. Take care not to push too hard, while also gently pushing out any air bubbles. Lift up a corner of the Sheer Heaven to see how well the image is transferring. Continue burnishing until you are happy with the results. Even when the image has only partially transferred, the results can be quite interesting.

STEP 3, OPTION B. Flip the wet Sheer Heaven onto your fabric. Burnish it with the heel of your hand while also pressing and pushing with your fingertips. This will push the ink around, giving a watercolor-like effect to your final transfer.

STEP 2

STEP 3 OPTION A

STEP 3 OPTION B

STEP 3, OPTION C. Spray your fabric lightly with the rubbing alcohol as well. Holding the fabric by two opposite corners, gently lay it down on the wet surface of the Sheer Heaven. Work slowly, allowing the opposite edge from where you're holding to touch down, then the middle, and then the remainder. Very gently push out any air bubbles with your fingertips (A). Drape a protective fabric or piece of paper over your fabric, then set a heavy pile of books on top. Wait several hours for it to dry (B).

Note: If you're working with dark or black fabric, carefully cut away any Sheer Heaven that goes beyond your image before applying the rubbing alcohol. The transferable surface of Sheer Heaven is white and will show on your fabric. If this happens, however, you can always paint over the white areas with heavy-body textile paints or acrylic paints mixed with the appropriate textile medium.

STEP 4. Carefully remove the Sheer Heaven. Allow fabric to dry thoroughly before handling, then heat-set.

STEP 3 OPTION C (A)

STEP 3 OPTION C (B)

STEP 4

EXPLORING THE POSSIBILITIES:
Sheer Heaven

- This close-up image of a cactus was transferred from the Sheer Heaven (A) to the cotton fabric (B) using rubbing alcohol and a bone folder. I then used Derwent Inktense water-soluble ink pencils to define the green and white areas of the plant.

PROJECT: **Golden Acrylic and inkAID Precoats**

Both inkAID and Golden Acrylics have developed a series of exciting products that enable an incredible variety of substrates to be printed on with an inkjet printer. These products do leave a hand that resembles a shower curtain, but your images will be sharp and vibrant, and you'll still be able to sew through them with ease.

With both inkAID and Golden Digital Grounds, use the White Matte precoat for the sharpest images. Use the Clear precoat for silk and sheer fabrics. InkAID also comes in red, blue, pearl, and bronze. The color of these precoats will show through your image. Prepare your fabric by prewashing it in hot water using Synthrapol or heavy-duty laundry detergent without scent or fabric softener.

After you've printed the fabric, allow it to dry. The truth is that I'm never quite sure how long to let an inkjet-printed piece cure before handling, so I always go with overnight. It seems safe. You know . . . sleep on it.

SUPPLIES NEEDED

Work surface covered with plastic sheeting

Foam brush

Golden Digital Ground or inkAID precoat

Prewashed fabric (see page 28)

Iron and ironing board

Freezer paper

Masking tape

Image, adjusted to the size of your fabric and set with a resolution of 200–300 ppi

Inkjet printer

Computer

STEP 1. Using a foam brush, apply several layers of the precoat to the prewashed fabric, waiting for each coat to dry before applying the next coat in the opposite direction. Allow to completely dry.

STEP 2. Iron the fabric to a piece of freezer paper cut to the correct size for your printer. To help the paper feed through the printer smoothly, fold a length of masking tape over the leading edge of the paper (the one that will feed through the printer first; see page 199). Lay the tape on the fabric side first, then fold it over onto paper.

STEP 3. Set paper-backed fabric in the printer tray, taking care to make sure it is positioned correctly so that you print on the fabric side, not the paper side. Print. Allow to dry.

STEP 4. Peel the paper backing off, then heat-set.

I created this image transfer by first digitally photographing a large, mixed-media collage on canvas (40" × 24"), then uploading the file to my computer and printing onto a Jacquard Cotton Inkjet Fabric Sheet using an HP desktop printer with DURABrite ink. The image transfer, The Gift, is 8½" × 11".

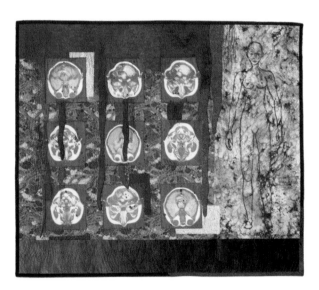

Karylee Doubiago's *Skull* (top, 17" × 18")
and *Brain Scans* (bottom, 24" × 18")

Karylee Doubiago's textile work has intrigued and fascinated me since I first saw one of her pieces. With each new example, my interest has continued to grow, as I find new ways to see her work and thus discover new personal meaning. It takes real courage to follow your creative muse and create artwork that isn't "pretty," especially when the medium is fiber art and quilts.

Karylee has recently become fascinated with x-rays and uses them very effectively on her quilts. She uses donated x-rays from friends and hospitals, rephotographs them on a light box, modifies them in Photoshop, and then prints them on fabric. At this stage, they are still in black and white, but Karylee then embellishes them with paint and pencils.

I love how emotionally raw they seem. They are unsettling and mysterious, and yet very personal, too. They speak to me in a voice I do not understand, tugging at me, drawing me in, and echoing a truth I can't speak of. My impulse is to look away, but my eyes are riveted.

Karylee's work has won numerous awards and is included in Patricia Bolton's *1000 Artist Trading Cards* (Quarry, 2007) and Cyndy Lyle Rymer's and Lynn Koolish's *Innovative Fabric Imagery for Quilts* (C&T, 2007).
www.kadstudio-lonewolf.blogspot.com

213

Profile: Linda Matthews

I think of **Linda Matthews** as the mixed-media artist extraordinaire. Of all her creations, however, it is her art bags that I enjoy the most. In them, she uses a combination of plain and textured fabric that is made by bonding fabric and paper together. The surface of the fabric is then prepared for either hand painting with acrylic paints or for printing using an inkjet printer.

When designing the surface of the bag for inkjet printing, Linda works in Adobe Photoshop with templates prepared in the shapes of the bags. Once the design is finalized, she prints it on the fabric, cuts the pattern pieces out, and then constructs the bags by machine and by hand. Linda is a creative and generous artist who always packs a wealth of technical information into her blog posts and tutorials.
www.linda-matthews.com

Linda Matthews's *Magnolia* (top) and *Geisha* (bottom) art bags (each about 12" wide × 9" high × 3" deep)

Profile: Wen Redmond

Wen Redmond's *Flown* (top, 40" × 30") and *Perception of Trees* (bottom, 35" × 36")

Wen Redmond's lifelong fascination with photography has found its own unique expression in the way she digitally manipulates then prints on fabric using inkjet. In *Flown*, Wen photographed a nest she found abandoned on her porch. Using her computer, Adobe Photoshop, and digital photographs of her own painted fabric, Wen divided the image then digitally fused it to images of her fabric. She printed these images onto pretreated fabric using an inkjet printer, then fused (with real glue!) the fabric to a stiff interfacing. She stitched the different segments together with a hand-tied bookbinding method. The result is mysterious, etherial, and magical! *Perception of Trees* is equally compelling.

Wen's work was featured in Ray Hemachandra's and Karey Bresenhan's *500 Art Quilts* (Lark, 2010) and in many other publications, including *Fiber Art Magazine* and *Craft Report*. Her work has been widely exhibited throughout the United States in galleries and juried and invitational shows, including at the Fuller Craft Museum, Rubin Gallery, Craft Boston, and Quilt National. She was also a Niche finalist in 2008 and 2010.
www.wenredmond.weebly.com
www.wenredmond.blogspot.com
www.fiberartgoddess.blogspot.com

CHAPTER 13

Marbling Methods

Marbling on fabric (as well as paper) is a single-print process that has its origins in twelfth-century Japanese *suminagashi* (ink floating). Another type of marbling, and the one that's a more direct antecedent of modern-day techniques, was being done in Turkey, Persia, and India in the eleventh and twelfth centuries. Called *ebru* (cloud art) in Turkish, the process used thickened water as the marbling base and produced the flowing, marbleized designs we are most familiar with today. It wasn't until the mid-eighteenth century that the techniques and much-cherished secret recipes finally found their way to the United States. By then, however, books were being produced by machinery rather than by hand, so the handmade marbleized paper that was often used on book covers was no longer in demand. In the 1970s, when the handcraft of bookmaking became popular, there was a resurgence of interest in the technique.

217

It is called *marbling* because the paint patterns resemble the grain of marble. There are a couple of ways to marble on fabric with paint. Both require suspending or floating paint on some kind of gel-like surface or thickened water. Traditionally carrageenan, a gelling agent extracted from seaweed, is combined with water to create the proper surface for a marbling base, but a synthetic product called methylcellulose (also known as methylcel) is also now available. Because carrageenan is a natural product, a mixture lasts only a day or two at the most in your refrigerator. On the other hand, methylcellulose can last as long as four months once mixed. Methylcellulose is also less expensive.

To marbleize, you float ink or paint on top of the base mixture, and then pull or rake a stylus of some kind through the paint to create patterns. To transfer the patterned ink or paint, you simply lay your fabric on the surface.

Shaving Cream as a Marbling Base

For this homespun version of marbling, I recommend Jacquard Airbrush Color, Golden Airbrush Color, Liquitex Professional Acrylic ink!, Daler-Rowney FW Acrylic Artists' Ink, or Tsukineko All-Purpose Ink. (See page 222 for additional paint suggestions.)

For the stylus, you can use skewers, chopsticks, bamboo skewers, toothpicks, wide-toothed combs, hair picks, forks, wire whisks, and/or knifes. Ready-made rakes specifically designed for marbling are also available. The smaller the tip of your stylus, the more delicate your marbling lines will be.

Light- to medium-weight fabric with a dense weave, such as cotton or silk broadcloth, silk crêpe de Chine, or rayon challis, is suitable for marbling. Cut 8-by-8-inch pieces and prewash them in hot water using Synthrapol or heavy-duty laundry detergent without scent or fabric softener.

PROJECT: Marbleizing with Shaving Cream

SUPPLIES NEEDED

Work surface covered with plastic sheeting

Can of foam shaving cream with aloe (the aloe type tends to be creamier than regular shaving cream)

Large plastic squeegee or plastic ruler

Three or four colors of marbling paints or inks

Eyedroppers, toothpicks, toothbrush, and/or spoons, for applying the paints

Tray or disposable pie tin to lay your messy tools on

Styluses (several; see Combs and Rakes, page 228)

Prewashed fabric (see page 28)

Iron and ironing board covered with a drop cloth

Cotton or muslin press cloth

STEP 1A

STEP 1B

STEP 2

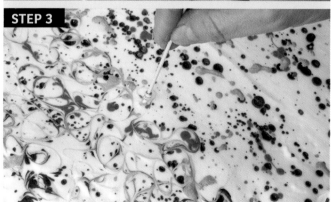

STEP 3

STEP 1. Spray shaving cream directly on the plastic sheeting. Use enough to cover an area 12" × 12" about 1½" thick (A). Smooth the surface with the squeegee or ruler (B).

STEP 2. Sprinkle several colors of ink or paint from the tip of a toothpick over the surface of the shaving cream. You can also drop the ink from an eyedropper, splatter it from a toothbrush, or dribble it from the end of a spoon or knife.

STEP 3. Drag or swirl a stylus through the paint-spattered shaving cream to create a design or marbled effect. Make smooth, graceful pulls and keep the stylus close to the surface of the cream rather than plunging in and touching the work surface. Fill in blank spaces with more paint as needed.

STEP 4. Lay a piece of prewashed, dry fabric on top of the shaving cream. Gently pat on it until the ink has saturated it.

STEP 5. Holding the two corners farthest from you, lift the fabric off the cream, and lay it down on your ironing board. If a really good layer of shaving cream remains on the piece, scoop it off with the squeegee, taking care not to touch the surface of the cloth.

STEP 6. Lay a cotton or muslin press cloth over the painted fabric and any shaving cream that may still be there. Then use your iron to heat-set and dissolve the last remaining bits of the shaving cream. Wash.

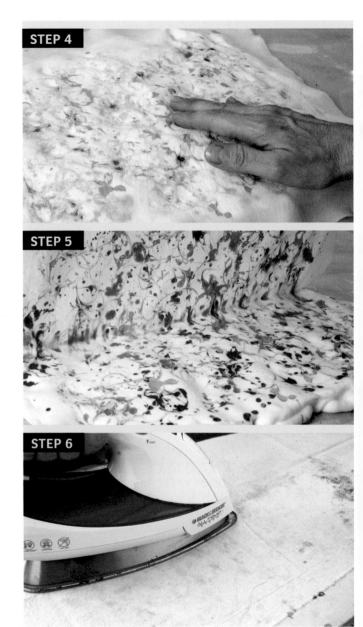

EXPLORING THE POSSIBILITIES:
Marbling with Shaving Cream

- **Second Prints.** You often can get a second print on the same surface, without disrupting the base or adding more ink or paint.

- **Reusing the shaving cream.** You can reuse the shaving cream several times. I like to fold it in upon itself **Ⓐ**, mixing the colors together as I do, which gives me a tinted base instead of white. I then smooth the surface and add more ink **Ⓑ**, using a multipronged stylus to spread the ink **Ⓒ**. Eventually, the color of the shaving cream muddies, at which point I dump it and start with fresh cream.

221

Traditional Marbling Technique

Your marbling pan or tray should measure 2 to 3 inches deep and several inches more in length and width than the fabric pieces you intend to marble. It should also be white (or light), so you can see the paint colors. You can use a cardboard box with the sides cut down and then lined with plastic. Do not line it with thin garbage bags, as the weight of the solution would tear the bags, leaving you with quite a mess to contend with. If you plan to marble large pieces of fabric, you may want to construct a bottomless pan or frame for the purpose.

Paints and Mediums

Marbling paints from PRO Chemical & Dye are my first choice for many reasons, the most important of which is that they don't have to be heat-set. The color selection, however, isn't that great. Add their Marbling Surfactant as a dispersant to thin the paints, as well as their Colorless Extender to thicken the paint, if necessary. (See Experimenting for Success, on page 229 for advice on how to use surfactants and extenders.)

Some other paints and inks I've used include Jacquard's Airbrush Color and Versatex Screen Printing Inks, which come in a great range of colors. Mix in Jacquard Versatex Dispersant to help the paint float better on your marbling base. Another possibility is Golden Acrylic Airbrush or Fluid Acrylic Colors, which should be mixed in equal parts (1:1) with Golden GAC 900 fabric/textile medium to make the paints compatible for use with textiles. You also need to prepare a solution of Golden Acrylic Flow Release and distilled water, which will be added to the paint mixture to achieve the right consistency so that the paints disperse correctly on the marbling base. Start with a ratio of about one part Golden Acrylic Flow Release to seven parts water; the mixture should be the consistency of whole milk or light cream; you may have to do some experimentation to find out what ratio works best.

Marbling Base

The base, methylcellulose, is available online from PRO Chemical & Dye, Dharma Trading, and other dye- or marbling-supply houses. You may choose instead to use carrageenan (available from Dharma Trading and ProChemical & Dye). If so, follow the directions on the package for mixing and use.

Water

Distilled water is recommended, particularly if you have hard water in your area. You can give regular tap water a try, but add some water softener: 1 tablespoon of softener per 1 gallon of water. Dissolve the softener before adding any other ingredients.

Stylus

Use the same tools described for marbleizing on a shaving cream base (see page 228).

Fabric

A light- to medium-weight fabric with a dense weave, such as cotton or silk broadcloth, silk crêpe de Chine, or rayon challis is suitable for marbling. Cut pieces at least 2 inches smaller than your marbling pan, and prewash in hot water using Synthrapol or heavy-duty laundry detergent without scent or fabric softener. In order to facilitate the fixing of paint or dye to the fabric, you'll need to pretreat the fabric with a mordant. You can use alum or aluminum sulfate, available from PRO Chemical & Dye, Dharma Trading Co., and other dye- or marbling-supply houses for this purpose.

PROJECT: **Marbling on Fabric**

SUPPLIES NEEDED

Two small buckets (for mixing the base and for the alum)

Work surface covered with plastic sheeting

Measuring spoons

Alum or aluminum sulfate (mordant)

Warm water

Prewashed fabric (see page 28)

Rubber gloves

Clothesline or drying rack and clothespins or clips (*Note:* If your drying rack is inside, spread sheets of plastic on the floor underneath it.)

Methylcellulose

Wire whisk

Clear household ammonia

Waterproof marbling pan or tray

Newspaper torn into 2" strips, as long as your marbling tray

Three or four colors of marbling paints

Eyedroppers (one for each color), toothbrush, knife, and/or spoon

Styluses, including toothpicks, chopsticks, appetizer picks, and so on: one for each color

Plastic needlepoint screen or drain board for a small piece of fabric, or 5-gallon bucket, for a larger piece of fabric

STEP 1. Prepare the mordant by dissolving 4 tablespoons of alum or aluminum sulfate in 1 quart to 1 gallon (depending on the amount of fabric you are using) of warm water. Soak the fabric in the mixture for 15 minutes, stirring occasionally to make sure the fabric is fully saturated. Oversoaking may cause the fibers of the fabric to break down, however, so set a timer if you may be distracted. *Note:* If your fabric pieces are small, you can lay them out on plastic and sponge them with the mordant instead of soaking them.

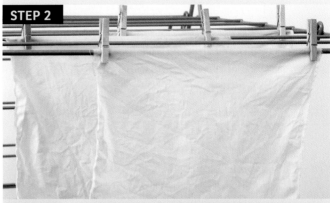

STEP 2. Using rubber gloves, squeeze out the excess liquid (do not rinse) and hang the fabric by two corners to dry, taking care not to fold back any corner. Line dry only — don't use a clothes dryer.

STEP 3. For the base, slowly stir 5 tablespoons of methylcellulose into 1 gallon of warm water using a wire whisk. Add 1 teaspoon of clear household ammonia to help the water and methylcellulose mix. Continue stirring until the mixture is clear, about 5 minutes.

STEP 4. Pour the base mixture slowly into your marbling pan to a depth of 1½"–2", and let it sit for at least 30 minutes. Although you can use it at this point, for best results, let it sit at room temperature for an additional 8–12 hours. The mixture will keep for 3–4 months at room temperature and still retain its original thickness.

STEP 5. Drag a 2" piece of torn newspaper over the top of the base to eliminate any air bubbles or dust and even out the surface tension. Don't fret too much about anything that clings to the edges of the pan.

STEP 6. Experiment before you actually begin! Shake the paints thoroughly before use and throughout the marbling process. Working with one color at a time, try out your paints, applying a few drops of each color on the marbling base. (See Experimenting for Success, page 229.) Drag more newspaper strips across the surface of your base to remove these trials before proceeding with step 7.

STEP 7. Using the eyedropper, begin dropping multiple colors of paint onto the base. To form concentric multicolored circles, drop colors on top of each other. The more colors you drop, the deeper and richer your finished product will be. Try splattering drops from a tooth-brush or from the end of a spoon or knife. Keep in mind that wherever there's no paint, the fabric will show through.

STEP 8. Use one of the styluses to draw designs in the paint or to lightly comb through it. Use clean, smooth strokes, and keep the stylus just below the surface, not letting it touch the bottom of the pan. Here, I demonstrate a traditional pattern called Bouquet, pulling first a hair pick down the base from top to bottom (A), then pulling a larger homemade comb across the base in a wavy pattern (B). (See page 226 for some suggested traditional patterning.)

STEP 9. Fold the fabric in half (without creasing the fold). Holding two corners in each hand, place the fabric just above the base so the middle will land on the paint first, then swiftly and smoothly let the two sides fall. Any hesitation may show up in the final result. Practice makes perfect. (If you're working with a large piece of cloth, you'll need a second set of

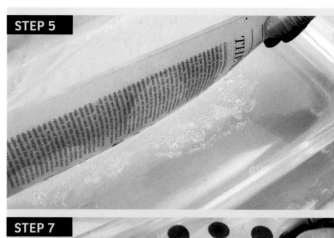

STEP 5

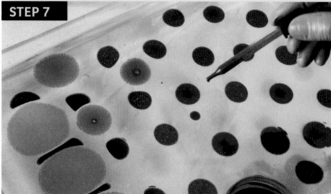

STEP 7

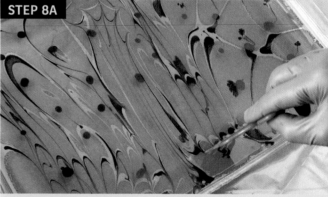

STEP 8A

STEP 8B

hands!) Gently pat the fabric to ensure that all parts of it contact the base.

STEP 10. Remove the fabric by holding the two top corners, then pulling it up and out of the pan.

STEP 11. Rinse very gently in cool water. Do not wring, twist, or rub the fabric or you may smear the paint. If your fabric piece is small, lay it on a drain board or a plastic needlepoint screen, and run cool water over it. If it is fairly large, you may rinse it in a 5-gallon bucket of cool water: lift it in and out of the water several times.

STEP 12. Hang the fabric on a line or clothes rack to dry. Wait 3 days before washing, then heat-set according to manufacturer's directions, if necessary.

STEP 13. Skim off any remaining paint with newspapers, and pour the base into a bucket to store for future use.

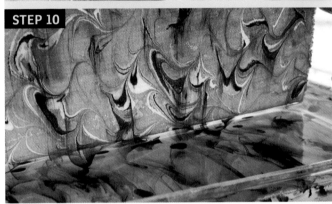

EXPLORING THE POSSIBILITIES:
Traditional Marbling Patterns

You can find many marbling patterns online and in books, or you can make up your own. Those shown on the facing page include traditional patterns, as well as more free-form designs.

- **Bouquet.** For this very traditional pattern, pull a hair pick vertically down the base, then pull a larger comb horizontally across in a wave pattern.

- **Stone.** Drop colors on the base, but do not rake. Completely cover the surface with drops of paint. Take your time, waiting for each drop to disperse before adding another next to it.

- **Banquet #1.** Rake horizontally across the base using a hair pick, then rake vertically using a banquet comb in a wave pattern.

- **Banquet #2.** Begin by pulling a fine comb or hair pick vertically down the entire surface of the marbling bed. With a stylus, draw horizontally across the marbling bed with parallel wavy lines, then crisscross these stylus-drawn lines with another vertical set.

- **Snail.** Use a bamboo skewer to make spirals or swirls across the surface. Try out different-size spirals.

- **Wave.** Use a large comb or rake to pull the paint vertically across the surface of the base. Using the same comb, pull vertically again in a zigzag pattern.

- **Wings.** You can create either small or large wings, depending on the size of comb you use. Pull a comb horizontally across the base, then use a stylus to draw continuous half-heart shapes running parallel to the combed pattern.

- **Feather.** Using a big comb, rake horizontally across your base. Then take a skewer or chopstick and comb up and down vertically through the horizontal lines about 1 inch apart.

- **Cascade and nonpareil.** These two patterns are basically the same, the only difference being that the lines in nonpareil are closer together. Using a large comb or hair pick, rake in one direction, then rake in the other direction. You can change the size of the comb for the second pass, if you like.

- **Flower patterns.** You can make lovely flower patterns by dropping colors in concentric circles, then using a skewer to pull the spaces between the petals in toward the center.

COMBS AND RAKES

You can make your own marbling tools, purchase commercial tools meant for the purpose, or simply use such items as hair, afro, or pet combs; chopsticks; small whisks; and so on. Along with the items shown below are two easy-to-make tools (a wide-toothed comb and a broom whisk) that I find useful.

Wide-toothed comb Ⓐ. Tape toothpicks, cocktail skewers, pins, or fine nails about 1½ inches apart to a base slightly narrower than the width of your marbling tray. Suitable bases include a ruler, heavy cardboard, foam core, or a lightweight strip of wood, such as lath. About 2 inches of toothpick should extend from the base. Completely cover the base with waterproof tape or gloss medium. If you use wood and nails, a coat of polyurethane will keep your comb looking nice for a long time.

Broom whisk Ⓑ. Cut a small handful of straw from a plastic whisk broom. Bind the strands of straw together at one end with a rubber band.

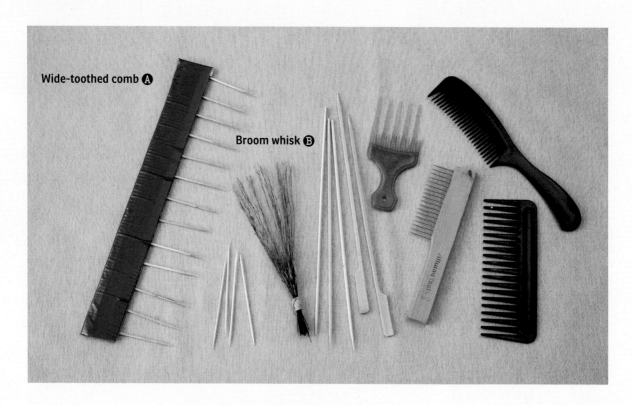

Wide-toothed comb Ⓐ

Broom whisk Ⓑ

EXPERIMENTING FOR SUCCESS

- **If the color sinks Ⓐ.** Different colors disperse or spread out on the surface of the base at different rates, so it's important that you experiment with them. Some colors may even sink. Ideally, all the colors should disperse as much as possible at the same rate. Colors sink because the paint is too thick and thus too heavy. If this happens, add a few drops of PRO Chemical & Dye's Marbling Surfactant, dish-washing liquid, or rubbing alcohol, and test again. Continue to add one drop at time until it disperses at the same rate as your other colors.

- **Getting the dispersal size right Ⓑ.** The thinner the paint, the wider it will disperse and hence the lighter the color will be. I like to have the paint spread in circles anywhere from 1½ to 2 inches in diameter. You may like a little less or a little more, depending on the kind of design you envision. Here, the gold paint is thinner than the purple.

  If the paint spreads too much, your marbling base may be too thin. You can either make a new base using a larger amount of methylcellulose, or try adding a drop or two of Jacquard Neopaque Flowable Extender to alter the surface tension and hopefully slow down the rate of dispersion.

CHAPTER 14

Fold and Color

In this chapter, you'll bind and tie cloth in a variety of ways, and then expose the bundle to paint. Where the fabric is bound, the paint can't reach it, resulting in a wide array of patterns and designs. Often referred to as shibori, this is another resist technique, and it's a procedure that has been used in many parts of the world dating back as far as 800 CE.

The possibilities for dyeing, clamping, and folding cloth are infinite. Although the process is really meant for dyeing large pieces of cloth, you can achieve exciting results using small pieces of fabric and paint. A piece of paint-dyed fabric can then be used as a wonderful base from which to apply many other surface design techniques and achieve complex, rich, and visually exciting fiber art.

In this chapter, you'll see some examples of ways to fold, tie, and clamp cloth. Some have their roots in Japanese *shibori* hand dyeing. Others may be familiar if you were tie-dyeing T-shirts in the 1960s, when they were widely popular! All can be altered in some way. Use your imagination.

Whatever the binding method, after you've made the fabric bundle, you soak it in water until fully saturated. Squeeze out the excess water as much as possible, and then pour paint on the bundles or, for more control, apply paint with eyedroppers or squeeze bottles. The fabric bundles can also sit in a container or pool of paint, as the wet fabric wicks up the paint.

Paint

Thin textile paint and/or transparent textile paint with 3 parts water to 1 part paint. For lighter shades, add lightening medium to the mixture. You can also use thinned artist acrylic paints with the appropriate textile medium, acrylic inks, and Tsukineko ink, although the paints are probably more cost effective for this technique.

Binders and Clamps

Rubber bands, synthetic sinew, string, clamps, clothespins, paper clips of all kinds, and hair clips all work. The reason for such a variety of clamps is because each resists the paint differently, resulting in different kinds of marks on the fabric. With each of the folding techniques, experience is going to dictate how tightly to clamp the fabric and how much paint to use.

Fabric

Prewash light- to medium-weight fabric in hot water using Synthrapol or heavy-duty laundry detergent without scent or fabric softener. Start with pieces that are on the small size; scarf lengths of lightweight silk and very lightweight cotton work as well. For large and/or densely woven fabric, you would really want to use dyes, unless you don't mind a significant change in the hand of the fabric.

PROJECT: **Basic Fold-and-Color Technique**

SUPPLIES NEEDED

Paint

String or rubberbands

Eyedroppers, squeeze bottles, small spray bottles, and small plastic cups to dispense the paint

Binders and/or clamps (see suggestions at left)

Bucket or container of water to soak the bundles

Prewashed fabric (see page 28)

Waterproof trays or dishes

Spray bottle filled with water

Salt

Starburst

Use a relatively square piece of fabric. Pinch the very center of the fabric and start turning your hand, while holding the center between your fingers. Keep turning until you have a disk of fabric. Bind it with string or rubber bands as shown (A). Soak the bundle in water to saturate, then squeeze out excess water and lay it on a tray. Use squeeze bottles to squirt the paint into the folds of the bundle (B). Be generous with the paint and the variety of colors you use. Allow to dry overnight before unwrapping the bundle. Heat-set with your iron, according to manufacturer's instructions and the appropriate temperature for your fabric (see page 22).

233

Accordion Folds

Do this at an ironing board. Fold the cloth in an accordion or fan style that is a couple of inches wide, ironing each fold as you go. Then fold again, accordion style, in the opposite direction, refolding over the same folds you just made so that the bundle will be in the shape of a square when you are finished. (See page 241 for illustration.) Bind with a clamp or rubber band (A). Soak the bundle in water to saturate, then squeeze out excess water and lay it on a tray. Pour a bit of paint into the tray and set one side of the bundle in it (B). Watch as it wicks its way up. When you're satisfied, turn the bundle over and soak the next side in a different color of paint. Continue in this fashion until all the sides are covered. Allow to dry overnight before unwrapping the bundle. Heat-set with your iron according to manufacturer's instructions and the appropriate temperature for your fabric (see page 22).

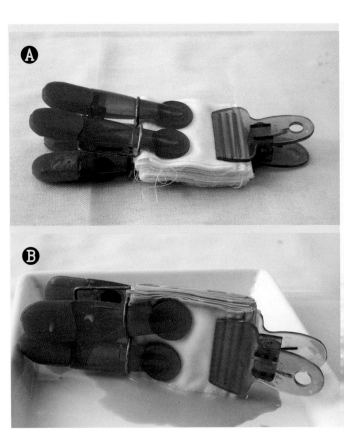

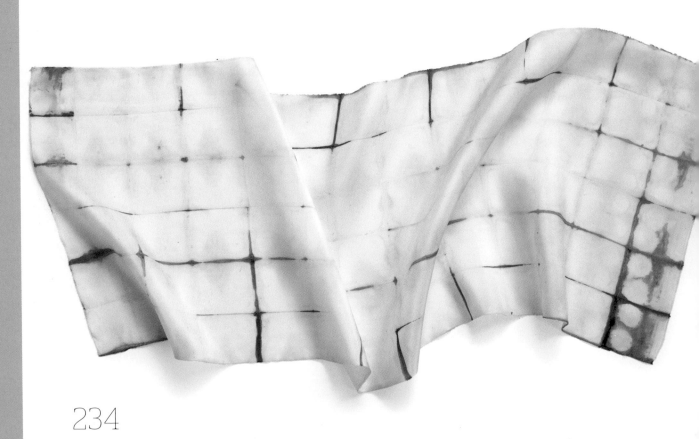

Jelly Roll

Fold the cloth in an accordion or fan style that is a couple of inches wide, ironing each fold as you go. Then roll it up widthwise, jelly-roll fashion. (See page 241 for illustration.) Bind with a rubber band (A). Soak the bundle in water until saturated, then squeeze out excess water and set the bundle down in a pool of paint. Allow much of the paint to wick up, then turn it over and set the opposite end into another color. You can also dispense the paint with an eyedropper or a squeeze bottle, sticking the tips right into the folds of the roll (B). Allow to dry overnight. Unclamp and heat-set (see page 22) if necessary.

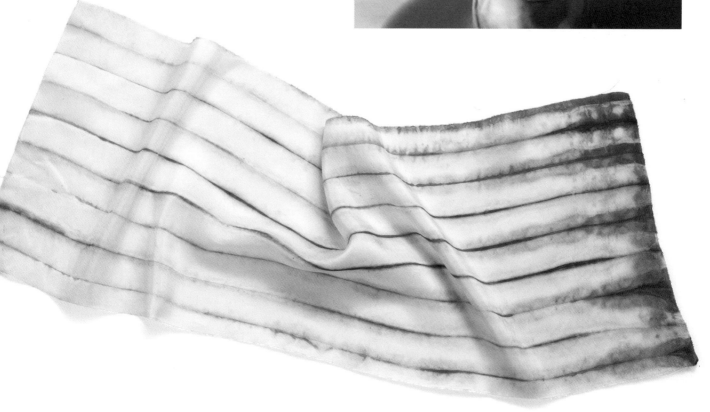

Twist

This works better if the fabric is a long rectangle, such as a scarf length. Gather together one end of the fabric and clip it to a table or shelf. With both hands, twist the fabric until the entire length is twisted. Fold the twist at the center and allow the whole thing to twist around itself. Unclip the end and tie the ends together with a rubber band or string (A). The tighter the twist, the stronger the resist will be. Soak the bundle in water until saturated, then squeeze out excess water and set the bundle down on a tray. Use a squeeze bottle or eyedropper to dispense paint throughout the bundle (B). Be generous with the paint and use a variety of colors. Allow to dry overnight. Unclamp and heat-set (see page 22) if necessary.

Lumpy Pancake

Lay your fabric out flat on the table. Spritz it a bit with water. Starting at the center, loosely gather the fabric in until it's disk-shaped, with lots of bumps in it (A). Carefully transfer it to a tray, then spritz it with water. For best results, spray on the paint (B). Allow to dry overnight (C). Open up and heat-set (see page 22) if necessary.

Flag Fold

Do this at an ironing board. Fold the cloth in an accordion or fan style that is a couple of inches wide, ironing each fold as you go. Fold over one short end to the adjacent edge, forming a small triangle. Turn the piece over, and fold up another little triangle. Continue in this way to the opposite end, folding from the front and then the back until the whole piece is a neat little bundle in the shape of a triangle. (See page 241 for illustration.) You can bind it with one clamp, several rubber bands, or several clamps, perhaps one on each corner (A). Soak the bundle in water until saturated, then squeeze out excess water and lay it on a tray. Pour three paint colors into small cups. Set each side of the triangle in a cup of color, one side at a time (B). Allow to dry overnight. Unclamp and heat-set (see page 22) if necessary.

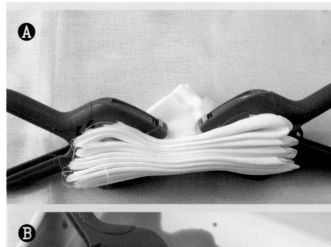

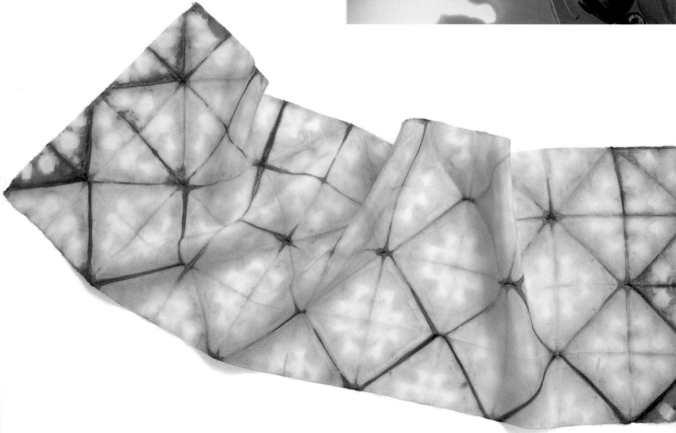

Chevron

Do this at an ironing board. Fold the cloth in an accordion or fan style that is a couple of inches wide, ironing each fold as you go. Fold your fabric in half, then make a fold from one corner at a 45-degree angle. Fold back up on the same angle, about 1½" away from the first fold. Continue to fold back and forth in this manner until you have a long narrow strip and the whole piece is folded. (See page 241 for illustration.) Bind with clothespins or bobby pins positioned at each fold (A). Soak the bundle in water to saturate. Squeeze out excess water and lay the bundle on a tray. Pour or drop paint onto it (B). Allow to dry overnight. Unclip and heat-set (see page 22) if necessary.

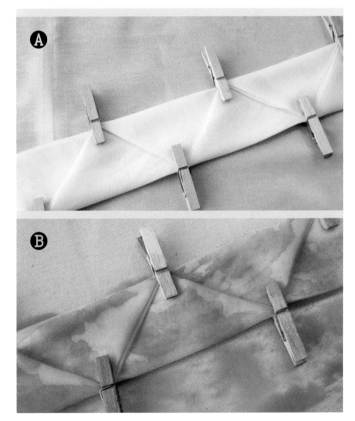

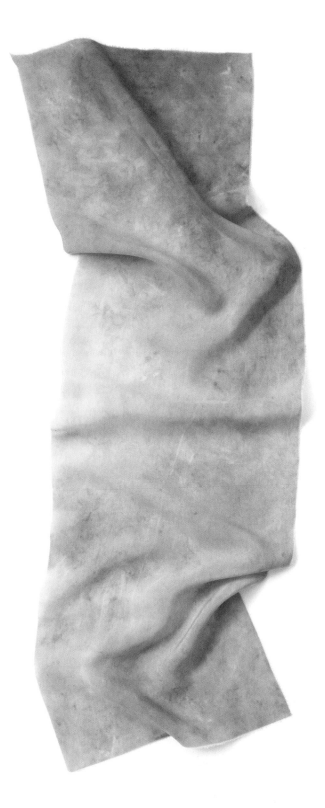

Scrunch

Scrunch a piece of fabric into a ziplock bag. Spray the fabric with water, then spray, pour, or drop paint into the bag (A). Squish it all around a bit; add some salt for good measure (B). This will create a starburst effect, similar to when you apply salt to direct-painted areas (see page 44). Allow to dry overnight in the bag before opening up the fabric. Heat-set by ironing according to manufacturer's instructions and the appropriate temperature for your fabric (see page 22).

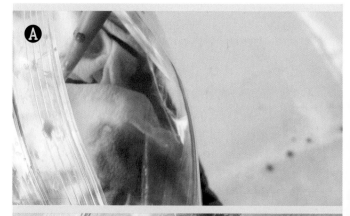

ACCORDION FOLDS

Begin each of the folds shown here by folding your fabric in an accordion **Ⓐ**, or fan, style that is a couple of inches wide, ironing each fold as you go. Then try these variations:

Double Accordion Ⓑ (page 234). Turn the accordion strip 90 degrees and fold accordion style again until you've created a folded square. Bind it as shown.

Jelly Roll Ⓒ (page 235). Roll up the accordion strip widthwise, jelly-roll fashion. Bind it as shown.

Flag Fold Ⓓ (page 238). Fold over one short end of the accordion strip to the adjacent edge, forming a small triangle. Turn the piece over, and fold up another little triangle. Continue in this way to the opposite end, folding from the front and then the back until the whole piece is a neat little bundle in the shape of a triangle. Bind it as shown on page 238.

Chevron Ⓔ (page 239). Fold the accordion strip in half, then make a fold from one corner at a 45-degree angle. Fold back up on the same angle, about 1½" away from the first fold. Continue to fold back and forth in this manner until you have a long narrow strip and the whole piece is folded. Bind it as shown.

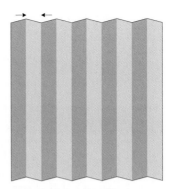

Basic Accordion Ⓐ

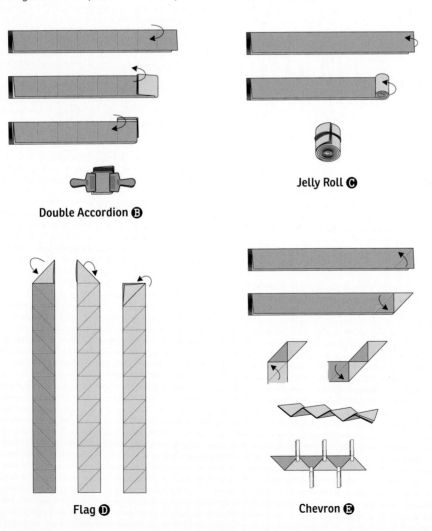

Double Accordion Ⓑ

Jelly Roll Ⓒ

Flag Ⓓ

Chevron Ⓔ

CHAPTER 15

Drawing on Fabric

I've always been in love with the simplicity of the drawn line. Whether using pencils, pastels, crayons, or even the kind of brush used in Japanese and Chinese calligraphy (often referred to as a *sumi* brush), one simple drawn line can hold a world of emotions in a single sweep across the page. The line can be jagged and harsh or elegant and flourishing, thin or thick, bold or delicate. A drawn line (referred to by many artists as mark making) can be used very functionally to emphasize an object by outlining it or, in contrast, as tiny, abstract scratch marks across a length of cloth.

Over the years I've tried numerous ways of incorporating the hand-drawn line into my fiber pieces. As an artist, I have always been concerned about longevity and the archival qualities of a given art piece — not for the purposes of ego (although I am sure that must be in there somewhere!) but for the concerns of my buyers. So I've looked for ways and materials to ensure that these lines drawn on cloth are as lightfast and permanent as possible.

You'll find many pencils, crayons, and markers to choose from. Like most art supplies, price can really determine quality. The more expensive brands tend to have a higher pigment base and are generally lightfast. Some of the products I describe here have been manufactured expressly for use with textiles. Those that have not can be adapted by adding a medium of some sort. Of course, most of these mediums do change the hand of the fabric, but I'll point those out as we come to them.

Pencils

Although as a rule, pencils are not designed for use on fabric, I have some favorites that I've adapted for use on fabric. If you plan to use pencil on fabric, choose fabric with a tight weave and a smooth, matte finish. If the fabric is thin and/or floppy, iron it to a piece of freezer paper before marking on it (see page 88). The reality is that most pencil marks are impossible to get out of fabric, so you usually don't have to worry about how long the marks will last. I generally err on the safe side with my art projects, however, and add a bit of protection over the drawing by dabbing a bit of Jacquard Neopaque Flowable Extender on the tip of a round paintbrush and then carefully painting over the pencil lines. I also heat-set the area once the extender has dried.

Graphite Pencils

The Prismacolor Ebony Graphite Drawing Pencil is my all-time favorite. It is a thick graphite pencil with an incredibly creamy hand and a satiny finish. It smudges beautifully but also holds a nice point for fine work. To protect the drawing, pick up a bit of Jacquard Neopaque Flowable Extender with the tip of a round paintbrush and carefully paint over the pencil lines.

Colored Pencils

Prismacolor colored pencils are the only way to go. Like Prismacolor's Ebony pencil, these colored pencils are unsurpassed for creaminess and blendability, even on fabric. Their range of colors is fantastic as well. They can be worked in layers to achieve depth of color and tonal range. If you use them for coloring in solid areas, begin with a light touch, gradually building up colors as you go along. For instance, if you are aiming for a nice blue color, use several shades of blue. If the blue is for water, add a bit of green or even pink. If you want to shade an area from one color to another, start out very light so you can see how the colors blend before getting too dark. Once the color is on the fabric, there's no turning back. Ideally, you should be using more than one color throughout the entire piece, gradually adding less of one and more of another as you make your way across. To protect the drawing, pick up a bit of Jacquard Neopaque Flowable Extender with the tip of a round paintbrush and carefully paint over the pencil lines.

TIPS FOR USING PRISMACOLOR PENCILS

- If you want just a hint of color, draw heavily on another piece of fabric, then rub the color onto the piece you're working on.

- As a general rule for all painting and color application, you should try to work from light to dark, if possible.

The photo (above) shows a practice print that I felt was rather faint and unclear. I worked on it with colored pencils to illustrate what you can accomplish with these tools, even on a print that's not so great.

245

Watercolor Pencils

I find that most watercolor pencils don't have the intensity of color on fabric that they have on paper. Because these pencils remain water soluble even after they've dried, any images you make with them are likely to be faded or lost if the fabric is washed or water spattered. There is, however, one exception: Derwent Inktense water-soluble ink pencils. These pencils give the fiber artist a wonderful range of possibilities. They have jewel-like, vibrant colors with a firm, creamy texture that blends beautifully. You can buy them singly or in boxes of 12, 24, 36, or 72 colors. They are also available without the wood pencil casing. Similar to a piece of chalk, these color blocks are great for working large areas. And best yet, although they're used with water, once dry, they're permanent. No heat-setting is required, so layering colors is a snap.

Fabric

For this process, choose any tightly woven, smooth fabric with a matte finish, cut to pieces about 12 inches square. If your fabric is thin or floppy, iron it to a piece of freezer paper, or place a nonslip mat, such as Grip-n-Grip (from Bear Thread Designs), under the fabric to hold it in place while you work. Prewash the fabric in hot water using Synthrapol or heavy-duty laundry detergent without scent or fabric softener.

PROJECT: Pencil Watercoloring on Fabric

SUPPLIES NEEDED

Work surface protected with plastic sheeting

A piece of muslin placed over the plastic to be used as a drop cloth

Painter's tape or pins (optional)

Prewashed fabric (see page 28)

Spray bottle for water

Derwent Inktense water-soluble ink pencils

Watercolor and/or foam brushes (optional)

Jacquard Neopaque Flowable Extender

STEP 1. Tape or pin the muslin and your fabric piece to your work surface, or put it on a Teflon mat.

STEP 2. Paint or spray water over the entire surface of the fabric: wet it, but don't saturate it.

STEP 3. Draw your design on the wet fabric with the color pencils (A & B), spreading the color around with a brush, if you'd like (C). Let it dry.

STEP 4. Again spray or paint water over the fabric surface, including over your design. Use a much smaller amount of water this time. Draw again. Notice how the colors bleed on the wet fabric, but not where it is dry. You can use your fingers to help blend the colors.

STEP 5. Repeat step 4 until you are happy with your piece.

STEP 6. The color will continue to blend and move as long as the fabric is wet. At any point, you can use a hair dryer on it to preserve the look. You can then work back into the piece with a dry pencil or one that has been dipped in water, or rewet the entire piece before working back into it. (See completed piece on page 248.)

STEP 7. Apply a coat of colorless extender, if desired.

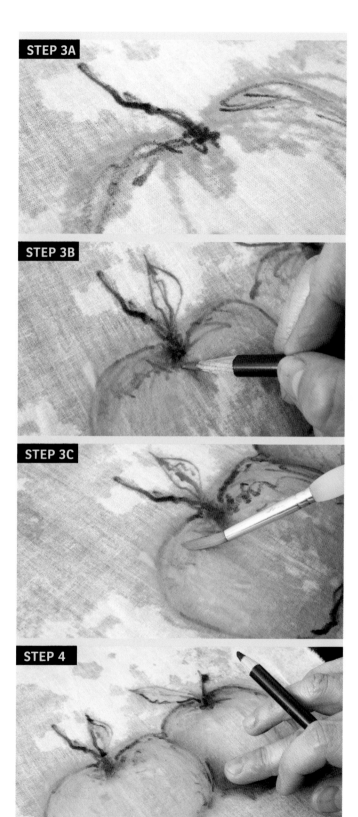

STEP 3A

STEP 3B

STEP 3C

STEP 4

EXPLORING THE POSSIBILITIES:
Derwent Inktense Pencils

• **Iron freezer paper** to the back of the fabric to stabilize it. Draw on dry fabric first and then wet it with water.

• **Dip the pencil tip in water,** then draw on dry fabric.

• **Spray or paint** Jacquard Neopaque Flowable Extender on the fabric instead of water to control bleeding. Go back into the piece with water and a brush to blend selected areas.

• **Use a water-soluble** gutta-like resist to totally contain areas of color. (See page 166 for information.)

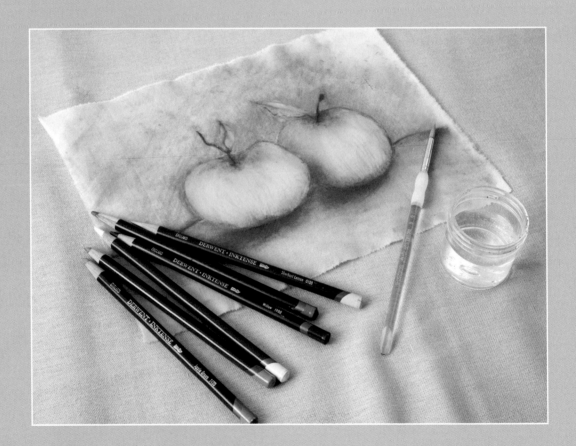

Crayons

Here I include anything that looks and handles like a crayon. Of the several varieties out there, I discuss only the brands that I use.

Pentel Fabric Fun Pastel Dye Sticks

These dye sticks are easy and great fun to use on natural fibers. Draw freehand or use them with stencils. Pentel Fabric Fun Pastel Dye Sticks work beautifully for painting on a piece that has already been quilted. The colors are vibrant, permanent when heat-set, and leave no trace of a hand on the fabric. Their limitation is that they come in only 15 colors. The price can't be beat, however, so they're especially convenient if you are working with kids.

Caran d'Ache Neocolor II Water-Soluble Crayons

Use these crayons as you would Inktense pencils (see page 246). They have a reputation for not being permanent, even if heat-set. I haven't had this problem, however I haven't used them on cloth that I've repeatedly washed. A thin coating of Jacquard Neopaque Flowable Extender applied over your design with a foam brush will protect them, but on thin fabric this product leaves a noticeable change in the hand.

Fabric painting with Caran d'Ache Neocolor II water-soluble crayons and freehand machine stitchery (see chapter 17).

Markers

You have many choices when it comes to markers! Experiment with various brands to see if they work well on fabric and are light-fast and permanent. As a general rule, I'm not that fond of markers, except maybe to sign my name, and certainly for any extended text I might want to add to an art piece. My reason is that the mark they make is, in and of itself, just an even application of uninteresting color: it is not painterly and lacks any kind of texture or nuance. If your project has a great deal of machine or hand stitching, however, you can achieve wonderful shadows and highlights by using markers among the stitching lines.

Jacquard Tee Juice Fabric Art Markers

These markers come in three sizes and 16 colors. The largest is fat and juicy, boasting a sponge head and a squeezable base with liquid ink. The fine point is great for writing text and signing your name. They need to be heat-set for permanence.

Tsukineko Fabrico Markers

Available in 31 colors, Tsukineko Fabrico Markers have a bullet end for writing and drawing details, as well as a brush end for fancier work. They don't need to be heat-set.

Tsukineko Fantastix

These nifty little devices consist of a plastic sleeve the size of a small marker surrounding a hard foam core. The end of the foam has either a bullet tip or a brush tip, with no color of its own. To use, you dip the tip in ink or thin textile paints to make your own markers. They are particularly useful if you need to match colors exactly to what you've already painted.

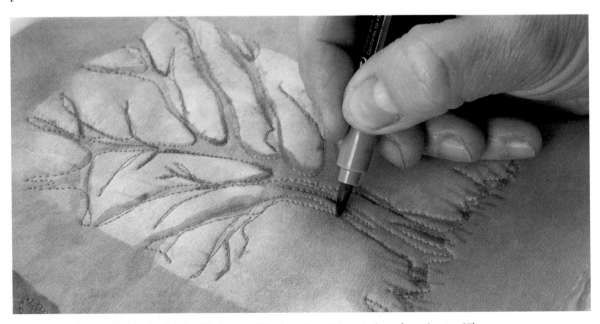

Fabric painting with Tsukineko Fabrico Markers and freehand machine stitchery (see chapter 17).

Shiva Artist's Paintstiks

I absolutely love Shiva Paintstiks! They tend to be pricey, but they're worth every penny. Don't confuse Shiva Paintstiks with other brands of paint sticks and oil bars. They're not the same! All oil-paint sticks consist of oil paint in stick form made with linseed oil. In contrast, the oil in Shiva Paintstiks has been refined in such a way as to make them less acidic, thus making them safe to use on textiles. Also, the percentage of linseed oil is much smaller than in other paint sticks.

Shiva Paintstiks are available in sets and individually; you can also find mini half sticks. They have a wonderful creamy texture, very much like lipstick, and come in a wide range of colors, including 22 iridescents and 55 matte colors. The iridescent colors are highly reflective, so they work beautifully on everything from dark fabrics to the sheerest of sheers. Mix them on a palette or directly on your fabric. Shiva offers a blender stick that helps you achieve lighter tones. Finally, each stick comes with its own protective "skin" that is self-healing after each use. What could be easier!

Because Shiva Paintstiks smudge so easily, and because you must wait three to five days before heat-setting, I recommend using them as one of the last layers of your piece. When used correctly, after heat-setting these little gems do not change the hand of your fabric.

PROJECT: **Stenciling with Shiva Artist's Paintstiks**

Shiva Paintstiks give fabulous results when used with stencils. The stenciled image looks as if it is sitting on the surface of the fabric, greatly adding depth and dimension to your work. You'll need some kind of palette for the colors if you stencil with these paint sticks. Look for something with a slight tooth. You can easily make one by adhering strips of masking tape or painter's tape on a plate or piece of cardboard, as shown in the photo below.

Fabric

To use Shiva Paintstiks to stencil on fabric, prewash your fabric in hot water using Synthrapol or heavy-duty laundry detergent without scent or fabric softener. If your fabric is lightweight and slippery, tape or pin it to your work surface before you can begin, or place a nonslip mat, such as Grip-n-Grip (from Bear Thread Designs), under the fabric to keep it from shifting. Another option is to spray the back side of the fabric with removable 505 Spray and Fix basting fabric adhesive; use rubbing alcohol to remove any adhesive that remains when you are finished.

SUPPLIES NEEDED

Hard, flat work surface covered with plastic sheeting

Pins, blue painter's tape, Teflon nonslip mat, or 505 Spray and Fix basting spray fabric adhesive

Shiva Artist's Paintstiks (several colors)

Paper towels or sharp knife

Palette or palette surface (see suggestions above)

Short, natural-hair stencil brushes or small, hard-bristle oil painting brushes

Stencil (from acetate or freezer paper; see pages 83–88 for information)

Prewashed fabric (see page 28)

STEP 1. Pin or tape your fabric to your work surface, or use a nonslip mat or adhesive spray to stabilize it as described above. If your stencil is large (anything you can't comfortably hold down with just one hand), tape it down on top of the fabric or use spray adhesive to hold it in place.

STEP 2. Remove the protective skin from the paint sticks by pinching the pointed end with a paper towel, rubbing it on a paper towel laid flat on your work surface, or carefully shaving it off with a sharp knife. (Be careful of the shavings though, as these are oil paint and will stain your floor or carpeting.)

STEP 3. Rub patches of color on the palette, using all the sticks you are working with. You can mix colors together on the palette if you desire.

STEP 4. With your stencil brush, pick up some paint from one of the color patches.

253

STEP 5. Place the stencil on the fabric and apply paint within the stencil, paying careful attention to the edges of each opening, so you get nice crisp edges on the fabric.

STEP 6. Put several different colors directly on the fabric, then blend them together with a stencil brush.

STEP 7. Lift the stencil.

STEP 8. Let the image dry for 24 hours; see the opposite page for finishing and care instructions.

TIPS FOR USING SHIVA ARTIST'S PAINTSTIKS

- Apply paint only at the edges of the stencil, carefully fading the paint in toward the center by pulling it out with a dry brush. This technique offers the illusion of a transparent shape.

- To produce an image that appears to have volume, use a darker color on one side of the image. Softly blend the dark and light colors together toward the center.

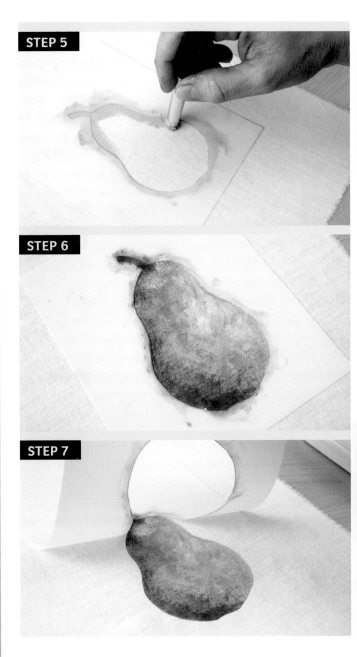

STEP 5

STEP 6

STEP 7

Heat-Setting, Cleanup, and Aftercare

Images made with Shiva Paintstiks will be dry to the touch in 24 hours, but, depending on the amount of paint you used, you should let it dry completely for three to five days, or sometimes longer. After this rest, heat-set the paint by ironing at the temperature setting appropriate for the fabric. Place a piece of baking parchment paper on your ironing board to protect the cover from oil stains, and another piece of parchment paper over the fabric to protect your iron.

Fabric that has been embellished with Shiva Paintstiks can be machine- or hand-washed in cool to warm water. It may *never*, however, be dry-cleaned.

EXPLORING THE POSSIBILITIES:
Using Shiva Paintstiks and Textile Crayons

- **Use textile crayons** for rubbings (see page 258).

- **To remove bits of unwanted paint,** place a piece of masking tape over the unwanted paint, and rub it with your fingernail or the edge of a credit card. Lift the tape off, removing most of the paint, or at least lightening the error.

PROJECT: **Stripes and Plaids with Shiva Artist's Paintstiks**

Instead of cutting a stencil, you can block out a pattern with painter's tape or even simply strips of paper to create interesting stripes and plaids with Shiva Artist's Paintstiks or textile crayons.

SUPPLIES NEEDED

Hard, flat work surface covered with plastic sheeting

Prewashed fabric (see page 28)

Pins, blue painter's tape, Teflon nonslip mat, or 505 Spray and Fix basting spray fabric adhesive

Shiva Artist's Paintstiks or textile crayons (several colors)

Sharp knife

Palette or palette surface (see suggestions on page 252)

Short, natural-hair stencil brushes or small, hard-bristle oil painting brushes

File folder, heavy stock paper, or paper towels (optional)

FOR A SOFTER LOOK

For a soft-edged stripe, tear a file folder, heavy stock paper, or even paper towel in a strip. Place the strip on your fabric, then brush paint across the torn edge onto the fabric (A). Reposition the paper or tear a new piece and make additional layers with different colors (B).

STEP 1. Pin or tape your fabric to your work surface, or use a nonslip mat or adhesive spray to stabilize it as described on page 252.

STEP 2. Use different widths of blue painter's tape to mark out a grid on your fabric.

STEP 3. Remove the protective skin from the paint sticks by pinching the pointed end with a paper towel, rubbing it on a paper towel laid flat on your work surface, or carefully shaving it off with a sharp knife. Be careful of the shavings though, as these are oil paint and will stain your floor or carpeting. (See step 2, page 253.)

STEP 4. Rub patches of color on the palette, using all the sticks you are working with. You can mix colors together on the palette if you desire.

STEP 5. With your stencil brush, pick up some paint from one of the color patches and use it to fill in the grid you made in step 2.

STEP 6. Remove the tape carefully and reposition it to make a new pattern. Use different colors, as desired, allowing the paint to overlap previously painted sections as well as cover bare areas. Continue to remove and reposition the tape until you're satisfied with your design.

STEP 7. Let the paint dry for 24 hours; see Heat-Setting, Cleanup, and Aftercare, page 255, for finishing and care instructions.

STEP 5

STEP 6

PROJECT: **Making Rubbings with Shiva Artist's Paintstiks**

Shiva Paintstiks are also ideal for making rubbings. To create texture, use any item with a relief or raised pattern, such as stamps, linoleum blocks, wood cuts, found objects, corrugated cardboard, and so on. Don't forget that you can glue all kinds of objects to a piece of cardboard or foam core to make a relief for rubbing purposes. Examples include yarn, rope or cording, washers, ceramic tile spacers, a piece of textured fabric, and so forth. You can even do a rubbing of tree bark on your fabric. The possibilities are endless!

SUPPLIES NEEDED

Work surface protected with plastic sheeting or newspaper

Textured item for your rubbing plate (see suggestions at left)

Spray adhesive (optional)

Teflon nonslip mat (optional)

Prewashed fabric (see page 28)

Shiva Artist's Paintstiks (several colors)

Sharp knife

Blue painter's tape

STEP 1. Spray the top of the item you're taking the rubbing from (your rubbing plate) with spray adhesive if you think the fabric may slip on it, then place it on your work surface, with a Teflon nonslip mat under it if needed. You may instead just tape it to the work surface. Lay your fabric on the rubbing plate. (You may spray the back of the fabric with removable adhesive also, if necessary.)

STEP 2. Open the cardboard sleeve that protects your paint stick, and push out the bottom end of the stick. Break off a small piece, and use a sharp knife to carefully cut a line down it, cutting just through the protective skin from top to bottom; peel off the skin. (See step 2, page 253.)

STEP 3. Using the side of your paint stick, rub over the fabric in a stroking motion, away from your body. Continue to cover the entire area of the rubbing plate, always rubbing in the same direction. Pay close attention to where the edges of your rubbing plate are. It's easy to fall off the sides, putting paint where you hadn't intended it to be. For multiple images, move your fabric so another area is over the rubbing plate, or move the rubbing plate.

STEP 4. Try overlapping the images using different colors. To remove unwanted paint, use painter's tape (see page 255).

STEP 5. Let the image dry for 24 hours; see Heat-Setting, Cleanup, and Aftercare, page 255, for finishing and care instructions.

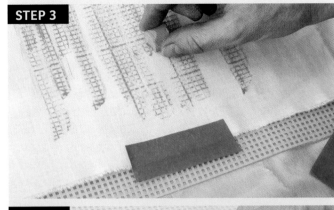

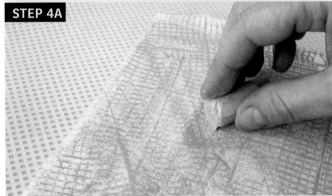

Profile: Peggy Brown

Peggy Brown taps into her wealth of knowledge and experience as a collage artist to create her gorgeous art quilts. Working with layers of watercolor and fabric, she creates a stunning illusion of depth. Sometimes she uses image transfer to reproduce one of her paper collages to fabric, where she will then further paint and collage. This is one of my personal favorite ways to work. When my son was a young teen he called it "making collages out of collages," and definitely saw it as an opportunity to worry about Mom.

I love the beautiful line work Peggy created with machine stitching in *Collaboration II*. It is a wonderful example of how the use of line can not only rein in a piece, but also merge the different elements with each other and with the outside edges of the work. The lines also create movement and give the piece a dancelike quality.

Peggy's work has been widely exhibited at shows and galleries throughout the United States, including in both private and corporate collections. Her work was included in Nita Leland's and Virginia Lee Williams's *Creative Collage Techniques* (North Light, 2000). *www.peggybrownart.com*

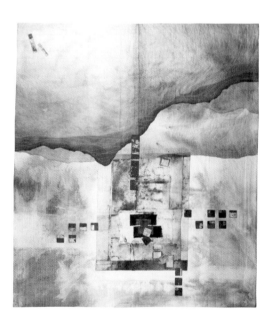

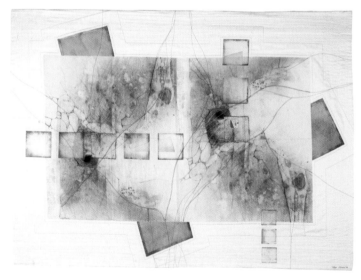

Peggy Brown's *Echoes* (left; 48" × 48") and *Collaboration II* (right; 40" × 30")

Profile: Kathleen Kastles

Kathleen Kastles pushes her mediums of choice to their fullest. Her work may start with an idea, a photograph, or a sketch, or sometimes with the simple desire of putting certain colors together. The whole cloth quilt titled *Elaine* was painted on white kona cotton fabric prior to quilting. She used acrylic inks mixed with aloe vera gel to give them the consistency of artist acrylics. Her *Texting in the Mall* (see page below) started as an enlarged drawing that was machine embroidered onto a length of gray fabric. The bench, planter, and plant were cut from nylon organza then appliquéd. The more subtle areas, such as shadows and details of the plant, were created directly on the cloth with Shiva Paintstiks. The whole piece was then quilted.
www.kathleenkastles.com

Kathleen Kastles's *Elaine* (top, 13½" × 24¾") and *Texting in the Mall* (bottom, 39¾" × 46")

CHAPTER 16

All That Glitters

There really is nothing quite like a little shine or glitter. Even if you think of yourself as a nonglitter sort of person, you'll find that sparkle, in modest amounts, can add a lift to your piece. It is also a fabulous tool for creating contrast, movement, and, of course, depth.

Since this chapter covers both foils and metal leaf, it's important to understand what each is and how they differ. *Metal leaf* tends to have a more delicate and richer quality to it; *foil*, on the other hand, has a tendency to be brighter and almost brassier. Simply because it's sturdier, I prefer foil when I'm working on fabric that I plan to make into garments. For wall-hung art pieces, I use whatever visually suits the piece. Each is applied in much the same way.

With all of the methods described here, it's important to remember to protect the metal leaf or foil with a sheet of baking parchment paper or a press cloth before ironing over it.

Textiles that have been embedded with foil can be washed by hand or in the washing machine on a gentle cycle. Metal leaf is more fragile and should be washed only by hand. Neither one can be dry-cleaned or put in a home dryer.

It's usual to save the application of metal leaf or foil to your textile art as a final, or close-to-final, step. Although visually similar, there are subtle and important differences between the two, but both mediums require the use of an adhesive. Of the several options for how to use these materials, some work better than others. I have my personal favorites, but I encourage you to try different methods and see which resonate for you.

Metal Leaf

Some five thousand years ago, Egyptians were the first artisans to use gold-beating — the process of hammering metal into thin sheets for decorative purposes. Metal leaf is metal that has been hammered to a thickness of 0.2 to 0.3 of a micrometer. To give you some context for this, a micrometer is a unit used for measuring wavelengths, so it's very, very thin! Metal leaf comes in a form called books, measuring approximately 5 inches square. The pages of these books are made of tissue paper, between each of which is a thin sheet of metal leaf. There are usually about 25 leaves in a book. Aluminum, copper, silver, brass, imitation gold, and pure gold are all available for purchase in leaf form from a number of companies. I have not found any one company's product to be different from others.

Foil

Foil is actually plastic embedded with color that has been adhered to a backing sheet of cellophane. You have a wonderful variety of colors to choose from, including some unusual, variegated metallic-like surfaces that are also fun to use. Foil comes in sheets 6 by 12 inches and 12 by 12 inches, as well as by the yard and in 50- and 200-foot rolls. You can also find starter packs that contain small samples of a variety of colors.

Foil manufactured specifically for textile applications is available from various online sources and some art- and craft-supply stores. The two I'm most familiar with are from Jones Tones and Screen-Trans Development Co. Jones Tones foil comes in 12-by-12-inch sheets and 12-inch-by-50-foot rolls. Screen-Trans foil comes in 12-inch-by-20-foot rolls; it can be purchased by the yard from Laura Murray Design, an online-only source (see resources, page 306 for more information). The latter is by far the most economical way to go. Both companies make their own adhesives, as well: Jones Tones Foil Glue and Screen-Trans foil Transfer Adhesive. You can also apply metal leaf and foil with fusible webbing. See Products Used for Applying Metal Leaf and Foil to Fabric, opposite, for other adhesive options.

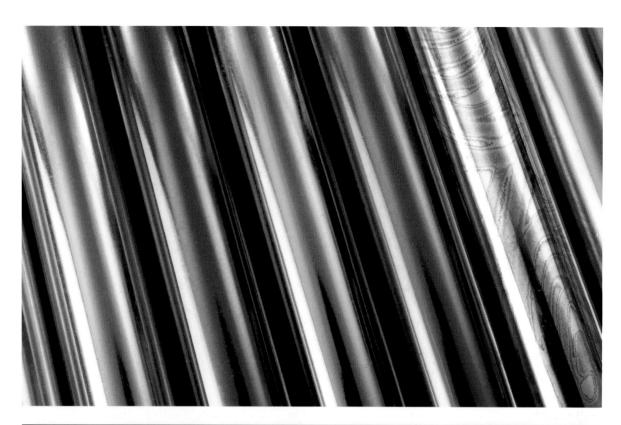

Products Used for Applying Metal Leaf and Foil to Fabric

Product	Foil	Metal Leaf
Wonder Under	x	x
Steam-A-Seam 2 or Lite Steam-A-Seam 2	x	x
Mistyfuse	x	x
Fusible thread (from most quilting shops and online)	x	x
Jones Tones Foil Glue, with heat	x	x
Jones Tones Foil Glue, without heat	x	
Screen-Trans Foil Transfer Adhesive	x	x
Bo-Nash Bonding Agent	x	x

PROJECT: **Applying Foil with Fusible Webbing**

SUPPLIES NEEDED

Prewashed fabric (see page 28)

Iron and ironing board or work surface prepared for ironing

Fusible webbing (such as Lite Steam-A-Seam 2, Wonder Under, and Mistyfuse)

Sheet of foil, 12" × 12"

Baking parchment paper, for use with Mistyfuse

Sewing machine, for use with fusible thread

Using Lite Steam-A-Seam 2 or Wonder Under for Foiling

STEP 1. Lay out your fabric on your ironing board or work surface.

STEP 2. Cut a small shape 1"–3" in diameter out of the Lite Steam-A-Seam 2 or Wonder Under.

STEP 3. Peel off *one* side of the paper backing from your shape.

STEP 4. Place the shape on your fabric with the webbing side facing down. (The remaining paper backing is facing up.) With the temperature of your iron set for cotton or the hottest your fabric can withstand, press for 10–15 seconds (A). Remove the paper backing (B).

STEP 5. Place the foil sheet over the shape with the color side facing up. This may seem counterintuitive; just keep in mind that if you can see the color, then it is in the right position.

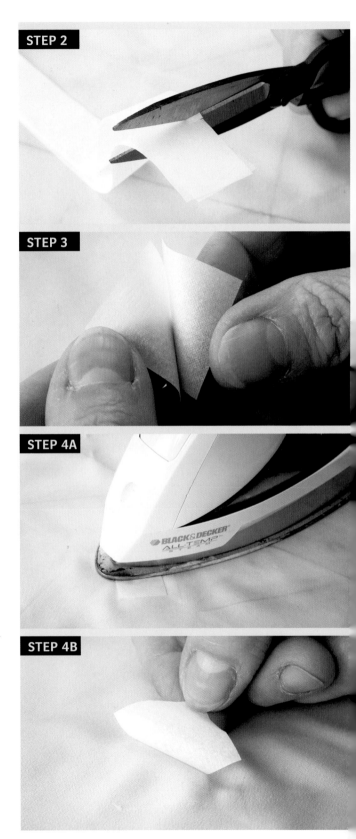

STEP 2

STEP 3

STEP 4A

STEP 4B

STEP 6. Using the edge of the iron, close to the tip, rub across the area where the webbing is. Use a firm hand and rub five or six times, always in the same direction. Because the foil and the cellophane sheet covering it are both plastic, take care not to melt them.

STEP 7. After cooling for a few minutes, remove the foil backing sheet. I have found that a quick snapping motion, not unlike when you remove an adhesive bandage, works best.

Using Mistyfuse for Foiling

STEP 1. Lay out your fabric on your ironing board or work surface.

STEP 2. Take a 4" × 4" piece of Mistyfuse, and tear it apart by holding it on opposite edges, then gently pulling outward. Repeat on the other edges, then continue to tear until the piece looks a bit like a spiderweb.

STEP 3. Place the Mistyfuse on your fabric. Place a sheet of foil, color side up, over the Mistyfuse.

STEP 4. Follow steps 6 and 7 for using Lite Steam-A-Seam 2 or Wonder Under, page 267, to iron on the foil and remove the foil backing.

STEP 2

STEP 4

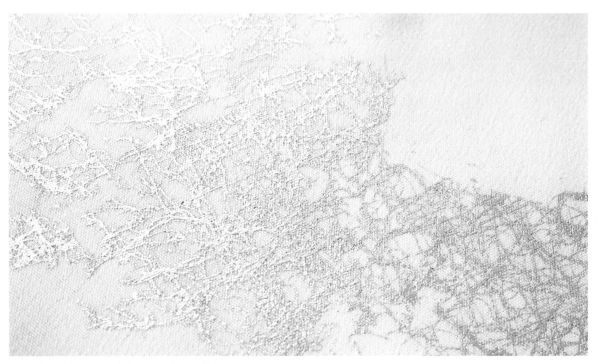

Mistyfuse adds some delicate, weblike glitz to a piece.

Using Fusible Thread for Applying Foil or Metal Leaf

STEP 1. Wind a sewing bobbin with fusible thread.

STEP 2. With your fabric facedown (so that the bobbin thread will be on the right side), machine stitch in whatever pattern you wish.

STEP 3. Follow steps 5 through 7 for using Lite Steam-A-Seam 2 or Wonder Under, page 267, to apply the foil.

EXPLORING THE POSSIBILITIES:
Fusible Thread

- Instead of machine stitching the fusible thread, lay a continuous length on your fabric in a random or planned design pattern, or cut individual pieces of thread and place them in a pattern

- Carefully hand stitch a design.

PROJECT: **Applying Metal Leaf with Fusible Webbing**

SUPPLIES NEEDED

Prewashed fabric (see page 28)

Iron and ironing board or work surface prepared for ironing

Fusible webbing (such as Lite Steam-A-Seam 2, Wonder Under, or Mistyfuse)

Metal leaf

Baking parchment paper

Soft paintbrush

STEP 1. Lay out your fabric on your ironing board or work surface.

STEP 2. Cut a small shape 2"–3" in diameter out of the fusible webbing. Peel off *one* side of the paper backing.

STEP 3. Place the shape on your fabric with the webbing side facing down and the paper backing facing up. With your iron set for cotton or the hottest your fabric can withstand, press for 10–15 seconds. Remove paper backing.

STEP 4. Gently slide a piece of metal leaf out of the book and place it on the fusible webbing. Take care: Even the slightest breeze can turn a sheet of metal leaf into a sail. Place a piece of baking parchment paper over the metal leaf to protect it.

STEP 5. Using the edge of the iron, close to the tip, rub across the area in the same direction five or six times where the webbing is, using a firm hand. Leaf is not plastic, so you can use the flat of the iron as well.

STEP 6. Remove the parchment paper, then use a soft paintbrush to gently brush away any metal leaf that didn't fuse to the fabric.

STEP 4

STEP 5

STEP 6

FINISHED

Special Glues or Adhesives for Foil and Metal Leaf Applications

Some adhesives offer the potential of combining other processes, such as silk-screening, stenciling, stamping, and direct painting with foil and metal leaf applications. Jones Tones Foil Glue and Screen-Trans Development Co. Foil Transfer Adhesive are two of these. If you consider others, keep in mind that the glue needs to be water soluble (for cleanup), but permanent when dry.

- **Jones Tones Foil Glue** can be used straight out of the squeeze bottle for drawing and writing purposes and without setting it with an iron. It dries clear, making it hard to see on some fabrics. The directions on the bottle tell you to wait from one to eight hours for the glue to dry after you've applied it to your fabric, before applying the foil or metal leaf. That's quite a discrepancy in waiting time! I've found, however, that drying time largely depends on how thickly you apply the glue. It should be clear in color, but still tacky to the touch. At that point you can lay the foil on the glued area, color side up. Although the product instructions say to rub it with your finger, I find that it really needs to be burnished on. I get great results putting the back of a spoon over the area to be foiled, then with my thumb in the bowl of the spoon, rubbing back and forth using a good amount of pressure. A bone folder would work nicely as well. If I don't cover all the glued areas on my first attempt, I just reposition the foil and burnish it again.

- **Foil Transfer Adhesive** is my personal favorite. Because it's gray, it's easier to see. I feel, too, that when it is silk-screened onto even the most delicate silks, it barely changes the hand of the fabric. Whatever method you use to apply this adhesive, once it dries, you apply the foil or metal leaf using the appropriate procedures described on pages 266 and 270.

- **Silk-screening** the glue on your fabric gives you by far the thinnest, most even of applications. It has the advantage of being able to add glitter to a large area with a complicated design. You apply the glue just as you would paint (see page 153). Let it dry, then apply the foil or metal leaf using the appropriate procedures described on pages 266 and 270.

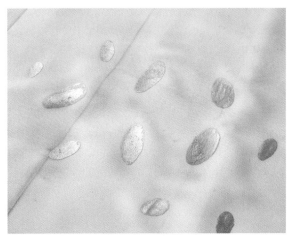

Silk-screened metal foil

Stenciling works well, too, although the glittery areas will be thicker (see page 84 for advice on stenciling). Use a sponge-type stencil brush to apply the glue. Allow the glue to dry.

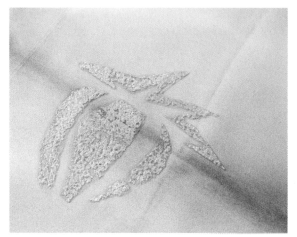

Stenciled metal foil

Stamping is more likely to give you spotty results, because it's hard to brush the glue evenly on the stamp. The effect can be used with great results, however, depending on your piece and what you're trying to achieve. (See pages 62–77 for information about stamping.) Allow the glue to dry.

Stamped metal foil

Direct painting the glue with a watercolor brush or a sponge brush gives similar results to stamping, although you can cover a larger area. Paint your design freehand or following a pattern, and then allow the glue to dry. As with stamping, you are likely to get spotty results, which you can repair by adding more glue, waiting for it to dry, and then burnishing on more foil or metal leaf. Or, you may like the painterly effect!

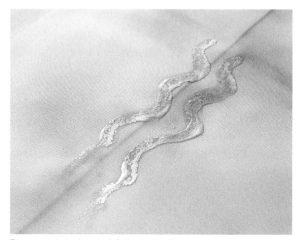

Direct-painted metal foil application

PROJECT: Applying Bo-Nash Bonding Agent

SUPPLIES NEEDED

Iron and ironing board or work surface prepared for ironing

Bo-Nash Bonding Agent powder

Prewashed fabric (see page 28)

Baking parchment paper

Foil

STEP 1. Randomly sprinkle the Bo-Nash Bonding Agent powder on your fabric.

STEP 2. Lay a piece of baking parchment paper over the powder. With your iron set for cotton, but without steam, press over the areas where you put the powder. Remove the parchment paper.

STEP 3. Place a sheet of foil, color side up, on the bonding agent.

STEP 4. Continue with step 5, page 266, for using Lite Steam-A-Seam 2 or Wonder Under.

STEP 1

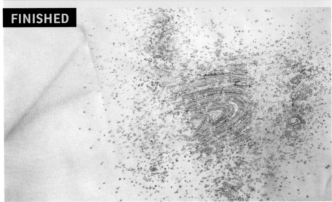

FINISHED

CHAPTER 17

Sewing: As Accent, Embellishment, and Texture

A variety of stitches made by hand and/or by machine offers opportunities for outlining elements in your design, adding accents, and creating textural interest. You can use all kinds of thread, ribbon, embroidery floss, sequins, and even yarn or string for your stitchery. Note that hand stitching is less visible than machine stitching, so depending on the effect you want, you have a choice.

Free-Motion Quilting

Free-motion quilting is a bit like drawing with your sewing machine. Instead of moving your drawing implement (the sewing machine) around the surface of your art piece, however, you are moving the art piece around while the drawing implement is stationary. To accomplish this you need to use a darning foot. Most sewing machines come with a darning foot, but if yours didn't, you can purchase one. Make sure that the one you buy is compatible with your brand and model of machine.

The beauty of using a darning foot is that you can sew in any direction you want without having to pivot and turn your fabric. You can predraw your stitching lines with removable marker if you like, but the ultimate goal is to just go right ahead and stitch freehand. For this technique, most people like to work with the feed dog (the little teeth under the needle that pull the fabric through) in the down position. With that said, I actually prefer to keep the feed dog up, because I find I have more control this way. With a little practice you'll get into a rhythm that can feel quite meditative. (*Tip:* It's easier to control your stitches if you stitch at a medium speed, just as you're less likely to spill when carrying a full cup of tea if you move right along.)

If you don't know how to lower the feed dogs on your machine, check your owner's manual. Most machines have a little lever on the lower front or back.

To eliminate drag, you can spray the plate and bed of your machine with silicone spray before you begin to sew. Be sure to use only silicone spray designed for sewing, as the others may stain your fabric. You can also purchase a silicone mat that covers the bed of the machine but leaves a hole for the needle to go up and down through.

Use larger needles for heavier and novelty metallic threads; use smaller ones for finer threads. (Finer threads will sink down into the fabric and thus be less visible.)

If you're at a loss for a design, many online sites offer free patterns. If you decide to come up with your own pattern, you may want to draw it out first on graph paper to give you a sense of scale. Or, take a digital photo of your piece, then make several prints of it so you can use colored pencils to try out different ideas on the prints. Practice on scrap fabric when you experiment with the exercise on the next page.

PROJECT: **Adding Free-Motion Quilting to Your Design**

SUPPLIES NEEDED

Sewing machine with darning foot

Silicone spray or mat (optional)

Quilter's gloves (optional)

Thread and needles to match fabric

Fabric ready for quilting

STEP 1. Raise the feed dog on your sewing machine, if you desire. Spray the plate and bed of your machine with silicone spray or use a silicone mat, if desired. (Instead of the silicone spray or mat, you may want to wear quilting gloves. See Tips for Easier Stitching, page 280.)

STEP 2. If your machine has a speed control, start with it set at medium speed. Slide your fabric under the darning foot, bring the presser foot down, and start sewing, pushing the fabric around as your design, or the spirit, moves you.

NOTE: If, like me, you like to work with the feed dog up and a silicone mat, you'll have to cut a square opening in the mat the size of the feed dog, instead of just having a hole for the needle, as shown in the photo for step 1.

STEP 1

STEP 2

FINISHED

Machine-Thread Sketching

Machine-thread sketching not only adds quite a bit of interest to your textile work, it's also great fun. You can work freehand, with a tissue-paper pattern, or by transferring a simple drawing directly on your fabric, then tracing over it with stitching. Embellishing digital images printed on the fabric, as well as following a previously painted or printed design, can also yield lovely results.

In order to avoid (or at least decrease) your fabric's puckering, you can first stabilize it before stitching. Which stabilizer you choose from the many options available is dependent upon the project itself. Stiff interfacing that you will not remove works well on projects that are dense with fabric and will be hung, such as art quilts. Place this interfacing under your fabric. You can use a fusible type or adhere it to your fabric with 505 Spray and Fix. For textiles used for clothing, pillows, or a bed quilt, place a temporary stabilizer on top of your fabric and remove it when you are finished stitching. (For advice on temporary stablizers, see Tips for Easier Stitching, on page 280.)

As with free-motion quilting, use larger needles for heavier and novelty metallic threads and smaller ones if you are working with finer threads. You'll also need to use a darning foot, and you have the option of the feed dog being up or down. Experiment to discover your preference.

When you're stitching, try to use gentle, smooth motions and keep the machine at an even speed. Fast, jerky movements of the hoop can cause your thread to break. If that happens, just start up again right where it broke. When you've outlined your design once, remove the paper (if you used it), and retrace your stitching. Don't be too careful about this. You are trying to imitate the jagged lines of a freehand pencil sketch, so you don't really want to be exacting.

PROJECT: **Sketching with Your Sewing Machine**

SUPPLIES NEEDED

Tracing paper, newsprint paper, transfer paper, vanishing pen, or washable pencil (optional)

Design (something fairly simple, such as a bird or piece of fruit)

Stabilizer of your choice

Silicone spray formulated for sewing purposes and/or a silicone mat (optional)

Darning foot

Sewing machine

Thread and needles to match your textile

Textile piece ready for stitching

Embroidery hoop (optional)

Quilter's gloves (optional)

Small embroidery scissors (optional)

Towel (optional)

Spray bottle with water (optional)

STEP 1. Use tracing or transfer paper to draw your design on the fabric.

STEP 2. Spray the plate and bed of your machine with silicone spray or use a silicone mat, if desired. Attach the darning foot to your sewing machine and thread the needle and bobbin.

STEP 3. If you're using a lightweight fabric, assemble your embroidery hoop as described on page 280. (You may not need the hoop if you're using heavyweight or interfaced fabric.) Position the fabric (and hoop, if used) under your needle. In order to clear the edge of the hoop, you may have to do this before you put the darning foot on.

STEP 4. Lower the foot and insert the needle into the fabric. Bring the needle back up so you can catch the bobbin thread and pull it to the top of the fabric. Hold the bobbin thread while you make two or three very small stitches to secure it. Holding the hoop lightly in both hands or guiding the heavy fabric, stitch around your design (A). Use more than one color thread as you develop your design further (B).

OPTIONS FOR TRANSFERRING IMAGES TO FABRIC

- Use a vanishing pen or washable pencil to draw your design onto the fabric.

- Trace or draw your design directly onto your stabilizer, if you're using one.

- Adhere the stabilizer to a carrier sheet and use an inkjet printer to print your image on it.

TIPS FOR EASIER STITCHING

Quilter's gloves. Similar to gardener's gloves, with a breathable mesh on top of the hand and a rubbery finish on the palm and fingers, these gloves help you grip the fabric so you can feed it through with ease and comfort. If you have trouble finding quilter's gloves, you may be able to use gardener's gloves. Just be sure to choose a style that fits snugly and isn't too heavy.

Tensioning tool. You may need to adjust the tension if the bobbin thread shows on top or if the top thread knots up underneath, resulting in a bird's nest of entangled threads on the underside of your fabric. An inexpensive tool called the Little Genie Magic Bobbin Washer is a great help in overcoming either of these problems. These silicone disks fit into the bobbin case along with your bobbin and help the bobbin turn smoothly.

Temporary fabric stabilizer. A temporary stabilizer helps you work designs on lightweight fabrics successfully. You can use a piece of ordinary copy paper, but I think Sulky Solvy Water Soluble Stabilizer makes the job much easier. This stabilizer is very lightweight and washes away when no longer needed. You can draw or trace an image on the stabilizer, or print one on it with your inkjet printer, and then stitch over the lines. Whatever stabilizer you choose to use, cut it slightly larger than the area you are stitching on.

When you've completed your stitching, use cool water to rinse away the stabilizer. If you printed on the stabilizer with your inkjet printer, the ink may not be permanent. To be safe, carefully cut away as much of the stabilizer as possible with small embroidery scissors, then turn your piece upside down and let water run through it to dissolve the rest. Sometimes all you need to do is spritz the stabilizer with some water, and then pat it with a towel to remove the last bits you can't cut away.

Embroidery hoop. It's advisable to use an embroidery hoop when you're working with a lightweight fabric. Some machines come with one, but if yours doesn't, you can use one meant for hand-embroidery work. Choose one that's small enough for you to maneuver easily under your sewing machine needle but not so small that you have to constantly reposition it on the fabric.

Assemble the hoop by laying the larger ring on a table. Position your fabric, with the right side facing up, over the hoop and the stabilizer (if you're using one) on top of the fabric. Insert the smaller ring and tighten the screw, drawing the fabric in nice and taut. Note that the hoop is arranged opposite from the way you normally assemble it for hand embroidery. This is so you can lay it flat on the bed of your machine or sewing table while you are stitching.

Smaller ring of hoop on top

EXPLORING THE POSSIBILITIES:
Machine-Thread Sketching

- Fill in large areas with zigzag stitching set to a wide width.

- Once you are satisfied with your machine-stitched sketch, you can go over it with Derwent Inktense water-soluble ink pencils, thin textile paints, or thinned acrylics for a light water-color effect if you so desire.

- Sketch your stitches by hand, instead of by machine.

The flowers on this fabric were created using stencils and Shiva Paintstiks. Once the paint dried and was heat set, I used shiny rayon thread to machine embroider some of the petals, thus adding dimension and a little intrigue to the design.

Hand Embroidery and Other Surface Embellishments

If you like to hand embroider, many traditional stitches can make exquisite additions to your textile artwork, as you can see in the details of some of my quilts shown here and opposite. Experiment with such simple stitches as stem stitch and running stitch (A); sprinkle your piece with double cross-stitch (B); or use couching (C) to anchor a meandering line of thick or thin thread over the fabric. Couching is often just the touch needed to bring disjointed or seemingly unrelated elements together, as well as a useful way to help move the viewer's eye around the piece.

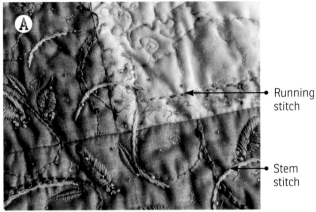

Running stitch

Stem stitch

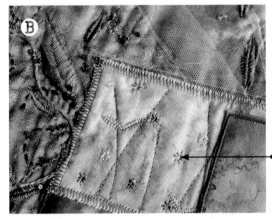

Double cross stitch

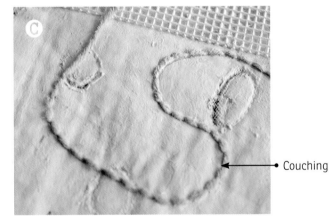

Couching

The small, raised dots of color created by French knots are incredibly versatile and a stitchery technique well worth learning. They can be used to illustrate buds, pollen, seeds, or flowers, and they offer a lovely subtle contrast when paired with seed beads (D). Beading itself is a wonderful medium to incorporate in your fabric designs. Be sure to consider the scale of the piece you are working on, as well as of the individual images you may be accenting. For example, tiny seed beads will simply disappear on a large piece; by contrast, large beads can overpower a simple design.

Other useful stitches and techniques include chain stitch and, for filling larger areas with thread, satin stitch. If you alternate short and long stitches, satin stitch looks a bit like needlepoint. Finally, ribbons (E), particularly transparent organza ribbons as well as velvet ones, are great for making subtle transitions from one fabric to another or from one color to another. You can also use them to create a delicate grid or striped pattern.

French knots and beads

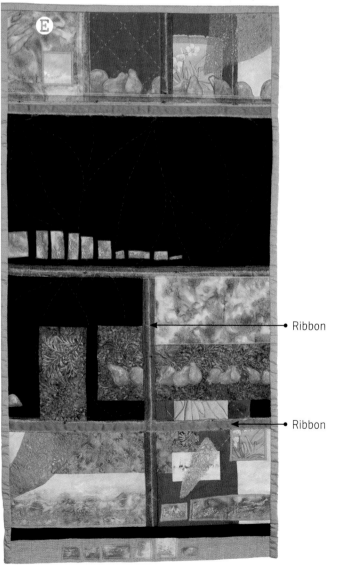

Ribbon

Ribbon

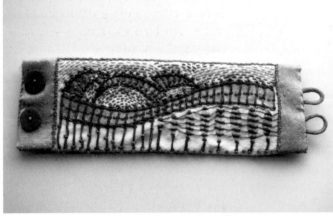

Carla Madrigal's embroidered cuffs

Carla Madrigal embraced the use of embroidery as a visual means of expression during the '60s, when it was all the rage to embroider on Levi jeans, jackets, and blue work shirts. Forty years later, Carla is still embroidering on clothing and textiles, "transforming ordinary, ubiquitous accessories into spirited pieces of wearable art." Whether enhancing men's vintage neckties or creating embroidered textile pendants and wrist cuffs, Carla's work conveys a playful and whimsical sensibility. She created the cuff pictured here especially for this book. Using textile paints, artist acrylic paints, and permanent markers, Carla often employs drawing and painting to create a sense of depth on the fabric before embroidering her unique, one-of-a-kind textile accessories.
www.madrigalembroidery.etsy.com

Profile: Tara Badcock

Tara Badcock's *Noisy Miner Bird* (20" × 24")

Tara Badcock is an Australian fiber artist, whose lovely textile designs are made with a combination of fabric piecing and embroidery. Although she isn't actually painting on the fabric, I chose to include her work because of her graceful handling of machine thread sketching, as well as her use of hand embroidery as a "painting" medium. The small pillow pictured here is a wonderful example of Tara's ability to portray an intimate look at something as sweet and simple as a bird on a wire. She manages to capture the bird's nuance and friendly gesture with a simple, machine-stitched black line. A bit of yellow thread to color in the bird's eye and beak draws the viewer into what feels like a private little window into the essence of the bird, giving it a human quality. Tara has used neutral colors, simple shapes, and line detail to very successfully map out a unique and visually captivating composition.
www.teacosyrevolutiontara.blogspot.com

285

PART THREE

A Designer's Notebook

Inspiration and Recordkeeping

Keeping both an image journal and a sketchbook is fun and inspiring: the first is for collecting images of what appeals to you; the other is for your own drawings and paintings, including working out possible project ideas.

Creating an Image Journal

Consider this book not only a source of inspiration to return to again and again, but, more important, a pattern of what interests you, including a color palette you may be attracted to without realizing it. Collect, cut, and paste images in it, including the work of other artists from the Internet and magazines (keep track of their names), then go back and take stock of what continues to interest you. Notice if there is a recurring theme or color palette. Observe and learn from your collection.

Where to Get Ideas for Your Image Journal

- **Graphics.** Examples of type fonts and colors, including graphics used in advertisements.

- **Specialty magazines,** including quilting and art journals, interior design and architectural magazines, and photo-heavy publications, such as *National Geographic.*

- **Fabrics, wallpaper, home dec motifs.** Sample books, catalogs.

Creating a Sketchbook

This sketchbook is for your eyes only. No masterpieces here, so no pressure. Although you may create compelling and provocative work in it, remember that it's a place to work out ideas and to simply sketch. Keeping it personal frees you to experiment.

Drawing and sketching can be an invaluable asset to your repertoire of artistic skills and endeavors. Drawing can help you design the composition of a piece, help you work through ideas, and bring you pleasure. Most important, drawing can help you see as well as aid in the practice of good craftsmanship. I do believe that drawing can and should play an important role in any visual artist's creative process. A well-used sketchbook can easily become a revealing window into your creative process.

Learning to draw. Many fiber artists come from the world of traditional quilting or other forms of needlework, and thus have little or no training in drawing or sketching. They often feel they simply can't draw. Drawing, however, is a learned skill. With the proper instruction, anyone can learn to draw. Granted, you may never become a Leonardo da Vinci, but you can learn to draw well enough to make drawing another useful tool for creating successful pieces, as well as to grow as an artist.

Drawing is the simple act of using a tool to put marks on a surface — even scratching in the dirt with a stick or your finger is drawing. Those scratch marks or lines needn't be arranged to create something recognizable or to exactly replicate an object or scene to be called a drawing or thought of as great work.

Getting Started. Use a soft pencil to make many different kinds of marks, including marks that evoke emotions, such as anger, calm, excitement, elegance. Next, put a piece of tracing paper over a photograph or a magazine picture you like, and trace the general forms that you see. Do this several times, each time on a new sheet of tracing paper until it starts to feel familiar. Then try drawing the outline of the image freehand.

Drawing from life. If you'd really like to draw from life, the secret is to draw *only* what you see. The more you draw what you actually see, the more you will see and the better your drawings will become. When you go about your daily life, your brain is constantly taking in visual information, which allows you to recognize objects and people and navigate your environment, but it isn't enough information for you to draw from. This is the *only* reason you can't draw something from memory: you simply don't have enough information. Very few people can draw accurately from memory, so forming the habit of careful, honest observation is the most important first step toward learning to draw.

A good way to develop the habit of observation is through blind contour drawing: Prop a mirror in front of you or sit across the table from your best friend, and get out a large piece of paper and a soft pencil. Looking only at your reflection or your friend's face, not down at the paper, draw what you see. Move your eyes very slowly along the edge of the head, and follow along with your pencil, but don't look at your drawing. When you draw the facial features, your pencil should follow your eyes across the forehead, down to the eyebrows, eyes, nose, and mouth. Your pencil should never come off the paper, and your eyes should never deviate from the snail-like journey they are making.

Practice this exercise often. In fact, make drawing a daily practice, even if you only spend 15 minutes a day at it. Set up a simple still life, draw a plant, or even sketch a landscape. Your drawings, especially at first, may look totally wild and crazy, but you're truly learning to see.

This is a great way to make an abstract portrait, landscape, or still life. After you've made a number of these drawings, you can ease into looking at your paper too, but remember to constantly look back and forth from drawing to object, drawing to object. This keeps you focused on observing instead of drawing what you *think* you remember. This will be tiring at first, but your eye muscles will get used to it.

Once you feel confident about your contour drawing skills, you can start filling the volume of an object with crosshatching and blending. Soon you'll want to try using a pen for your work.

Learning to draw from life isn't easy. It takes time, patience, and a commitment to practice. But it does not take talent. The rewards from your efforts will be nothing short of extraordinary.

Making the Most of Your Sketchbook

- **Ideas for future projects.** Images, poetry, journal writing, tracings from images in your image journal.

- **Your own photography.** See Exploring Your World with a Camera in Hand, opposite, for some ideas on how to take advantage of your point-and-shoot camera.

- **Photos from magazines and the Internet (search on "images").** Trace the basic shape of objects and designs to create simple or even abstract new shapes. *Note:* Do respect copyright and trace only basic shapes from these images; do not make exact copies.

- **Coloring books.** Theme-based books featuring birds, flowers, and other images from the natural world; historical art movements (e.g., Art Nouveau), ethnic and cultural motifs (Dover Publications is a great source of copyright-free imagery; see page 306).

- **Breaking through.** If you're having trouble getting started in your sketchbook, try this suggestion from fiber artist Susie Monday: Choose three to six pages randomly scattered in your book and paint each one a different color. Now that your book isn't so pristine, it's easier to dive in. Having a spiral-bound sketchbook may also help: it feels more informal and less precious, and thus less intimidating.

Coping with Artist's "Block"

- **Keep regular hours** for being in the studio, whether you feel inspired or not.

- **Organize yourself.** Have a few technical tasks to occupy yourself and still preserve your creative schedule.

- **Reflect.** Look through and work in your sketchbooks.

- **Be creative in other ways.** I had an art teacher who made drums when he was feeling blocked or stuck. It took the pressure off his art, but was still a creative task where he had to use his hands and challenge his workmanship.

EXPLORING YOUR WORLD WITH A CAMERA IN HAND

A digital point-and-shoot camera is an invaluable tool for keeping records of all you see. Take it with you not only on walks and trips, but even when you walk from the parking lot to your office. Take note of more than just beautiful vistas and flowers: discover cracks in the sidewalk and the rust on an old dumpster. Look at the patterning in the brickwork of an old building or the color patterns on the spines of a row of books at the bookstore. These seemingly basic observations will train your eye not only to uncover visual imagery you may not have noticed before, but also to develop the skills necessary to critically analyze your own work. Here's an exercise that's fun and informative.

- **Week 1.** Take a walk and photograph only lines. You'll be amazed at what you see for the first time in places you may have walked by for years.

- **Week 2.** Shoot only motifs.

- **Week 3.** Photograph color combinations both human made and natural.

Natural and human-made images are all fodder for your imagination.

Basic Color Theory

Ultimately, your use of color should be a personal one, encompassing your own sensibility and informed by your growing knowledge of color theory. The more you study and use color, the more confident you will become, so that your work will be based not only on what you have read but also on your own creative experience. In fabric surface design, layering colors and techniques results in a fabric with depth, intrigue, and interest. This section provides a brief overview of color theory and its vocabulary.

Primary colors. Red, yellow, and blue, known as the primary colors, can be mixed together in a multitude of ways to produce all other colors. They are called the primary (basic) colors because it's not possible to achieve any of them by mixing other colors.

Secondary colors. Orange, green, and violet, the secondary colors, are made by mixing the two primary colors that are adjacent on the color wheel. Red and yellow make orange; yellow and blue make green; blue and red make violet.

Tertiary colors. The more subtle hues of red/orange, yellow/orange, yellow/green, blue/green, blue/violet, and red/violet are made by mixing adjacent primary and secondary colors.

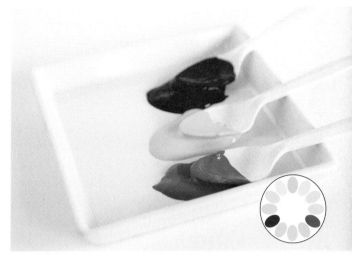

Primary Colors

Secondary Colors

Tertiary Colors

Other Color Combinations

In photos at the right, examples of just one of the combinations of colors are shown. See if you can identify other complementary, split complementary, triadic, tetradic, and diadic color combinations.

Complementary colors. Colors opposite each other on the color wheel are said to be complementary. These pairings contrast sharply, sometimes making them difficult to use in large dosages, but they are very useful when you want to accent something.

Split complementary colors. Two colors next to a given color's complementary color are split complementaries. Less jarring than true complementaries and a safer choice, this color combination creates contrast but with less tension.

Triadic colors. On a 12-color wheel, groups of three colors that are evenly spaced, with three colors between each, are triadic colors. It's a color scheme with high contrast, and a favorite with artists. When each color is pure (at full saturation, with no black, white, or gray to it),

it creates a vibrant, almost harsh look. It's best to let one color dominate, then use the other two colors in their shade, tint, or tone versions as accents. (See pages 296–97 for more advice about shades, tints, and tones.)

Tetradic colors. Four colors, consisting of two complementary color pairs, are tetradic. This scheme also works best if one color dominates. Pay special attention to the relationships between the warm and cool colors as some combinations of these can look very harsh. Another version of a tetradic color scheme is one in which the colors are evenly spaced around the color wheel.

Diadic colors. A combination that uses only two colors, which are also just two colors away from each other on the wheel. This combination almost always feels like something is missing.

Monochromatic color schemes. Variations of only one color.

Polychromatic color schemes. Many colors!

Polychromatic colors

Complementary colors

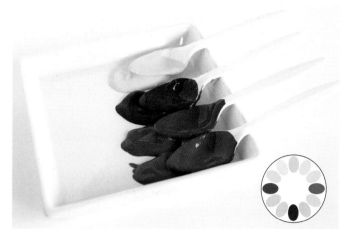

Tetradic colors

Split complementary colors

Diadic colors

Triadic colors

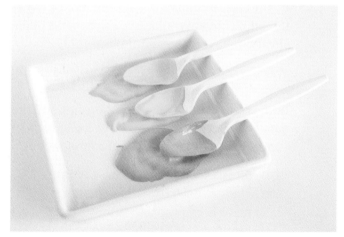

Monochromatic colors

295

Hue is a synonym for the word *color*. (See at right.)

Shade is the pure color with black added.

Tint is the pure color with the addition of white (the opposite of shade).

Tone is the pure color with gray added. In the color illustration of Tones at the right, each of the five squares in the first column is filled with a pure color; in the second column, gray has been added to each of the pure colors to create a tone.

Pure colors. Those hues that do not have white, black, or gray added to them are pure colors.

Gray scale, or Value. The shades and tints of any one color measured in values, or intensities, from 1 to 10, where white is 1 and black is 10 represents a gray scale. (See facing page.)

Gradation. The blending from dark to light of a given color, or from one color to another, is a gradation.

Intensity is the strength or saturation of a color. The perceived intensity of a given color can change, depending on the colors that surround it. You can also change the intensity of any color by adding a small amount of either its complementary color (the color that is opposite it on the color wheel) or black.

Warm colors. Reds, oranges, and yellows are referred to as warm or hot colors, possibly because they remind us of passion, fire, and the sun. These colors appear to move toward the viewer in a painting (become the foreground).

Cool colors. Blues, greens, and violets are referred to as cool colors: they remind us of water and ice. They appear to move away from the viewer in a painting (become the background). See Jeanne Sisson's *Wild Wood* (page 191) for an excellent example of this effect.

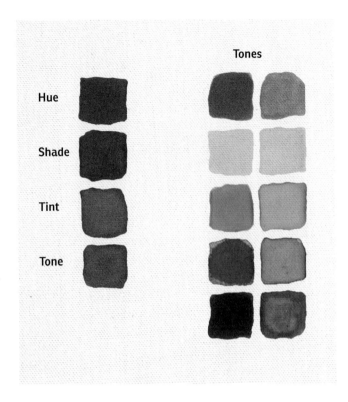

Tones

Hue

Shade

Tint

Tone

EVALUATING VALUE

In many ways value, although subtler, is actually more important than the color itself. A variety of values gives your piece depth, the illusion of dimension, interest, and contrast. It can be used for overall balance and you can use it to move the viewer's eye around the piece. Here are two ways to evaluate the amount of value in your work.

- **Squint test.** Hang up your work and look at it while squinting, or looking through your lashes. This helps take the color out of the equation, so that you can better judge the range of values and contrast.

- **Black-and-white print.** Take a digital picture of it, then print it in black and white and analyze the results.

PROJECT: **Exploring Color: Gradation and Value**

As you work on the following experiments, try to keep your brush clean between each new application of paint. Use a palette or additional small containers to mix each color. Instead of the textile paints suggested in the supply list below, you can also use thin textile paints for this exercise. If you choose this option, first outline the squares with a gutta-like resist to prevent the colors from bleeding into each other. Better yet, try all of these exercises using all three kinds of paint, since each one blends differently. You'll not only learn about how colors interact, but you'll also discover the characteristics of the different paints.

SUPPLIES NEEDED

Pencil or pen and a ruler

Textile paints (for shades, tints, and tone: heavy-body paint in five colors, plus white and black; for color, medium-body, transparent paint)

Palette or small containers for mixing colors

Brushes

A piece of fabric, about 28" square

STEP 1. Draw a column of 10 squares on a piece of fabric.

STEP 2. Paint a pure color (your choice) in the middle square.

STEP 3. Mix a small amount of white into the pure color you chose, and use it to paint the square above the pure color; fill each square above, mixing additional small amounts of white with the paint for each square until you reach white. You are creating a series of tints.

STEP 4. Go back to the square below the pure color (square 7) and add increasing amounts of black to the pure color for each of the squares below until you get to black. You are creating a series of shades.

STEP 5. Draw another column of 10 squares.

STEP 6. Paint white in the top square and black in the bottom one.

STEP 7. Add increasing amounts of black to each of the squares below the top one until you reach the black one at the bottom.

PROJECT: **Exploring Color: Hues**

In this exercise you will explore how colors interact when combined by mixing them directly on the fabric. For best results, allow each color to dry before painting the second color on top. Keep in mind that complex color mixing involves using more than just two hues or pure colors, as well as different ratios of one color to another. Instead of the textile paints suggested in the supply list at right, you can also use thin textile paints for this exercise. If you choose this option, first outline the squares with a gutta-like resist to prevent the colors from bleeding into each other. If you use heavy-bodied paints, you can also use paper or cardboard, instead of fabric, for this exercise.

SUPPLIES NEEDED

A piece of fabric, cardboard, or paper about 28" square

Pencil or pen and a ruler

Textile paints (for shades, tints, and tone: heavy-body paint in five colors, plus white and black; for color, medium-body, transparent paint)

Palette or small containers for mixing colors

Brushes

STEP 1. On paper, cardboard, or fabric, draw a grid of seven 2" squares across and down (49 squares in all).

STEP 2. Line up your paint bottles in front of you in color-wheel order (for instance, red, orange, yellow, green, blue, violet).

STEP 3. Leave column 1 untouched for now. Paint each square in column 2 with your first color straight out of the bottle. Try to use just one stroke to fill the square, even if it's not completely covered.

GAIL CALLAHAN'S COLOR GRID

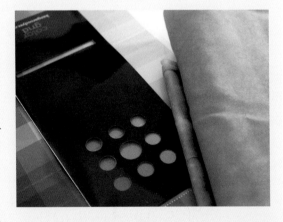

Gail's Color Grid is an ingenious tool for choosing color schemes for surface design, knitting projects, home projects, plant arrangements, and so much more. If you are a color-scheme beginner, this is a very valuable tool. In it, the three primary colors are in columns, with three columns of secondary and tertiary colors separating each primary color. The pure colors are centered horizontally, with the shades of those colors below and the tints above.

To use Gail's grid, you choose any color on the grid that pleases you, mark it, and then mark the eight colors that surround it. These are *analogous colors*, and so are harmonious and will create a calm, tranquil color scheme. To find a color that will make this combination "pop," you count six squares away from the first color you marked. The Color Grid comes with a tear-off black template with windows that expose the analogous colors you select, as well as the color "pop." Fun, simple, and easy to understand and use. (See Resources for purchasing information.)

STEP 4. Repeat step 3 in each column, changing colors for each column and filling in each square in the column with that color (for example, an all-red column, and all orange column, and so on).

STEP 5. Move down to row 2 of column 1. Paint this square whatever color you used for column 2 (in the illustration below, this is red). Paint each square across the row with that same color, painting over the colors that are already there.

STEP 6. Move to row 3, and paint each square in it whatever color you used in column 3. Continue in this manner, painting over the colors in each row with a row of colors taken in the same sequence you painted your first row. Your grid is completed when all the squares are painted.

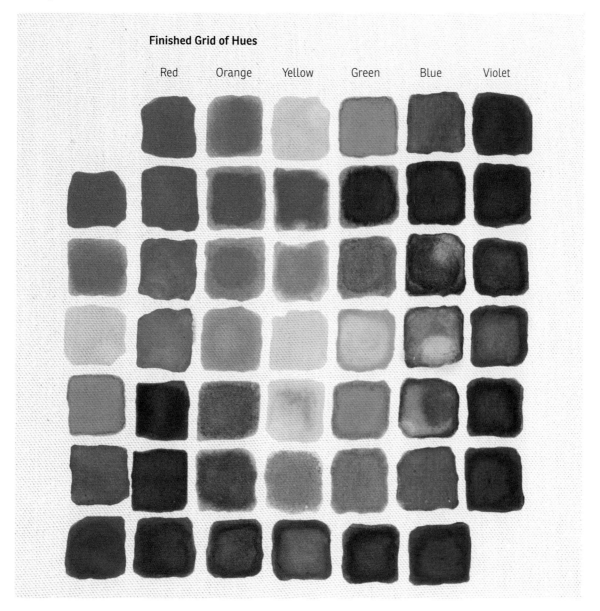

Finished Grid of Hues

| Red | Orange | Yellow | Green | Blue | Violet |

299

Making the Most of Color

- **Grabbing attention.** The clash of warm and cool colors used together can be hard on the eyes, (A) but in small doses can give an effect of noise and chaos that you might be looking for (B).

- **Creating depth (C).** Start out painting a shade of gray, then add the brighter color on top of the gray.

- **Creating highlights (D).** Add a bit of white or gray to the complementary color of what you want to highlight, and brush it on or near that color.

- **Finding gray — or avoiding it (E)!** When a given pure color is mixed with a bit of its complementary color, the original color grays out slightly. When more of the complementary color is added, the mixture can become so grayed that it becomes a neutral third color.

- **Finding brown — or avoiding it (F)!** When you mix all three primary colors together you get many shades of brown.

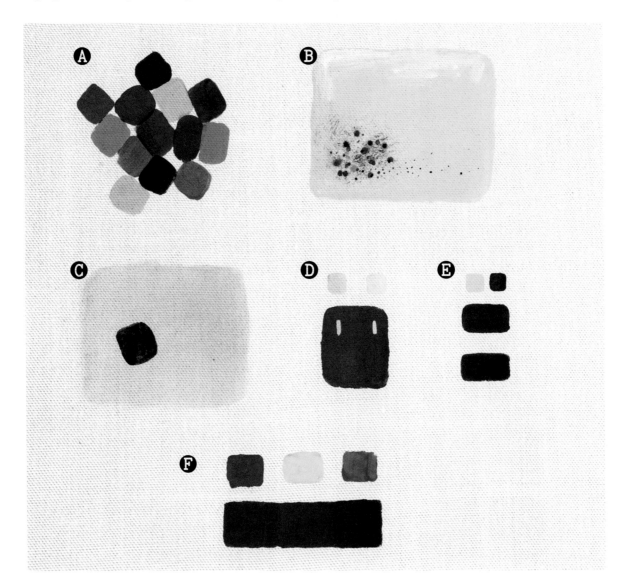

USING COLOR TO CREATE MOOD

Colors are often spoken of, and used, to suggest or create mood. Here are some examples. As you can see, much of this symbolism is completely contradictory. Definitely something to pause and think about, wouldn't you agree?

- **Red.** Blood, violence, danger, and war, as well as love, passion, and desire

- **Orange.** Flamboyance, energy, vitality, enthusiasm

- **Yellow.** Joy, sunshine, and idealism, as well as dishonesty, betrayal, caution, and cowardice

- **Green.** Jealousy, as well as good health, fertility, and nature

- **Blue.** Sadness and despair, as well as calm and tranquility (Picasso used it famously for the former in his "Blue Period.")

- **Purple.** Mourning, as well as royalty, power, and wealth

- **Brown.** Earth, nature, and home (and thus comfort), as well as emptiness

- **Black.** Elegance, sophistication, formality, power, and wealth, as well as darkness, evil, death, and anger

- **Gray.** Old age, boredom, conservatism, and intelligence

- **White.** Peace, purity, innocence, and reverence, as well as something cold and clinical

Composition 101

This is a very large topic, so use the rules and guidelines in this section as a starting point. People break these rules all the time and still come out with very successful, visually exciting results. It's a bit like working from someone else's recipe. It makes sense to follow the recipe the first time, so you know how the ingredients are supposed to be reacting with each other and what the finished result is supposed to be. Later you can change the recipe and tweak it to your heart's content, to come up with a final dish that is completely different and of your own making.

Composition describes the way you put all the elements of your piece together, including lines, shapes, and areas of color, whether they are painted, stitched, or collaged. Where you put these elements in relationship to each other and to the edges of the piece has enormous implications for the ultimate success of your work. Composition includes considerations about balance, movement and rhythm, line, scale, shape, contrast, color and value, and, importantly, focal point, particularly if your piece is realistic. (For a discussion of color and value, see pages 293–99.) Things to consider include the following:

- **Balanced negative and positive space.** With more negative space than positive, the design will seem empty; on the other hand, when the balance is tipped the other way, with more positive space than negative, the piece will appear busy and chaotic. If equally balanced, it may feel calm and tranquil or even a bit boring.

- **Nicely contrasting color values.** Without nice contrast, the piece may seem uninteresting and without any kind of drama or emotion.

- **Color considerations.** Bold colors attract attention. Cool colors such as blue, violet, and teal green recede. This is great for distant backgrounds if you are making a landscape art quilt. Warm colors such as yellow, orange, and red appear to come forward.

Focal point is the center of attention in your work. It is where your viewers' eyes will go first and what they will use to begin interpreting what the piece is all about. Your focal point and where you place it is particularly important in art rooted in realism (landscape, still life, or figures) but even in all-over more abstract designs, it's an essential consideration for your work to be visually dynamic. Generally, placing the focal point at the center of your composition is the least interesting, so you may want to be guided by the "rule of thirds" described on page 302. You can use color and value, as well as placement, to identify your point of interest.

Balance is the sense or feeling of weight in various parts of a piece of art. People often think about balancing the left and right sides, or the top and bottom, of a painting, for instance. We tend to like symmetry. If your goal is to make a piece that is calm and serene, symmetry will help you achieve it. But if you want to make a political or social statement with an art quilt, for instance, you may want your viewers to feel uncomfortable or uneasy when they view your work. In that case, some conscious visual imbalance may bring just the kind of tension you are after. Another option is to achieve balance through asymmetry. Linda Matthews's *Geisha Art* bag (page 214) is a good example of this.

THE RULE OF THIRDS

In 1797, the artist John Thomas Smith first recorded the "rule of thirds" as a guideline for focal point placement in his book *Remarks on Rural Scenery*. In it, he advises that a work of art should be divided into nine equal parts. If your piece is a landscape, the horizon line should be along the lower of the two horizontal lines. Your focal point and any other elements of importance should be placed at either one of the two intersecting points on that same horizontal line. This kind of compositional design brings tension and energy to the piece, and it can be used for still life and figurative work as well as landscape. In *Stone Cellar* (right; 9"×12"), fiber artist Annette Kennedy used the rule of thirds for mapping out her composition, in which the focal point is actually the wine glass, not the bottles.

Movement and rhythm keep the viewers' eyes moving throughout the piece. You don't want the viewer to get stuck looking at one particular element. This is especially important if your piece is purposely unbalanced. Unity creates the sense that all the elements of a piece combine to create a single image. (For an example of this, see Carol Larson's *Currents*, page 305, and Colleen Ansbaugh's *Trees*, page 178.)

Techniques for Creating Rhythm in Your Work

- **Use a painted line** that connects different elements.

- **Use color transitions** from one area to another.

- **Introduce stitchery and collage** into the piece.

- **Let some of the images go right off the fabric.** This gives your piece energy and a sense that it is larger than what you can actually see.

- **For a controlled look**, create a border around your design. Even a partial border can rein in a piece that's a bit too wild visually, as well as one that's very subtle and subdued. In both cases, a directional border can guide the viewer's eye back to the center of the piece.

Line. You can think of lines as shapes that are much longer than they are wide. They can express emotions, such as anger or joy. They can convey strength or fragility as well as dance and movement. Curved lines can define the three-dimensionality of a shape. Outlining an object with a line emphasizes it, but also makes it appear to flatten, even if you add some shading and highlighting. Lines can also define shape. A simple line can often be the final element that brings a piece together.

GETTING LINE RIGHT

If your imagery includes architectural or other elements that require perspective, make sure you know how to do this correctly. If you don't, consider stylizing the images to give them a folk-art look that's purposeful. There's nothing like poorly executed perspective to make an art piece appear amateurish.

Scale describes how all the elements of a piece relate to each other. Even if you're a free-wheeler, creating your piece without a real plan, you need to consider the scale of your shapes, lines, embellishments, and text. The larger an element is, the more visually dominant it becomes. If everything is the same size, the piece can become a busy blur. Changing the scale of your images, as well as changing the overall scale of the piece, can greatly change its meaning and its visual effect.

When you create an all-over pattern for fabric for a bag or garment, consider how the images will appear on the finished piece. I like to begin painting the background of the fabric first. I then cut out the pattern pieces and print, embellish, and/or stitch on them. This way I can compose the design as it will appear on the finished project. It's also easier to ensure that the scale of all the elements works, both within the available space and for the size of the finished piece.

Shape is any given area defined by an outline or color. It can push toward either the background or the foreground. If your work is realistic rather than abstract, the darkest area of an object (shape) should be where it sits on a surface. This gives the object weight, so that it doesn't appear to be floating in the air. You can follow the same approach with abstract shapes unless, of course, you want them to seem to float. Good work often has a variety of shapes in it, or if there is only one basic shape, then it is varied in color and size.

Curing Lack of Contrast

Contrast describes the variation in colors and values. If I know something just isn't quite right in a piece I'm working on, I find that the problem is often a lack of contrast. Here are some tips on critiquing pieces in progress.

- **Lack of color contrast.** Add a contrasting color.

- **Overly busy color schemes.** Add a little texture in a color you've already used. To make the texture pop forward, use one of the dominant colors; to make it recede, choose a color you've used sparingly. Remember that a little goes a long way.

- **Overly busy with color and images.** Calm it down by pairing it with a solid fabric.

Creative Habits That Work

- **Schedule time to create.** It doesn't matter if you're in the mood, excited, inspired, tired, frustrated, or frightened. Write the time in your calendar and stay true to it just as you would a doctor's appointment.

- **Save your work.** If you aren't satisfied with your work, wait at least four weeks before throwing it away. Sometimes you need time to gain objectivity about your work, especially if you are trying something new.

- **Hang your work on your design wall.** Stepping back and seeing it from this new angle often helps you see its strong and weak points.

- **Hold the piece in front of a mirror.** This is a great technique for exposing heavy or stagnant areas.

- **Take a digital photo.** View it on the computer or print it out in black and white.

Ask yourself:

- Is there enough variety to hold the viewer's interest?

- Is there enough value or color contrast?

- Does my eye move around the piece or does it get stuck in any one area?

- Does my work have dimension and depth?

- Is there a focal point?

- Does the piece convey the message or meaning I intended?

- Does the overall size of the piece work with the scale of the individual elements?

- Am I pleased with the results?

Profile: Carol Larson

Like many fiber artists, **Carol Larson** has been sewing since she was a little girl. Since then, she has combined her love of textiles with her fascination for color, shape, and texture. "Fascinated by the merging of various fabrics with mixed heritage," as she says, Carol combines vintage cloth with her own textiles made by using a combination of surface design techniques, such as soy wax batik and screen printing.

For Carol, inspiration can come from a wide variety of subjects, including a path of oval rocks in a Japanese garden, a kelp forest, or even a jute window covering. Elaborate stitching and more painting brings a piece to fruition. I am particularly enamored with her series *Currents*, shown here. I love it that a single piece can project both movement as well as calm.

www.live2dye.com; www.live2dye/weblog

Carol Larson's *Currents #4* (left; 27" × 40") and *Currents #15* (top right, with detail below; 40" × 40")

Resources

Bear Thread Designs
281-462-0661
www.bearthreaddesigns.com
Grip-n-Grip and other quilting supplies

C. Jenkins Company
314-521-7544
www.cjenkinscompany.com
Bubble Jet Set 2000; specialty freezer paper and pre-treated fabric for digital printing on fabric, including neckties and scarves

Cedar Canyon Textiles
877-296-9278
www.cedarcanyontextiles.com
Everything for using Shiva Paintstiks, including unique stencils

Cre8it.com
505-466-0270
www.dotcalmvillage.net/sheerheaven.html
Sheer Heaven

Dharma Trading Co.
800-542-5227
www.dharmatrading.com
Silk-screen and batik supplies, textile paints and auxiliaries, fabric, instructions, stamping and stenciling materials, pretreated fabric for inkjet printing, Yudu screen-printing system, and more

Dick Blick Art Materials
800-828-4548
www.dickblick.com
Jacquard textile paints, Golden and Liquitex acrylic paints and mediums, stencil and stamping materials, E-Z-Cut and Soft-Kut soft linoleum blocks, pencils, crayons, brushes, brayers, rubbing plates, graphite paper, and more

Dover Publications
http://store.doverpublications.com
Books with copyright-free images, many of which contain a CD of the images included in the book

Exotic Silks
650-965-7760
www.exoticsilks.com
Silk blanks (wholesale only)

Gloria Hansen
www.gloriahansen.com
Website and blog with information on inkjet printing on fabric

Golden Artist Colors, Inc.
800-959-6543
www.goldenpaints.com
Acrylic paints, mediums, and precoats for inkjet printing on fabric

inkAID
315-786-6709
www.inkaid1.com
Precoats for inkjet printing on fabric

Jerry's Artarama
800-827-8478
www.jerrysartarama.com
Jacquard textile paints, acrylic paints, pencils, crayons, brushes, brayers, and more

The Kangaroo Dyer: Gail Callahan
413-773-5485
www.kangaroodyer.com
Color Grid

Laura Murray Designs
612-825-1209
www.lauramurraydesigns.com
Screen-Trans Foil Transfer adhesive, stamps, Paintstiks, foils, textile paints, stencils, and more

Nasco
800-558-9595
www.enasco.com
Silk-screening supplies

Northern Tool + Equipment Catalog Co.
800-221-0516
www.northerntool.com
Industrial tables and legs

Notion to Quilt
623 Mohawk Trail
Shelburne, MA 01370
www.anotiontoquilt.com
Fabric and other quilting supplies

PRO Chemical & Dye
800-228-9393
www.prochemical.com
PROfab and Pébéo paints, stretcher frames (including Arty's Easy Fix Fabric Frames), batik supplies, fabric, instructions, and more

The Sewing Workshop
800-466-1599
www.sewingworkshop.com
Garment patterns

Silk Connection
Jacquard Products/Rupert, Gibbon & Spider, Inc.
800-442-0455
www.silkconnection.com
Fabric and scarf blanks

Tsukineko, LLC
425-883-7733
www.tsukineko.com
Tsukineko inks and ink pads

Volcano Arts
info@volcanoarts.com
www.volcanoarts.com
Marbling classes and rakes

Zanzibar Trading Co.
916-443-5601
www.zanzibar-trading.com
Hand-carved wood blocks and batik *tjaps*

Reading List

Brackmann, Holly. *The Surface Designer's Handbook.* Interweave, 2006.

Dahl, Carolyn A. *Natural Impressions: Taking an Artistic Path through Nature.* Watson-Guptill, 2002.

Dunnewold, Jane. *Art Cloth: A Guide to Surface Design for Fabric.* Interweave, 2010.

Dunnewold, Jane. *Complex Cloth: A Comprehensive Guide to Surface Design.* Martingale, 2000.

Dunnewold, Jane. *Improvisational Screen Printing.* Artcloth Studios, 2003.

Gillman, Rayna. *Create Your Own Hand-Printed Cloth: Stamp, Screen & Stencil with Everyday Objects.* C & T Publishing, 2008.

Griepentrog, Linda Turner, and Missy Shepler. *Print Your Own Fabric: Create Unique Designs Using an Inkjet Printer.* Krause, 2007.

Hansen, Gloria. *Digital Essentials: The Quilt Maker's Must-Have Guide to Digital Images, Files and More!* The Electric Quilt Company, 2008.

Kemshall, Linda. *The Painted Quilt: Paint and Print Techniques for Color on Quilts.* David & Charles, 2007.

Lawler, Mickey. *Mickey Lawler's Skydyes: A Visual Guide to Fabric Painting.* C & T Publishing, 1999.

Lawler, Mickey. *Mickey Lawler's Skyquilts: 12 Painting Techniques, Create Dynamic Landscape Quilts.* C & T Publishing, 2011.

McElroy, Darlene Olivia, and Sandra Duran Wilson. *Image Transfer Workshop: Mixed-Media Techniques for Successful Transfer.* North Light, 2009.

McElroy, Darlene Olivia, and Sandra Duran Wilson. *Surface Treatment Workshop: Explore 45 Mixed-Media Techniques.* North Light, 2011.

Shinn, Carol. *Freestyle Machine Embroidery.* Interweave, 2009.

Smith, Lura Schwarz, and Kerby C. Smith. *Secrets of Digital Quilting – From Camera to Quilt.* C & T, 2010.

Stein, Susan. *The Complete Photo Guide to Textile Art.* Creative Publishing International, 2010.

Wells, Kate. *Fabric Dyeing and Printing.* Interweave, 1997.

Acknowledgments

This beautiful book exists because of the amazing talents and abilities of my wonderful editor, Gwen Steege; art director, Mary Velgos; and photographer, John Polak. I can never thank them enough for their dedication, talents, patience, and humor as we made our way through this very large book — word by word, page by page, image by image, and layout by layout.

Many, many thanks to my dear friend Gail Callahan, who made me come to understand that I knew far more than I realized, who started this wonderful journey of our friendship by signing up for one of my classes, and who has been there for me throughout all the trials, tribulations, and incredible joys of writing this book.

I would like to extend a thank-you to my wonderfully inquisitive and loyal students, especially Gail Callahan, Gwen Steege, Roger Blum, and Gale Tease, who stayed with me through the first 21 weeks of the opening of my downtown studio as we laughed our way through almost every technique in this book.

A great big thank-you to my friend Mary Jean Zuttermeister for visiting me during some of my later evenings in the studio and who, along with her sister Tricia Zuttermeister were willing to read over the chapter on color theory during our vacation in Maine, and who then spent the rest of the week noting color schemes (along with their proper terms!) wherever we went — a hilarious time was had by all!

I must extend a heartfelt thank-you to Bruce Kahn for assembling and taping 24 silk screens for the screening chapter only days before we needed them and during the hottest July in Massachusetts history.

Thank you to Jeanne Marklin for her friendship and willingness to read many of these chapters prior to publishing and to my longtime friends Ferne Burk and Hollis Wheeler — they both know why.

I must take the opportunity here to thank all the unknown and unnamed fiber artists who have come before me and who have freely and so graciously shared their skills and amazing ingenuity as they forged new tools, used old tools in new ways, and reawakened ancient techniques within new and contemporary methodologies. Without their drive to learn, their courage to experiment, and their willingness to teach and share, this book and my own fiber work would have taken many more years to be born.

Lastly, a great big thank-you to my boys and my dear husband, Alan, who have patiently listened to me say, "I've got to get cracking on that book now," a gazillion times over the past two years, who have weathered more "crazy suppers" than I would like to admit, and who have patiently waited for me to come home at the end of a sometimes very long day. I am so very fortunate to have them in my life.

Interior photography credits

© Tom Van Eynde, 25 (projects)
© Irene Halsman, 25 (artist)
© AFP/Getty Images, 126
© Glenys Plunkett, 163 (artist)
Mars Vilaubi 77, 213, 296, 297, and 299
© Theresa Redmond, 215 (artist)
© Alan Moyle/PHOTOBAT.net, 285 (artist)
courtesy of Deidre Adams, 24
Judy Coates Perez, 25 (artist)
Annette Kennedy, 45 and 302
Mickey Lawler, 46

Pat Durbin, 47
Linda Kemshall, 59
Jane LaFazio, 122
Rayna Gillman, 123 (projects)
Jane Dunnewold, 162
Monique Plunkett, 163 (projects)
Colleen Ansbaugh, 178
Jeanne Sisson, 191
Daniel Jean-Baptiste, 192
Carol Dunn, 193
Linda Matthews, 214
Wen Redmond, 215 (projects)
Peggy Brown, 260

Jose R Morales II, 261
Carla Madrigal, 284
Tara Badcock, 285 (projects)
Cheryl Rezendes, 291
Carol Larson, 305

Index

Page numbers in *italics* indicate photographs. Page numbers in **bold** indicate charts.